The League of Nations and the Organisation of Peace

The League of Nations and the Organisation of Peace

Martyn Housden

Longman
is an imprint of

Harlow, England • London • New York • Boston • San Francisco • Toronto
Sydney • Tokyo • Singapore • Hong Kong • Seoul • Taipei • New Delhi
Cape Town • Madrid • Mexico City • Amsterdam • Munich • Paris • Milan

PEARSON EDUCATION LIMITED

Edinburgh Gate
Harlow CM20 2JE
United Kingdom
Tel: +44 (0)1279 623623
Fax: +44 (0)1279 431059
Website: www.pearson.com/uk

First edition published in Great Britain in 2012

ISBN: 978-1-4082-2824-1

British Library Cataloguing in Publication Data
A CIP catalogue record for this book can be obtained from the British Library

Library of Congress Cataloging in Publication Data
Housden, Martyn, 1962–
    The League of Nations and the organisation of peace / Martyn Housden.
        p. cm.
    Includes bibliographical references and index.
    ISBN 978-1-4082-2824-1 (pbk.)
    1. League of Nations—History.   2. Peace—International cooperation.   I. Title.
    JZ4871.H68 2011
    341.22—dc23
                                                                    2011033604

10   9   8   7   6   5   4   3   2   1
15   14   13   12   11

Set 10/13.5pt Berkeley Book by 35
Printed in Malaysia (CTP-PPSB)

Introduction to the series

History is narrative constructed by historians from traces left by the past. Historical enquiry is often driven by contemporary issues and, in consequence, historical narratives are constantly reconsidered, reconstructed and reshaped. The fact that different historians have different perspectives on issues means that there is also often controversy and no universally agreed version of past events. *Seminar Studies* was designed to bridge the gap between current research and debate, and the broad, popular general surveys that often date rapidly.

The volumes in the series are written by historians who are not only familiar with the latest research and current debates concerning their topic, but who have themselves contributed to our understanding of the subject. The books are intended to provide the reader with a clear introduction to a major topic in history. They provide both a narrative of events and a critical analysis of contemporary interpretations. They include the kinds of tools generally omitted from specialist monographs: a chronology of events, a glossary of terms and brief biographies of 'who's who'. They also include bibliographical essays in order to guide students to the literature on various aspects of the subject. Students and teachers alike will find that the selection of documents will stimulate discussion and offer insight into the raw materials used by historians in their attempt to understand the past.

Clive Emsley and Gordon Martel
Series Editors

To the usual suspects

Contents

PART TWO   DOCUMENTS

Acknowledgements

I must acknowledge John Hiden's part in getting me interested in the League of Nations in the first place, also his helpful comments on an earlier draft of the text. David Smith helped stimulate my interest in Russian history and Gaynor Johnson has taught me a lot about international history between the wars. Patricia Clavin first told me about the UN's Human Security agenda, and I am very grateful that she looked over the sections of the book dealing with economics. Bernhardine Pejovic (formerly of the United Nations Library, Geneva) introduced me to the work of Fridtjof Nansen. Naturally I am happy to recognise the assistance of all her colleagues in the archive – including Jacques Oberson for his helping identify some of the images used here. The staff at the British Library, Boston Spa were very helpful when it came to tracking down old League of Nations reports; the holdings at the J.B. Priestley Library at the University of Bradford were often invaluable; and the National Media Museum in Bradford must be acknowledged for letting me see its fine collection of inter-war photographs. Thanks are also due to Pearson Education, in particular to Christina Wipf Perry, for having faith in this project and to the series editor, Gordon Martel, for his helpful comments. The British Academy funded much of the research that stands behind this book. Obviously the errors in the text are my responsibility alone.

And, of course, I must not forget the usual suspects: Gillian, Patrick and Alexander. Without their support, nothing would ever get done.

Martyn Housden, Penistone, 2011

Publisher's acknowledgements

We are grateful to the following for permission to reproduce copyright material:

Plates 1, 2, 3, 5, 7 and 8 courtesy of UNOG Library, League of Nations Archives; Plate 4 © Mary Evans Picture Library/Alamy; Plate 6 courtesy of the National Media Museum/SSPL.

In some instances we have been unable to obtain copyright permission, and we would appreciate any information that would enable us to do so.

Chronology

A detailed timeline about the League of Nations is hosted by Indiana University. The web address is www.indiana.edu/~league/timeline.htm. An extended timeline is also available in A.H.M. van Ginneken, *Historical Dictionary of the League of Nations* (Lanham, MD: Scarecrow Press, 2006).

1919

January Paris Peace Conference opens.

April The conference adopts the Covenant of the League of Nations.
Sir Eric Drummond becomes the first Secretary General.
The Secretariat of the League begins working in Sunderland House, London.

June The Covenant is signed as part of the Treaty of Versailles.

1920

January The Treaty of Versailles enters into force, as does the Covenant.
Official opening of the League of Nations.
First session of the Council of the League.

February League begins to administer Danzig (Gdańsk).
Council accepts responsibility for protecting national minorities.
International administration of the Saar is established.

March US Senate rejects the Treaty of Versailles.

April The Council of the League turns to Fridtjof Nansen to repatriate POWs.

June Britain refers the Åland case to the Council.

October Polish General Zeligowski occupies Vilnius, sparking the dispute with Lithuania.

November League of Nations transfers from London to Geneva.
Danzig declared a free city under League administration.
The First Assembly begins sitting.

1921

June   The Council decides the Åland Islands remain part of Finland.

August   Fridtjof Nansen becomes High Commissioner for Russian Refugees.

September   The Permanent Court of International Justice is created.

1922

March   Health conference in Warsaw addressing the typhus epidemic.

September   The Third Assembly establishes the Health Committee.
Waves of refugees begin arriving in Greece from Turkey.

November   Lausanne Conference opens.

1923

January   Lithuania occupies Memel (Klaipeda).

March   Conference of Ambassadors recognises that Vilnius is part of Poland.

July   Lausanne Conference yields the Lausanne Treaty.

Aug.–Sept.   Italian occupation of Corfu.

1924

March   Convention on Memel is accepted by Lithuania and the Allied Powers.

August   Mosul question referred to the Council.

September   Protocol for the Pacific Settlement of International Disputes is placed
before the Assembly.

1925

January   Convention agreed on Opium and Other Dangerous Drugs.

October   Greek troops invade Bulgaria.

December   Greco-Bulgarian dispute settled.
Mosul question settled.

1926

May   Preparatory Disarmament Commission meets for the first time.

September   Anti-slavery convention adopted.
Germany admitted to the League as a permanent member of the Council.

1927

May   International economics conference in Geneva attended by 50 states.

September   General Act for the Pacific Settlement of International Disputes is agreed
by the Assembly.

1928

August   Kellogg–Briand Pact signed.

1929

October   Wall Street crash.

1930

Feb.–March   International economics conference.

November   International economics conference.

1931

September   Explosion on the railway at Mukden; Japanese hostilities begin in Manchuria.

1932

January   Lord Lytton is chosen to head the commission investigating events in Manchuria.
               Manchuria is declared an independent state, Manchukuo.
               Japanese attack on Shanghai.

February   World Disarmament Conference opens.

July   Turkey joins the League of Nations.
               Germany leaves the disarmament conference temporarily.

September   Lytton report is completed.

1933

January   Hitler becomes Reich Chancellor in Germany.

February   World Disarmament Conference reopens.
               The Assembly accepts the Lytton report.

March   Japan announces her decision to leave the League.
               Agreement signed in Geneva ending dispute between Peru and Colombia.

May   Chaco war between Bolivia and Paraguay.

June   Sir Eric Drummond resigns as Secretary General.

July   Joseph Avenol becomes Secretary General.

October   Germany withdraws from the World Disarmament Conference.

1934

September   USSR joins the League.

December   Wal-Wal incident involving Italy and Abyssinia (Ethiopia).

1935

January   Plebiscite in the Saar leads to its reincorporation into Germany.

March   Hitler announces the reintroduction of conscription.

October   Italy invades Abyssinia.
            Sanctions conference meets to discuss Italy; imposition of sanctions.

1936

May   Mussolini proclaims sovereignty over Abyssinia.

June   Haile Selassie, Emperor of Abyssinia, travels to Geneva to address the Assembly.

1939

December USSR excluded as member of the League, having invaded Poland and Finland.

1940

August   Joseph Avenol stands down as Secretary General. Sean Lester starts acting as his successor.

1944

Nov.–Dec. Charter of the United Nations drafted at the Tehran Conference.

1945

November First meeting of the United Nations Educational, Scientific and Cultural Conference (UNESCO).

1946

January   United Nations General Assembly opens in London.

April   Winding up of the League of Nations.

Who's who

Avenol, Joseph (1879–1952): With a background as a French banker, was engaged with the League's economic projects during the 1920s. When Drummond resigned, he took over as Secretary General, a post he held until 1940. Like Drummond, Avenol was no high-profile leader, but probably had more of a conservative caste of mind than the Scot. He came to believe that the strength of the League of Nations lay in its social and economic work.

Cecil, Lord Robert (1864–1958): Was Britain's Minister of Blockade during the First World War. Thereafter, he led the British delegation to the Paris Peace Conference and helped draft the Covenant of the League of Nations. At the First Assembly he was not chosen to represent Britain, but was a member of the South African contingent instead. He engaged consistently and strongly with the League, in 1923 becoming British Minister for League Affairs and representing Britain in the Council. He was awarded the Nobel Peace Prize in 1937. His memoirs were published as *A Great Experiment* (London: Jonathan Cape, 1941).

Crowdy, Dame Rachel (1884–1964): Before the First World War worked as a nurse and qualified as a pharmacist. During the conflict, she played a leading role for the Red Cross providing medical assistance to injured troops in France. When the League was set up, she was identified to lead the Social Affairs section, which she did until 1930. She showed a particular interest in health and the illegal trafficking of narcotic drugs. At the time, she was the most senior woman active in the League.

Drummond, Sir Eric (1876–1951): Born into the Scottish aristocracy, worked as a civil servant in the Foreign Office before being appointed Secretary General of the League of Nations in April 1919. The post was given to him after statesmen such as Woodrow Wilson and the Greek premier Eleftherios Venizelos had turned it down. In keeping with his personality, he developed the role as more of an administrative functionary than as high-profile, charismatic leader. He resigned in June 1933.

Madariaga, Salvador de (1886–1978): Spanish diplomat who served as director of the Disarmament Section of the League for a period in the 1920s.

Murray, Gilbert (1866–1957): A classics scholar from Oxford University, he became active in various League of Nations organisations. In 1922 he represented South Africa in the Assembly, as did Robert Cecil.

Ludwik Rajchman (1881–1965): was a medical doctor from Poland who was active in the Epidemics Commission fighting especially typhus in his home country. From 1921 until the end of 1938 he served as Director of the Health Section of the Secretariat.

Nansen, Fridtjof (1861–1930): the Norwegian made his reputation as a polar explorer, although he also travelled in Siberia before the First World War. He was commissioned by the League first to repatriate prisoners of war from Siberia and subsequently to explore how best to deal with Russian refugees. In the latter capacity, in 1921 he became High Commissioner for Russian Refugees. During his career, he also assisted Greek and Armenian refugees, for instance travelling to the Soviet Socialist Republic of Armenia to investigate the possibility of settling homeless Armenians there. He also took an interest in relieving the Russian famine of the early 1920s. His books include *Russia and Peace* (New York: Macmillan, 1924) and *Armenia and the Near East* (New York: Da Capo Press, 1976).

Smuts, Jan (1870–1950): A leading participant in the Boer War, he helped create the Union of South Africa. Having participated in the British War Cabinet during the First World War, he became a member of the British Commonwealth delegation to the Paris Peace Conference. He wrote the famous book, *The League of Nations: A Practical Suggestion* (1918).

Wilson, Woodrow (1856–1924): US President from 1913 to 1921. He took the USA to war in 1916 and championed the idea of a just peace that would benefit all inhabitants of the world. In particular, he wanted the German and Austro-Hungarian Empires to be reconstructed on the basis of self-determination. He formulated his liberal and democratic war aims in the 'Fourteen Points' which were unveiled to Congress on 8 January 1918. At the Paris Peace Conference, he chaired the committee which drafted the Covenant of the League of Nations. He could not, however, persuade the US Senate to approve the Treaty of Versailles and so his country never joined the League of Nations.

Glossary

Arbitration: The method of settling a dispute by negotiation, investigation and compromise rather than force. When faced with a quarrel between states, for instance, the Council of the League of Nations would set up committees to look at the situation in detail, would discuss the issues with representatives from the states involved and would make recommendations on how to proceed without recourse to war.

Assembly of the League of Nations: Established by Article 3 of the Covenant of the League of Nations, this was the organisation's parliament. Member states each sent up to three representatives to sit in the Assembly where they debated the issues of the day. The Assembly met once a year, generally in September.

Balance of power: A traditional technique for trying to keep the peace in the international arena. States arm themselves and create alliances such that the force of weapons and manpower at their disposal at least balances that of their potential enemies. The balance is assumed sufficient to dissuade a potential aggressor from starting a war, particularly for trivial reasons.

Collective security: The idea is founded in the Covenant of the League of Nations, particularly the Articles between 8 and 18. It implies that the peaceful states of the world will combine their forces to counteract aggression wherever it might occur. Ways to do this include moral pressure, economic sanctions and even military intervention.

Conference of Ambassadors: A temporary organisation sitting in Paris in the early 1920s and consisting of ambassadors from France, Britain, Italy, Japan and the USA. It was created by the Supreme Council in the wake of the First World War and addressed especially undecided matters arising out of the peace treaties.

Council of the League of Nations: Established in Article 4 of the Covenant of the League of Nations, this was the main decision-making and executive body of the organisation. Its permanent members initially were Britain, France, Italy and Japan. These were supplemented by the same number of temporary members. In later years, the membership of the Council was reformed and expanded. So Germany, for instance, when it joined the League, received a permanent seat in the Council. Its decisions were supposed to be made unanimously.

Covenant of the League of Nations: This was the blueprint of the League of Nations. It was part of the Treaty of Versailles, but was included in the other treaties ending the First World War.

Secretariat of the League of Nations: Established by Article 6 of the Covenant of the League of Nations, this was the civil service which supported especially the work of the Council. It had an international staff and was permanently active.

Self-determination: The idea that different national groups should be able to govern themselves – that they should be able to determine their own fate. The idea became popular with statesmen such as Woodrow Wilson during the First World War as it could help justify the fight against imperial powers like Germany and Austria-Hungary. It meant the Allies could promise that Poles in Germany or Czechs in Austria-Hungary would be allowed to establish their own nation states and govern themselves once the Allies were victorious. The idea, of course, was an over-simplification because the geographical distribution of national populations in Central and Eastern Europe was so complicated that it was quite impossible to form 'pure' nation states. This reality did not prevent the aim being popular, however.

Supreme Council: This was set up at the Paris Peace Conference and comprised the leaders of the main Allied Powers – USA, France, Britain and Italy. It was the ultimate body deciding international political questions immediately after the First World War.

Part 1

ANALYSIS

Introduction

Organising the Peace of the World

Despite only ever having a limited budget, the League of Nations became a massive, complicated organisation. Amongst other things, it sought to facilitate intellectual co-operation around the world, promoted good health globally, did its best to ensure freedom of transport wherever you wanted to go, helped provide the basis of international law, and (drawing on immense international expertise) tried to orchestrate a response to the Great Depression. In the first instance, however, it was a security organisation supposed to prevent anything like 1914 happening again.

One of the best-known phrases applied to the League of Nations is '**collective security**'. The words, apparently, were first used in 1924 by Czech statesman Eduard Beneš (1884–1948) while he was working on the Geneva Protocol (see Chapter 6). In particular Beneš was building on Article 8 of the **Covenant of the League of Nations** which committed the League's members to 'the enforcement by common action of international obligations' (Archive 0.1). Other articles, from 10 to 18, explained the mechanisms by which this would be achieved, that is to say, by discussion, **arbitration**, economic persuasion and perhaps even military intervention. But one idea stood out in collective security: that the peacefully inclined members of the League of Nations would work together to stop war wherever it looked likely to occur.

When conceived narrowly, therefore, 'collective security' included the following elements:

- public debate in the Council and the Assembly of actions carried out by statesmen;
- arbitration of disputes organised by the Council of the League;
- economic sanctions against an aggressor state;
- the possible supply of military units by members to stop war.

In truth, however, there was far more to the League of Nations' security agenda than this. Other strategies it used to try to prevent war included:

Collective security: The idea is founded in the Covenant of the League of Nations, particularly the Articles between 8 and 18. It implies that the peaceful states of the world will combine their forces to counteract aggression wherever it might occur. Ways to do this include moral pressure, economic sanctions and even military intervention.

Covenant of the League of Nations: This was the blueprint of the League of Nations. It was part of the Treaty of Versailles, but was included in the other treaties ending the First World War.

Arbitration: The method of settling a dispute by negotiation, investigation and compromise rather than force. When faced with a quarrel between states, for instance, the Council of the League of Nations would set up committees to look at the situation in detail, would discuss the issues with representatives from the states involved and would make recommendations on how to proceed without recourse to war.

- referring an international legal dispute to the Permanent Court of International Justice;
- the pursuit of disarmament;
- guaranteeing the rights of national minorities in new and enlarged states;
- the independent international administration of territories which posed particular security problems;
- removing the causes of instability and war through humanitarian action, for instance managing refugees;
- removing the causes of instability and war through international social and economic initiatives;
- promoting international harmony by fostering a spirit of co-operation and fellow feeling among states.

On balance, the League's work which related to its wider security mission is discussed much less in history books than the high politics revolving around the classic events of 'collective security'. Of course there are good reasons for this. The Manchurian and Abyssinian (Ethiopian) crises were critically important world events, and the way collective security was applied to them (deficiently in both cases) is part of the established narrative of the confrontation between democracy and dictatorship in the inter-war period. One of the purposes of this book, however, is to look beyond these certainties and to propose a wider appreciation of the humanitarian, social and economic initiatives which the League sponsored – including an explanation of how these constituted security work in their own right. By the late 1930s, in fact, within the League itself this wider security agenda was regarded as centrally important for the future (see Chapter 6).

Unsurprisingly, therefore, in the 1920s and 1930s some voices preferred not to speak of 'collective security' as the main focus of the League of Nations. The phrase was too narrow and failed to suggest the ultimate aim of eradicating violence completely from international politics (Bourquin, 1936: 10). Instead, some people preferred to talk of 'the organisation of peace' (*League of Nations*, 1930: 49; Rappard, 1931: 69). This highlighted the idea that the League would not just address international disputes as they arose, rather it would manage the world in such a way that disputes became unlikely at all. Humanitarian ventures, as well as progressive social and economic initiatives, were interpreted as ways to achieve this end. Hence the title this book is *The League of Nations and the Organisation of Peace*.

The League of Nations was a reaction against the suffering and waste of the First World War. As such, it was both building on foundations established by figures from previous periods and laying the basis for something we take for granted today: a rough sense of global community based on the idea that no state can exist in isolation. Given the complexity of the League's work, obviously a short introductory study cannot cover every aspect of what it did. Unfortunately here we will not be able to touch on, say, disputes which the League mediated in Latin America or the detail of its administration in the Saar and Danzig (today Gdańsk). Despite such gaps, this book will show why the history of an organisation that disbanded in 1946 is still of vital interest.

Its efforts to create international stability in ways that were more creative than military force or the **balance of power** are still relevant to the twenty-first century. It had to grapple with globalisation – another topic relevant today. And the text will highlight a number of names which deserve to be better known by students of the inter-war period. Lord Robert Cecil (1864–1958) helped draft the Covenant of the League of Nations and was active in Geneva as a representative of both South Africa and Great Britain. Time and again he spoke out for moral behaviour in international politics. Dame Rachel Crowdy (1884–1964) was the senior woman in the League during the 1920s and took a special interest in both health affairs and illegal traffic in drugs. Ludwik Rajchman (1881–1965) did sterling work in pursuit of a global health system. And we cannot overlook Fridtjof Nansen (1861–1930), the former polar explorer who worked tirelessly on behalf of refugees. The lives of these people begin to open up an alternative way of looking at the inter-war period: as an era of optimism that believed in the human potential to make the world a better place.

This book begins by describing the key characteristics of the League and its most notable historiographical controversy: was it a success or failure? It moves on in the second chapter to look at the organisation's roots and how it grew out of the First World War. The third chapter deals with the international disputes the League mediated during the 1920s, supplemented by its protection of national minorities in central and eastern Europe – which was a major security concern of the time. Next we discuss the League's more general security work, first by looking at its humanitarian projects involving refugees and then in terms of its social and economic projects. Finally we examine the marginalisation of the League during the 1930s as a result of the collapse of its disarmament conference and its deficient responses to the crises in Manchuria and Abyssinia. In the conclusion we ask: 'Where does this story leave our assessment of the League of Nations now?'

Balance of power: A traditional technique for trying to keep the peace in the international arena. States arm themselves and create alliances such that the force of weapons and manpower at their disposal at least balances that of their potential enemies. The balance is assumed sufficient to dissuade a potential aggressor from starting a war, particularly for trivial reasons.

1

What was the League of Nations?

WHAT WAS THE LEAGUE OF NATIONS AND WHY STUDY IT TODAY?

The League of Nations was an ambitious venture aiming to capitalise on some of the best possibilities of mankind. According to Sir Eric Drummond, the first Secretary General, it involved 'the creation of permanent institutions and the building up of a system of international co-operation, permanently to maintain the peace of the world' (Barros, 1965: 312). Lord Robert Cecil, an early champion of the League and Nobel Prize winner in 1937, believed (sometimes at least) the goal could be achieved by 'moral force' alone (*New York Times*, 15.1.1919). For individuals such as these, the League of Nations was the first institution which would have a truly global membership and which would organise global peace comprehensively for the long term.

Secretariat of the League of Nations: Established by Article 6 of the Covenant of the League of Nations, this was the civil service which supported especially the work of the Council. It had an international staff and was permanently active.

A book published by the **Secretariat of the League of Nations** in 1930 talked explicitly about 'the organisation of peace' (*League of Nations*, 1930: ch. 2). As such, it reflected a widespread belief that international disorganisation, including chaotic competition among nations, had been a major cause of war in 1914 (Sweetser, 1943a: 149). The League was supposed to replace hostile competition for individual power with constructive and friendly co-operation. To this end, the League was not just an organisation supposed to fight the fires of conflict as they broke out, or threatened to do so; it was supposed to promote peaceful international conditions so advantageous to people that their governments would be unwilling to throw them away. And if any given statesman did seem ready to provoke war, he would face a phalanx of politicians and peoples prepared to make sacrifices to stop him.

The League of Nations attempted to address the traditional security areas of military competition between states, diplomatic relations, alliance-building and the peaceful settlement of international disputes by negotiation; but it also aimed to remove the very causes of war by promoting social and economic justice among its members, and by addressing the needs of vulnerable people. This latter approach corresponds to a very modern idea of security, one which in some respects anticipated the UN's 'Human Security' agenda of 2003 [**Doc. 1, p. 116**]. In a sense, therefore, the League of Nations was eighty years ahead of its time. It presupposed that the harder nations worked together to address humanitarian, social and economic issues, the more likely they were to establish mutual interests and habits of partnership which would provide a bulwark against future conflict (Jones and Sherman, 1927: 140). In his memoirs, Robert Cecil maintained that although the League of Nations ultimately failed to keep the peace in Europe, its social and economic work was 'extensive and successful' (Cecil, 1941: 321).

As it examines how the League of Nations went about its work, this book will show that exciting stories and charismatic individuals are not (as the history of the twentieth century too often seems to suggest) the sole preserve of dictatorships and the battlefield. During its life, the League of Nations witnessed moments of high drama – such as Haile Selassie arriving to give a speech in Geneva as Abyssinia (Ethiopia) was being annexed by Italy – and dealt with issues of life-and-death importance to ordinary people. Obviously crises relating to war are an important part of the picture, but the League also dealt with fascinating, purposeful and life-affirming issues such as the management of refugees, the fight against infectious diseases, the abolition of slavery and people trafficking, and the campaign to stop opium abuse. The study will highlight some of the adventures that went along with the League's humanitarian enterprise. For instance, we will see how Fridtjof Nansen and his staff saved lives through dramatic actions in the Baltic and Black Sea regions, how medical institutions responded to the infection of millions with typhus, and how some women were 'salvaged' from virtual incarceration in Turkey.

This book will also attempt to show that although the central and eastern parts of Europe were sites of war, revolution and genocide, they were also – from the perspective of the League – laboratories for important humanitarian experiments. Nansen, for example, was the first High Commissioner for Refugees – and his efforts are still commemorated by the annual award of Nansen awards by the United Nations High Commission for Refugees to individuals responsible for outstanding work with vulnerable people. By telling stories such as Nansen's, this introduction to the League of Nations may motivate readers to look more closely at the organisation's good work. There are thousands of boxes of documents barely touched in the Geneva archive, all supplemented by similarly relevant and massive holdings in national archives around the world. In other words, the League of Nations is a fascinating but neglected topic of research. Perhaps for a handful of students at least, this will be a starting point for deeper learning about the League, and ultimately for studies of their own.

A COMPLICATED CHARACTER: SUPER-STATE, COMMONWEALTH, UTOPIA?

At the 1919 Paris Peace Conference, Woodrow Wilson, president of the USA and a major force behind the League of Nations, announced the creation of the organisation with the words 'a living thing is born'. By this he meant the League should be vital and energetic, a body that would get things done rather than become bogged down in interminable meetings and bureaucracy; it had to make an impact in the world – but how could it do this and what sources of power could it rely on? Even those actively engaged in setting up the League did not always agree.

Some tried to interpret the League as a 'super-state' or federation, that is to say a body with extensive powers and direct jurisdiction over its members. Others saw things differently. Robert Cecil, for instance, felt a super-state was unattainable in the early twentieth century because most states would not surrender their national sovereignty, certainly not to the extent necessary if the organisation was to set up, say, an international army (Cecil, 1923: 21). People like Cecil thought the League should be an instrument of voluntary co-operation: a partnership of states relying on discussion to yield decisions and leaving individual members to implement them (Mowrer, 1931: 398–400). As one commentator put it, the difference in the points of view was the same as asking whether the world should be organised centrally or regionally, universally or autonomously, through coercion or collaboration (Sweetser, 1943a: 153–4).

The League relied on its members for its very existence, so it could not take decisions that were too unpopular or they might leave. But if it was to inspire respect, it had to stand for *something* to which all members could commit themselves. This was why French politician Léon Bourgeois said the organisation had to be 'a third way'. So although the League was not supposed to become a super-state which would impinge on the sovereignty of its individual members, nonetheless it had more federalist characteristics than any prior international organisation (Rappard, 1931: 34–5).

The fact that the League could only expect direct orders to be respected by member governments up to a point helps us understand why some League supporters were aware of the importance of public opinion. If the League could convince ordinary people that its vision was correct, a groundswell of popular support might produce pressure on governments to commit more firmly to the organisation. This is why early theorists of the League accepted that innumerable tribunals and conferences often based in Geneva were unlikely to deliver peace on their own: whatever institutions the League set up, they had to reach out from Geneva and influence ordinary people as a means to the realisation of global community and fraternity (Woolf, 1916: 83).

This thinking can be seen in the writings of Robert Cecil and Jan Smuts, both of whom also agreed the League had to concern itself with more than security seen from a strictly military point of view. As Cecil put it, the League had to ensure that the 'products essential to the welfare and prosperity of mankind . . . be made available to all', and that peoples unable to defend themselves would not be exploited or oppressed (*New York Times*, 28.12.1918). With people living satisfied, peaceful lives on this basis, Cecil felt it unlikely that they would ever knowingly opt for war – and hence it made sense to assume that public opinion would constitute a force for good in the world [**Doc. 2, p. 116**]. As he once put it: 'What we rely upon is public opinion . . . and if we are wrong about it, then the whole thing is wrong' (Sharp, 1991: 62). Admittedly this emphasis on the feelings of 'the masses' was unpopular with some other League proponents, especially those wanting the organisation to be more of a super-state ruled from the centre. To French President Clemenceau, for instance, history showed that the voice of the people could become 'the voice of the devil' (Sharp, 1991: 62). Cecil, however, remained more optimistic.

Jan Smuts (1870–1950) had fought against Britain in the Boer War (1899–1902), helped establish the Union of South Africa and served in Lloyd George's Imperial War Cabinet before joining the Empire delegation to the Paris Peace Conference (Ginneken, 2006: 172). In late 1918 he wrote one of the most famous pamphlets, *The League of Nations: A Practical Suggestion*, outlining what a League of Nations should be. Smuts wanted the organisation to be an 'ever visible working organ of the great polity of civilisation' which would 'function so strongly in the ordinary peaceful intercourse of States that it becomes irresistible' (Smuts, 1918: 8). It would be founded in 'human ideals, in principles of freedom and equality, and in institutions which will for the future guarantee those principles against wanton assault' (Smuts, 1918: 14). Apart from heading off international tensions as they arose, Smuts believed the organisation had to work to remove the very causes of war – not least by addressing the conditions of life affecting the ordinary masses of the world [**Doc. 3, p. 117**].

A number of early League supporters, including Smuts and Cecil, not to mention the British foreign minister, Lord Curzon, thought one model for the League existed already. Given that the post-war settlement had broken up old empires, creating many atomised nation states in central and eastern Europe, there needed to be an international organisation arching over all of them, just as the British Empire did its member states (Cecil, 1923: 7; Smuts, 1918: 10; *The Times*, 27.6.1918). Not everyone, of course, appreciated the parallel between the League of Nations and the British Empire. Woodrow Wilson's 'Fourteen Points', for instance, spoke of common purpose 'against the Imperialists', but still there was a germ of an idea here which at least members of the British Empire could relate to.

In France, Léon Bourgeois saw things differently. He wanted to create an international community of common interest: a collective of states in which benefit for one would provide benefit for all. Co-operation would bring great advantages: peace, prosperity and social advancement beyond anyone's dreams (*The Times*, 6.9.1919). Under such circumstances, the threat of exclusion from the group would be powerful. The possibility of no longer sharing the advantages conferred by group membership would ensure that everyone adhered to the League's expectations. Robert Cecil appreciated this way of thinking. He agreed that co-operation between states would lead to an ever-greater sense of international community and to benefits all could enjoy (Cecil, 1923: 38). At a time when technology was advancing very rapidly, this vision of the League foresaw that the discoveries made by its most advanced members would be communicated more quickly to those members who needed them.

The League of Nations, then, was not only caught between understanding itself as super-state or partnership, it was also caught between looking to the past or the future. Inspiration in the British Empire, of course, provided a conservative motive for supporting the League: but ideas of developing an international community of common interest were more future-oriented. The latter contradiction helps explain why League supporters considered themselves to be practical and idealistic at one and the same time. They wanted to build on foundations which existed in the world already, but aimed to construct something new and better. They would not have appreciated a chapter about the League entitled 'The Geneva Dream' (Steiner, 2005). As one League official, Salvador de Madariaga, put it:

> We are not cranks. We are no 'enthusiasts'. We are as coldblooded as any political old-hand and as hard-boiled as any financier. We do not advocate the League because it is a religion; we advocate it because it is the only reasonable way to solve a definite problem, the terms of which can be put clearly to every man and woman with senses to observe and sense to judge. We believe that no business man would 'run' his business as the world is run to-day, letting every one of its departments steal a march on every other one, allowing them to work in utter lack of co-operation in a spirit of enmity and distrust. We do not advocate holiness. We advocate sense.
>
> (Greaves, 1931: 16)

League advocate Leonard Woolf believed that 'utopias' had to be consigned to the libraries (Woolf, 1916: 8). Smuts denied the League was 'Utopian' (Smuts, 1918: 7). Léon Bourgeois said, 'We are not dreamers of Peace. We mean to realize Peace' (*The Times*, 6.9.1919). To minds like these, the creation of an organisation of international unity was the only practical way to respond to the most pressing global issues of the day.

THE COVENANT OF THE LEAGUE OF NATIONS

The main principles of the League of Nations were laid down in the Covenant which was agreed at the Paris Peace Conference in 1919. Given that the document was produced by a committee, and that different people had different ideas about what the organisation should be, naturally it was a compromise. Unsurprisingly, it had imperfections and loopholes (not least, it omitted French demands that the organisation have an international army), but the Covenant marks the start of the story of the League of Nations.

The Covenant was divided into 26 articles. The first defined the conditions of membership, admission and withdrawal. The next group was also organisational, since Articles 2 to 5 defined the character and powers of the League's **Council** and **Assembly**. Articles 6 and 7 created the post of Secretary General and established a staff, the foundations for funding and set up the headquarters. The serious business of the organisation was taken up in Articles 8 and 9 which committed members to promote disarmament to the lowest levels commensurate with national security; but the stipulations which followed were, arguably, more important still.

Article 10 demanded respect for the territorial integrity of member states and promised protection by the League membership as a whole in the face of aggression, while Article 11 enabled any member to ask the Council for assistance if it feared attack. Articles 12 to 15 outlined acceptable ways by which League members could settle disputes, namely by having the issue investigated and discussed by the Council or Assembly, by placing it before an international court, or going to an additional form of arbitration. Members also pledged not to go to war until three months had passed from the date at which a dispute was brought to the League's attention. This delay, incidentally, was supposed to provide an opportunity for 'public opinion, properly organised and properly applied' to be heard, leading to the settlement of the dispute without violence (Cecil, 1923: 28–30). Through Articles 16 and 17, members agreed to take prompt action against anyone (i.e. member or non-member of the League) going to war in violation of Article 16. They could be asked to break all economic links with a transgressor, or perhaps to take appropriate military action.

In an attempt to make diplomacy more honourable and open, Article 18 demanded that, in future, all treaties signed by a state be sent to the Secretary General who would make them public. Article 19 empowered the Assembly

Assembly of the League of Nations: Established by Article 3 of the Covenant of the League of Nations, this was the organisation's parliament. Member states each sent up to three representatives to sit in the Assembly where they debated the issues of the day. The Assembly met once a year, generally in September.

Council of the League of Nations: Established in Article 4 of the Covenant of the League of Nations, this was the main decision-making and executive body of the organisation. Its permanent members initially were Britain, France, Italy and Japan. These were supplemented by the same number of temporary members. In later years, the membership of the Council was reformed and expanded. So Germany, for instance, when it joined the League, received a permanent seat in the Council. Its decisions were supposed to be made unanimously.

to recommend changes to the treaties and Article 20 said that treaties at variance with the Covenant could be abrogated at once.

More specifically, Article 21 specified that the Covenant was not at variance with the Monroe Doctrine, i.e. the idea, dating back to the early nineteenth century, that external Powers (especially European ones) should not interfere in the Americas' internal affairs. Article 22 established the mandates system, whereby formerly colonial lands of Turkey and Germany could be allowed differing degrees of autonomy under international supervision.

Social and economic affairs appeared in Article 23 which specified that the League would promote progressive ends in related areas. Article 24 continued in this vein, stating that already-existing international organisations (many of which dealt with relevant social issues) would henceforth be brought under the League's umbrella; meanwhile, in Article 25, member states promised to promote the activities of the Red Cross, and to act to prevent disease and in the 'mitigation of suffering throughout the world'. Finally, Article 26 outlined how the Covenant could be amended [**Doc. 4, p. 118**].

STRUCTURE OF THE ORGANISATION

Central to the implementation of the Covenant were the three key organisational bodies established in the League. These were the Council, the Assembly and the Secretariat.

The Council

The Council was arguably the most important institution of all. It was the small executive body responsible for supervising the implementation of the Covenant and dealing with any international disputes as they arose. It was to do this by agreeing to a course of action based on a unanimous decision.

The Treaty of Versailles and the Covenant of the League of Nations came into force on 10 January 1920, and the Council first met in Paris just six days later. Its membership was supposed to include the five victorious Great Powers, but when the US Senate refused to ratify the Treaty, the number was reduced to four (Britain, France, Italy and Japan). In addition, the Council had four non-permanent members who were elected by a two-thirds vote of the Assembly. Initially these were Belgium, Brazil, Greece and Spain. In 1922 the number of non-permanent members was increased to six, but the composition was overhauled more drastically still in 1926 when Germany was given a permanent seat and two semi-permanent seats were created for Spain and Poland. In 1933 Germany left the League, but the Soviet Union became a member of the Council the next year. At first the Council held four main sessions a year, but these were decreased to three as of 1929. It met for the last time on 14 December 1939 (Ginneken, 2006: 64–5; *Aims, Methods and Activity*, 1935: 32–4).

The Council had numerous important responsibilities. Under Article 11 of the Covenant, it was the body to which states appealed if they became involved in a serious international dispute, and as such it was expected to provide arbitration. In addition, it was responsible for setting up committees to address the affairs of national minorities, it supervised the work of various technical committees and it took an interest in the administration of mandate territories (see p. 86).

The Assembly

The Assembly was a kind of international parliament. Each member state sent three representatives to sit in it. In all, there were 42 member states in 1920 and 55 in 1927. Across the history of the organisation, some 63 states belonged to the League at one time or another and so were represented in the Assembly (Ginneken, 2006: 38).

As with the Council, major decisions had to be reached unanimously, but in the Assembly everyone was equal (i.e. there was no distinction between permanent and non-permanent members). Hence there was a kind of balance struck between the needs of the Great Powers which were guaranteed in the Council (by their permanent seats and disproportionate numbers), and the needs of the other states which could be pursued in the Assembly (where all were present on the same footing). Also there was a balance between the small body which was more effective when it came to getting things done (the Council), and the forum underlining that the League should really be about the participation of all (the Assembly) (Mowrer, 1931: 387).

The Assembly's agenda was drawn up, in the first instance, by the Secretary General, although it could revise the list of issues it wanted to discuss so long as two-thirds of the house agreed. Although the Assembly met only once a year, it was nonetheless a powerful institution. Not only could it elect the non-permanent members of the Council and admit new members, but it could debate the most urgent issues of the day. As a result, the Assembly's proceedings always aroused the interest of the world's press – even of states which were not League members. Consequently words uttered by Assembly members really were heard by a global audience. Robert Cecil rightly described the Assembly's first meeting on 15 November 1920 as a 'turning point' for the League (*New York Times*, 15.11.1920). What happened in the Assembly was supposed to be an important source of moral pressure on statesmen in general.

A number of committees were attached to the Assembly. They dealt with the organisation of the League, economic, social and technical issues, international justice, budget and staffing, the admission of new members, and political questions.

The Secretariat and Secretary General

The Secretariat of the League of Nations was something completely new. Initially based in Sunderland House, London, before moving to Geneva, it was an international civil service – a collection of about 700 officials drawn from different countries who served and facilitated the work of the Council, Assembly and the League's manifold committees and technical sections. Never before had such a body of people been drawn together – a group supposed to owe loyalty to no specific state, but to an international governmental organisation. Furthermore, because the Secretariat was at work all year round, it gave the League of Nations a continuous existence – the international civil servants were always in Geneva, even when the Council and Assembly were not in session.

The Secretary General was chief of the Secretariat. He appointed the staff and oversaw their work. Initially it was hoped that the post of Secretary General would be held by a major statesman who would provide a substantial and motivational figurehead for the League. As it turned out, first Woodrow Wilson and then Greek Prime Minister Venizelos turned down the post and so it fell to Sir Eric Drummond (1876–1951) (Plate 1). He was a British career diplomat and 15th Earl of Perth who had a very cautious, low-key personality and who did not really intervene directly in Council or Assembly initiatives. He resigned at the end of June 1933, handing over to Frenchman Joseph Avenol (1879–1952) who, although more obviously conservative than Drummond, was equally uncharismatic. He held the post until August 1940, when long-time League official and Irishman Sean Lester (1888–1958) took over until the organisation was finally wound up on 18 April 1946.

So, although the post of Secretary General sounded grand, its main incumbents at most hoped to influence international affairs in relatively subtle ways. Rather than seek publicity personally and put forward clear lines of policy, they tried to work behind the scenes and encouraged others to solve problems in their own ways.

The most senior woman in the League of Nations, initially at least, was a Briton called Dame Rachel Crowdy (1884–1964) (Plate 2). She was trained as a nurse and had served in the Red Cross during the First World War. During the first decade of the League she headed the Committee on Social Affairs and Opium.

The organisation and its cost

One author likened the structure of the League to a car. The Council was the steering wheel; the Assembly was the fly-wheel regulating the internal speed of the whole device; the committees and technical bodies were like the cylinders and pistons working away steadily; the Secretariat was the crankshaft connecting the motor to the wheels and making them turn; specialist bodies, such as the Minorities Section, were likened to shock absorbers dealing with specific problems as they arose; the members of governments were like a collection of actual drivers; while public opinion was the fuel making everything run (Zilliacus, 1929: 14–15). Adherents of the League soon were maintaining that had such an entity existed in 1914, the drift to war would never have happened. The organisation's systems of dealing with conflicts that allowed for delay, investigation, discussion, conference and the opportunity for reconciliation would have permitted the difficulties to be solved peacefully [**Doc. 5, p. 120**].

Perhaps surprisingly, since the League was clearly a complicated organisation with an important contribution to make to international life, it was always run on a shoestring. Between 1921 and 1927 its expenses were just $4 million per year. Britain was the largest contributor of funds, donating about $550,000 per year, while other states contributed what they could – even if it was just a few thousand dollars (Mowrer, 1931: 399). Although some newspaper articles gave the impression that the League was a lavish institution, with staff enjoying a kind of high life in offices which had once been hotel rooms overlooking Lake Geneva (formerly the 'Hotel National' and today 'Palais Wilson'), this was hardly fair (*New York Times*, 3.10.1920) (Plate 3). The staff had to work somewhere, and an organisation demanding the respect of the world could hardly be hidden away in backstreets.

Given such modest funding, as different crises arose, the League had to issue calls for extra resources. Since it took governments a long time to respond, and because sometimes their offers came with strings attached, time and again the League had to rely on charities such as the American Red Cross, Near East Relief and Save the Children to produce quick responses to humanitarian disasters. A contemporary commentator was quite right that without 'the co-operation of voluntary agencies, intergovernmental organisation [i.e. the League] can never proceed very far' (Zimmern, 1936: 8).

HISTORIOGRAPHY: THE LEAGUE AS SUCCESS OR FAILURE?

The main debate

So how has the League of Nations been treated by historians? Over half a century ago, the former Deputy Secretary General of the League, F.P. Walters was clear that his organisation was worth studying:

> Although the League's span of life was short and troubled, its success transitory, and its end inglorious, it must always hold a place of supreme importance in history. It was the first effective move towards the organization of a world-wide political and social order, in which the common interests of humanity could be seen and served across the barriers of national tradition, racial difference, or geographical separation.
>
> (Walters, 1952: 1)

Not everyone would agree with this assessment. Even early on it was noticeable that the organisation's work divided people passionately into groups 'for' and 'against' it (Alexander, 1924: 9). The literature about the League reflects this division: there is a split between those who see it as a success, and those who regard it as a failure.

A plethora of early texts argued strongly in favour of the League. Many of the authors had personal connections with the organisation and their work sometimes seems almost a semi-official report of what happened in Geneva. Apart from Walters's book, also significant (if older) was *League of Nations: Ten Years of World Co-operation* which was published by the Secretariat in 1930 and provided an almost heroic overview of what the organisation had done in the first decade of its existence. *Problems of Peace* was a series of edited collections of essays published annually by Oxford University Press in which League staff and activists commentated (usually positively) on the most pressing issues facing them. Even as late as the 1940s, Harriet Davis produced a collection of articles, including ones by League staff, emphasising the good work they had achieved during the 1930s. For instance, Arthur Sweetser, of the League's Information Section, and James McDonald, a former High Commissioner for Refugees coming from Germany, both made contributions (McDonald, 1944; Sweetser, 1944).

Like Walters, other participants in the League wrote full-length studies. C.A. Macartney was a historian and League activist who wrote in praise of its treatment of refugees (Macartney, 1930). Fridtjof Nansen was High Commissioner for Russian Refugees and published a number of books, not least a study of the planned settlement of Armenian refugees to the desert around

Yerevan in the Armenian Soviet Socialist Republic (Nansen, 1976). His collaborators, such as T.F. Johnson and Philip Noel Baker, added to the literature (Johnson, 1938; Noel Baker, e.g. 1926). William Rappard worked on mandates issues, but subsequently publicised the work of the League more generally too (Rappard, 1931).

This extensive praise was, however, quickly balanced by much more critical voices. A text, written by a number of authors who published under the name 'Vigilantes', came out soon after the Abyssinia crisis. It carried the title *Why the League has Failed* and argued that the organisation needed to be re-invigorated through greater work with the Soviet Union (Vigilantes, 1938: 91). The journalist Robert Dell was less overtly political in his critique. For many years he had commentated on events in Geneva, and not long after the outbreak of the Second World War wrote *The Geneva Racket*. This attempted to expose everything corrupt about the organisation. From an early point he was 'cynical' about this 'fraudulent institution' which betrayed public confidence. It was a centre of 'international intrigues' and displayed a childish attitude towards politics (Dell, 1941: 7–8). He went on:

It is by its success or lack of success in achieving its ends for which it was primarily created that the League of Nations must be judged and, judged by that test it must be held to have failed . . . It has failed in every important case in which a Great Power was directly or indirectly interested.

(Dell, 1941: 25)

To Dell's mind, the organisation had failed to challenge the primacy of national sovereignties, had exhibited systematic bias towards Europe over the rest of the world, failed to treat all states equally and, of course, failed to prevent the outbreak of the Second World War [**Doc. 6, p. 122**].

Critical opinion did not disappear with the passage of time. In 1975 Elmer Bendiner repeated Dell's accusation that the League was insubstantial to the point of deceit, saying that the 'Assembly ran on words. Many of them without consequence, but uttered grandly and solemnly for the record or for a constituency' (Bendiner, 1975: 171). He added criticisms that the League was not adequately democratic and that the inhabitants of some mandate territories were treated like children (Bendiner, 1975: 96).

Starting to balance the views

The two sides of a debate such as this have to be balanced. During the inter-war period, the League of Nations was generally treated by statesmen as only one organisation in the very complicated arena of international relations. As such, it remained a supplement to, rather than a complete replacement for, traditional diplomacy as pursued by the Great Powers – hence what it could achieve would always be limited (Steiner, 2005: 349). By necessity, it was also liable to be affected, either beneficially or detrimentally, by developments beyond its immediate sphere of influence (Zimmern, 1936: 284). At the time, in fact, on some occasions at least the public realised this was the case and asked whether a given crisis owed more to the League or the actions of national statesmen (Zilliacus, 1929: 15).

In the end, as the analogy with the car suggested, the League was a mechanism that always needed the active involvement of national politicians to give it direction and purpose. They had to participate in the organisation and help turn the idea of international fraternity into reality. But, as a British commentary on the Covenant of the League of Nations said, there was no necessity they would do so:

> If the nations of the future . . . are in the main selfish, grasping and war-like, no instrument of machinery will restrain them. It is only possible to establish an organisation which may make peaceful co-operation easy and hence customary, and to trust in the influence of custom to mould opinion.
>
> (Northedge, 1988: 54)

Under the circumstances, it was logical that politicians and commentators found there could be no foolproof guarantee of peace. Lord Grey, Britain's foreign minister in 1914, believed no organisation could provide complete security (*The Times*, 11.10.1918). Lord Curzon, Britain's representative at the first meeting of the Council, agreed that choosing war could be made more 'risky', but that the possibility of war could never be eliminated entirely (*The Times*, 27.6.1918). Even League stalwart Philip Noel Baker wondered if the organisation would have time to establish itself before war swept it away (Noel Baker, 1926: 129).

In other words, a final assessment of the success and failure of the League will have to be realistic. It will have to locate the organisation in the context of inter-war international relations and recognise its intrinsic limitations.

CONCLUSION

The League of Nations was a highly ambitious undertaking, but was neither perfect nor perfected. It was always a compromise between a model of a super-state and a model of a loose association of nations. It was a mixture of conservatism and idealism. The League sought to apply its best intentions in practical ways. It tried to balance the needs of Great Powers against those of small states. It was neither universal, nor the sole means of conducting international relations. With a meaningful lifespan of barely twenty years, it hardly had time to become a finished product; it was always a work in progress. It did not have time to mature before it faced the most challenging circumstances.

Perhaps the League suffered from coming into existence at a time of flux. A change was under way from a world of states governed by narrow self-interest, to one that was more willing to pursue conciliation and co-operation (Rappard, 1931: 115). As such, it was a time of hope, but of serious challenges too. Nonetheless, while it remains true that the League of Nations was dealt a fatal blow by the outbreak of world war in 1939, its central pre-occupations would live on.

2

How New was the League of Nations?

INTRODUCTION: DISILLUSIONMENT WITH THE BALANCE OF POWER

Prior to 1914, war was a well-established tool of international politics. There was no credible supra-national organisation available to prevent states going to war at any time they chose. Aggressive patriotism enabled political leaders to carry their people with them into a conflict. Under these circumstances, at least some (often British) minds believed peace was maintained by the creation of balances of power, that is to say, states were supposed to make sure that the strength of their armaments, supplemented by those of alliance partners, matched the strength of potential enemies. The threat implicit in such an arrangement was supposed to deter statesmen from military action, particularly if based on trivial or opportunistic grounds. For years before the First World War, the Triple Entente of Britain, France and Russia faced the Triple Alliance of Germany, Austria-Hungary and Italy. Although the reality of the outbreak of war in 1914 proved more complicated than the strict implementation of the Alliance system would have predicted (since, for instance, Italy did not actually fight on the side of the Triple Alliance), nonetheless a perception took hold that once war did start, the alliance system made sure that state after state was pulled into the catastrophe.

The determination to avoid another war like that of 1914–18 led statesmen to consider new methods of keeping the peace. As Lord Bryce put it in summer 1918, they had been at war for four years and did not want to live in the shadow of anything similar happening again (*The Times*, 27.6.1918). This implied a fundamental reappraisal of the concept of the balance of power, as Robert Cecil once explained:

> The Balance of Power was purely negative. It did not aim at improving the common life of nations. It accepted the proposition that every nation was

the potential enemy of every other nation, and it merely sought to limit the consequences of that disastrous assumption.

(Northedge, 1988: 22)

The preferred solution of Cecil and others was to create the League of Nations. But how new was this idea?

DISTANT ORIGINS

Thinkers had long tried to conceptualise how peace could be maintained. Early in the seventeenth century, Émeric Crucé published *The New Cyneas* (1623–24) which recommended the creation of a continuous assembly of ambassadors addressing international tensions as they arose and which would include the states of Europe, Persia, China, Abyssinia, the East and West Indies and Turkey (Hinsley, 1978: 20). In 1638, the memoirs of Maximilien de Béthune, Duke of Sully, described a Grand Design which was only slightly less ambitious. Here, a federation of Christian states would come together in a kind of European Union. Meanwhile, in *The Rights of War and Peace* (1625), Dutch jurist Hugo Grotius (1583–1645) sought to differentiate just from unjust conflicts, and maintained it was better to solve international problems through arbitration (or even drawing lots!) than by force.

A few decades later William Penn (1644–1718), the Quaker libertarian and founder of Pennsylvania province, wrote his *Essay towards the Present and Future Peace of Europe* (1693). He proposed creating a European assembly in which statesmen could meet to resolve their disputes peacefully. Benefits, he felt, would include a more effective use of money, ease of travel, less spilling of Christian blood and greater security against Turkish aggression (Jones and Sherman, 1927: 37, 46–8; Walters, 1952: 5–6).

Early in the next century Abbé de Saint-Pierre, Marquis of Normandy (1658–1743), published the *Project for Perpetual Peace in Europe* (1712–13). Apart from favouring constitutional monarchy, equitable taxation and education for all, the Abbé recommended founding a union of European monarchs. There would be a chamber of commerce ensuring fair trade, an international senate in a city of peace, and action taken against any monarch who threatened to breach the tranquillity of the world. Saint-Pierre's work influenced Jean-Jacques Rousseau (1712–1778) who, in *A Lasting Peace* (1761), foresaw a permanent international congress guaranteeing the territories of its members and able to take common action against any state threatening war.

Although the British philosopher Jeremy Bentham (1748–1832) also theorised about an international body managing relations between states, the inspirational German thinker Immanuel Kant (1724–1804) is the most frequently cited source of ideas about international peace. His essay *On Eternal Peace* (1795) argued that relations between European states were anarchic and that the balance of power could not solve the problem. Consequently he offered a new set of principles to govern international relations. For instance, treaties should be completely public and lacking in secret clauses. An independent state should never be annexed by any other, and no state should ever try to interfere in the domestic affairs of another. There should be no permanent armies and, if states did go to war, they should refrain from actions that would make it impossible to trust each other in the future. To all of this, Kant added that the chances of peace would be best if every state in the world was a republic, if an international 'law of nations' was created along with a 'federation of free states' to supervise it, and if people acted towards each other according to principles of 'universal hospitality' (Jones and Sherman, 1927: 49–52; Mowrer, 1931: 364; Rappard, 1931: 16–19).

In other words, for centuries thinkers had agreed on a number of points related to the idea of a League of Nations. There was a longstanding desire to create an international body to replace international chaos, with relations based on predictability and law. Following the rules was expected to maintain peace, but if the status quo were threatened, the united weight of all members of the organised international community could be brought to bear. Those working in Geneva in the 1920s would have recognised all of this, but the foundations of the League also existed beyond the pages of philosophy books.

NINETEENTH CENTURY: THE CONCERT OF EUROPE AND ARBITRATION

The Concert of Europe

During the nineteenth century, various practical developments occurred that supported international peace initiatives. With contacts between states multiplying across the century, steps had to be taken to reduce the risk of inevitable international disagreements leading to war. So, for example, the number of bilateral and multilateral agreements between states grew and the states met with increasing frequency in conferences.

The Concert of Europe was formed by virtue of the Congress of Vienna (1814–15). With the continent coming to terms with the heritage of the Napoleonic Wars, it aimed to maintain existing governments, territorial borders and the status quo more generally. Initially its core members belonged to the Quadruple Alliance, namely Britain, Prussia, Austria and Russia, with France expanding the group in 1818. Its peace function involved the members meeting for negotiations, should any dispute threaten to disturb the continent. The Concert met on about thirty separate occasions across the nineteenth century but only really functioned effectively for a couple of decades after its inception. In any case, its workings have been called 'slow, cumbrous and uncertain'. Symptomatic of its imperfections, no state had a clear right to call a meeting of the Concert, it had no clear rules of procedure and imposed no definitive obligations on its members (Walters, 1952: 9). Moreover, the Concert had no permanent existence – that is to say, when it was not in conference, there was no representative body which kept working away in the background. Understandably, then, it has been termed 'too often merely a machine at rest' (*Aims, Methods and Activity*, 1935: 15). So, although to some extent it managed to limit the consequences of the disintegration of the Ottoman Empire, it was not convened before the wars between Germany and Denmark (1864), Austria (1866) and France (1870), before the Russo-Japanese War (1904–05) or, most important of all, before the First World War. In the last instance, although British foreign minister Sir Edward Grey did try to convene a conference in 1914 to avert war, he did not suggest it was part of 'the Concert', the meeting would have had only a limited membership and it did not take place anyway, because Germany refused to participate (Northedge, 1988: 24).

The Concert was also hamstrung by the conservatism of the monarchs of the Holy Alliance (i.e. of Russia, Prussia and Austria). Their attitude was particularly unfortunate for a continent experiencing rapid social and economic changes and led to the Concert becoming rather a tool for reaction, for instance combating the growth of popular democracy and national identities. Nonetheless, it did function as an advisory body which, from time to time, formulated opinions on issues of international law and mediated situations where the interests of its members diverged. In this light it has even been called 'a precursor' of the Council of the League of Nations – although, given the nature of some of the monarchs involved, this comment has its limits (*Aims, Methods and Activity*, 1935: 16).

The rise of arbitration

By the late nineteenth century, the Concert of Europe was increasingly marginal to the conduct of international affairs; but as the Concert declined, so an interest in arbitration increased – that is, the settlement of disputes by referring them to impartial adjudication. States increasingly turned to this mechanism to deal with the minor issues of international life. Some 200 disputes were settled by arbitration between 1815 and 1900. As a rule, the terms of the arbitration were implemented quickly and none of the cases treated in this way subsequently became a cause of war. Arbitration became so popular that in 1890 a Pan-American Treaty of Arbitration was signed by 11 American republics, and in 1897 the USA and Britain signed an arbitration treaty (Walters, 1952: 9–10).

The most important development in the field of arbitration grew out of the Hague Peace Conference. This was proposed by Tsar Nicholas II in 1898 to promote disarmament and the peaceful settlement of disputes. When it met the next year, the President of the conference explained why it was becoming important to discover a way to solve disputes peacefully: 'there is a community of material and moral interests between nations, which is constantly increasing . . . If a nation wished to remain isolated it could not . . . It is part of a single organism' (Armstrong *et al.*, 1996: 11). The fact that nations were increasingly becoming financially and economically inter-dependent made it imperative that an alternative to force should become the accepted way of sorting out difficulties. It also implied that aggression by a single player in the international system could damage more than just the direct object of attack. Negative consequences would be felt by other states as well.

The effectiveness of the 1899 conference has, however, been questioned. Its discussions are said to have 'consisted of a curious amalgam of idealistic statements of purpose and careful disavowals by everyone that they were undertaking any binding commitments' (Armstrong *et al.*, 1996: 11). Its agenda was poorly thought out (Zimmern, 1936: 104). Even its creation of a Convention for the Pacific Settlement of International Disputes and a Permanent Court of Arbitration has been interpreted as marginal. Nonetheless, 26 states (including the USA) supported the permanent court and, when a second Hague Conference was convened in 1907, 44 states sent representatives (Jones and Sherman, 1927: 57). Furthermore, the court settled roughly two disputes per year from 1907 to 1914, not to mention the Behring Sea dispute between the USA and Russia over fishing in 1902, and the Dogger Bank incident of 1904 (when Russian warships shelled British trawlers).

Perhaps, however, the last two examples hint at a criticism of the application of arbitration before 1914. It was used for relatively minor issues, certainly not ones of vital interest for those concerned. Consequently, when statesmen gathered at the Paris Peace Conference in 1919, they largely ignored the experiences of the Permanent Court of Arbitration. Instead, too often statesmen reverted to old-fashioned solutions relying on national armaments, alliances and balance of power thinking.

NINETEENTH CENTURY: GLOBALISATION, HUMANITARIANISM, PACIFISM AND NATIONAL MINORITIES

Globalisation

In the nineteenth century the world was drawing closer together and at an accelerating pace – a process now referred to as 'globalisation'. With industry growing rapidly and communications improving, the world's economy was becoming a single unit. The developments only enhanced the possibility of friction between states and implied a growing need for the regulation of many features of international relations. As Jan Smuts put it later:

> All these matters, and many more, are rapidly, unavoidably becoming subjects for international handling. Questions of industry, trade, finance, labour, transit and communications, and many others, are bursting through the national bounds and are clamouring for international solution. Water-tight compartments and partition walls between the nations and the continents have been knocked through, and the new situation calls for world-government.
>
> (Smuts, 1918: 43)

Gradually, new practices began to emerge as administrative bodies began to regulate issues beyond the competence of single states (e.g. concerning international communications) and periodic conferences addressed issues of common interest (e.g. to do with trade and welfare). Some steps were taken to align different countries' laws in a number of fields as well (e.g. regarding the rights of workers) (Woolf, 1916: 102–3).

Many of these developments look mundane. In 1856 the Danube Commission was established to regulate river transport; in 1864, the Universal Postal Union was set up; the International Telegraphic Union followed the next year. Although certainly not dramatic, these steps showed that, in some areas at least, states were prepared to arrange their affairs by international agreement.

Humanitarianism and welfare

As well as practical and economic need, the humanitarian desire to promote common welfare also enhanced international co-operation. The International Committee of the Red Cross (ICRC) grew out of a committee founded in Geneva in 1863 which had Henri Dunant (1828–1910) as its secretary. In time, it grew into an impartial international organisation assisting victims of war and a powerful lobby promoting humanitarian values. Informed by

Dunant's experience of the aftermath of the battle of Solferino (1859), as early as 1864 the committee convened a conference attended by European governments plus the USA, Brazil and Mexico which agreed the Geneva Convention for the Amelioration of the Condition of Wounded in Armies in the Field. The humanitarian agreement was to be applied as widely as possible and marked the start of modern international humanitarian law.

In 1864, the embryonic ICRC sent delegates to care for the wounded in the war between Germany and Denmark. It was also active in the Balkans during the Eastern Crisis of 1875–78, the Serb-Bulgarian War (1885–86) and the Balkan Wars (1912–13). It was an international organisation with global ambitions which accomplished good works in many locations and received international respect and the support of numerous governments.

Slavery also drew an international response. Although national governments had taken steps to stamp out the practice these were inadequate, since demand and supply for slaves were both too widespread. As a result, the Declaration Relative to the Universal Abolition of the Slave Trade was made in 1815 and added to the General Treaty of the Congress of Vienna. It was the first genuinely international condemnation of slavery and encouraged all signatory states to prohibit the practice (Hinks et al., 2006: 186). The resilience of slavery, however, meant that it was still the subject of international agreements decades later. The Treaty of Berlin (1885) was signed by the Great Powers and included Article 9 which banned the slave trade in the Congo basin. Five years later an international conference was held in Brussels that addressed slavery not just in Congo, but also in the region around the east coast of Africa, the Persian Gulf and the Red Sea, and around the Indian Ocean too.

'White slavery', which involved the trafficking of women and children for sexual and domestic exploitation, was the subject of an international conference staged by charitable societies in 1890, and nine years later a congress of interested groups set up an International Bureau for the Suppression of Traffic in Women and Children. In 1902 the French government held another international conference which yielded a convention in 1904 according to which states would exchange information about the problem, watch railway stations for signs of trafficking, repatriate foreign prostitutes and supervise the activities of employment agencies. This was updated in 1910, with the convention now including provision for the punishment of anyone enticing women and girls into prostitution. When the First Conference for the Protection of the Child was held in 1913, 42 states were represented along with large numbers of private organisations (Greaves, 1931: 219–20; Castendyck, 1944: 210).

But just as economic forces, war, slavery and people-trafficking all cut across national borders to cause international problems, so did disease.

Smallpox, tuberculosis, influenza and even sexually transmitted diseases did not recognise a difference in the nationality of a victim, and the intensification of communications and transport around the world increased the opportunities for them to spread over large distances. Consequently they had to be treated internationally.

Health co-operation dated back at least to the first International Sanitary Conference of 1851 which was hosted by the French government and addressed quarantine restrictions to deal with cholera, yellow fever and plague. A whole series of international conferences followed, not least to do with sanitation and maritime transport through the Suez Canal, in the Persian Gulf and along the Danube. An outbreak of plague in 1896 made India the subject of discussion. The eleventh conference, held in Paris in 1903, was attended by 24 different states and led to a codification of all the previous health agreements. In December 1907, an International Health Office was created in Paris to centralise many aspects of health administration and to record relevant information (Greaves, 1931: 85–92; Huber, 2006: 453–76).

Closely related to health was the matter of opium. A product which could be grown in one country, refined in another but consumed in a third, this was regarded as an international problem from early in the twentieth century. A strong anti-opium movement in China led to the convening of a conference in Shanghai in 1909, by which time the USA was administering the Philippines, where there was a drugs problem too, and so it became involved at Shanghai. American concerns helped generate a further conference at The Hague in 1912 which produced the International Opium Convention. This recognised the need to limit opium production according to the requirements of legitimate medical markets and eventually was signed by 40 states.

Pacifism

Not unrelated to the growth of humanitarianism was the gradual increase in the influence of pacifism. Actually 'pacifism' is a surprisingly complicated term which has had various meanings over time. The word was first used in 1901 by Emile Arnaud who applied it to describe a movement to solve conflict through the application of arbitration and mediation. It did not refer to 'conscientious objection' to war as such, and many self-described pacifists believed in the right to apply force as a means to self-defence. Nonetheless, pacifism commonly is associated with one particular group, even if its influence pre-dated the creation of the term.

The Society of Friends (or Quakers) was established in the seventeenth century but their peace-oriented values became influential in the eighteenth and nineteenth centuries. The later period, for instance, saw a number of Quaker businesses in the UK gaining financial success (e.g. Rowntree and

Cadbury), which then funded good works such as prison reform and pro-tests against the death penalty. But Quaker values had implications for the international sphere too. Quakers were responsible for establishing the first Peace Society in New York in 1815 and one in London the following year. Similar organisations followed in Geneva and Paris (Hinsley, 1978: 93). The members 'for the most part followed the Quaker example and condemned all war, even in self-defence against unprovoked attack' (Walters, 1952: 7–11). Soon the different memberships began corresponding and held international conferences. Little by little their values began to percolate through to at least a few circles of government.

The rise of nations and the treatment of national minorities

The nineteenth century also saw the rise of a rather different social force: the idea of the nation. It was apparent in the ideas of philosophers such as Johann Gottfried Herder (1744–1803), who thought membership of a specific linguistic community helped make us what we are. Others, like Alexis de Tocqueville (1805–59) and John Stuart Mill (1806–73), began to agree that a common sense of nationality helped bind society together (Auer, 2004: ch. 1). Nor was the growing appreciation of the nation confined to thinkers: wider social changes were under way which spread a national consciousness among ordinary people (Gellner, 1983; Smith, 2000). These trends began to find political expression in nation-making projects such as the revolutions of 1848, the Italian Risorgimento and, in 1871, the founding of the German Empire.

Self-determination: The idea that different national groups should be able to govern themselves – that they should be able to determine their own fate. The idea became popular with statesmen such as Woodrow Wilson during the First World War as it could help justify the fight against imperial powers like Germany and Austria-Hungary. It meant the Allies could promise that Poles in Germany or Czechs in Austria-Hungary would be allowed to establish their own nation states and govern themselves once the Allies were victorious. The idea, of course, was an over-simplification because the geographical distribution of national populations in Central and Eastern Europe was so complicated that it was quite impossible to form 'pure' nation states. This reality did not prevent the aim being popular, however.

The peacemakers of 1919 were well aware of the growing importance of national identity and accepted the principle of '**self-determination**'. Woodrow Wilson and Jan Smuts believed that national groups should govern themselves. This theory justified the break-up of old empires, such as tsarist Russia and Austria-Hungary, and their replacement by new nation states like Poland, Czechoslovakia, Latvia, Lithuania and Estonia [**Doc. 7, p. 123**].

But the rise of national awareness also enhanced the recognition that not everyone living on a given territory belonged to the same national group. In particular, there were national minorities living among national majorities, and increasingly it was recognised that the former groups sometimes needed special protection. To give examples, we are talking about Poles who lived in Germany, Germans who lived in the Russian Empire or Christian Armenians living among Muslim Turks in the Ottoman Empire. As the nineteenth century progressed (and ideas of nationhood developed), it became increasingly clear that the position of these people was just too sensitive and important to be left to the host state alone. Put simply, ill-treatment of a national minority in one country could lead to an outcry elsewhere and endanger good international relations, perhaps to the point of war.

Consequently, the Congress of Vienna (1815) gave Poles the right to maintain their own national institutions, a stipulation that affected Russia, Austria and Prussia. Sixty years later, the Treaty of San Stefano (1878) included provisions for Armenians to have their communities guaranteed on Ottoman lands (Simpson, 1939: 523). The same year, the Congress of Berlin (1878) recognised that states should act according to a 'standard of civilisation', which included decent treatment of national minorities (Jackson Preece, 1998: ch. 4). Perhaps most important of all, however, the peacemakers of 1919 were well aware that the crisis of July 1914 had begun over minority Serbs living in Austria-Hungary's Balkan territories.

THE LEGACY OF WAR

Introduction

By the start of the twentieth century, most of the prerequisites for a fresh approach to international relations were present. Systems of international conferences had been established, arbitration had been applied voluntarily, economic and technological forces were pulling the world together, humanitarianism and pacifism were fostering ideas of international fraternity, and some national minorities were understood to need international protection. Before 1914, however, these characteristics did not realise their potential because something was still absent from the minds of most statesmen. The dire experiences of the First World War began to fill the gap, as the following extract argues:

> The abstract logic of the situation was clear. In a world of interrelated, inter-dependent states, war is antisocial and intolerable. Therefore, to make war cannot be the unconditioned right of any nation, because peace is vital to the whole community of states. It follows, then, that the community has the right to assure its own well-being by common action, to substitute peaceful measures for the coercion of war, and to back up those measures by force, if need be. This logic was not new, to be sure, but it gained unprecedented emphasis from the World War, which threw the delicate mechanism of international intercourse out of gear, and demonstrated that the nations had outgrown such a method of settling their disputes.
>
> (Mowrer, 1931: 363)

War mobilised the will to make a real change to the practice of international relations.

The idea the League gains currency

It is not certain who first used the term 'League of Nations'. It probably owes something to Léon Bourgeois who published *La Société des Nations* in 1908 (Armstrong *et al.*, 1996: 13). Lowes Dickinson used the phrase in August 1914, but no matter who invented the phrase, the idea of a union of states designed to prevent conflict gained popularity quickly in the opening years of the First World War. Popular anti-war groups sprang up, as politicians, authors and interested citizens everywhere began discussing better ways of organising international life in the future (Henig, 1973: 19).

In the USA, the League to Enforce Peace was set up in June 1915 and later supported the construction of a League of Nations (*New York Times*, 27.2.1919). From an early point, the concerns of this organisation mirrored those of the later League. So although some leaders in the League to Enforce Peace equated peace with the punishment of Germany, the organisation also favoured the application of law to international relations, the creation of an international court and the use of sanctions against aggressive states (*New York Times*, 24.2.1918; Mowrer, 1931: 365–6).

In Britain, Henry Brailsford wrote *A League of Nations* which called for the rejection of violence between states in favour of conferences, arbitration and disarmament (Brailsford, 1917). But no organisation was more thoughtful than the Fabian Society. International lawyer Leonard Woolf prepared two essays for its Research Department which were published as *International Government* (Woolf, 1916). He argued forcefully that a new international system should be built on foundations that existed already, with international disputes being solved by either a judicial tribunal or an international conference of states.

The interest of politicians

Individuals within government began pushing comparable ideas. In London, Robert Cecil served in the Foreign Office and as Minister for Blockade. In 1916 he wrote *Proposals for the Maintenance of Future Peace* which pressed for an international system dedicated to solving problems through arbitration and negotiation (Henig, 1973: 20). Around the world, politicians began thinking along similar lines, and in 1917 a Fabian pamphlet carried quotations supporting a League of Nations from the US president, Wilson, former British foreign minister Grey, former British prime minister Asquith, British prime minister Lloyd George, Russian prime minister Kerensky and French prime minister Ribot (Woolf, 1917). It was hardly surprising that, when Lloyd George outlined British war aims on 5 January 1918, they included

'The creation of some international organisation to limit the burden of armaments and diminish the probability of war' (*The Times*, 7.1.1918). Three days later Woodrow Wilson announced his Fourteen Points to Congress, which included: 'A general association of nations must be formed under specific covenants for the purpose of affording mutual guarantees of political independence and territorial integrity to great and small States alike' (*Wilson elibrary*).

A League of Nations had become fundamental to the way democratic statesmen responded to the First World War, and on 3 January 1918 Lloyd George established a commission headed by the high court judge Lord Phillimore to look at the question. It submitted its first report in March, recommending the creation of an alliance of states determined to preserve peace. The report proposed that no state should go to war before seeking arbitration, that states should impose pressure on an aggressor through economic sanctions and that war against one member of the organisation would constitute war against all (Sharp, 1991: 45–6; Zimmern, 1936: ch. 2; Henig, 1973: 25–32).

As the war ended, the ideas of Jan Smuts became especially well known in Britain. In December 1918, the South African member of Britain's war cabinet completed *The League of Nations: A Practical Suggestion*. It was the first plan originating in government circles intended to popularise discussion about a League. To Smuts's way of thinking, the Great War had destroyed all the old certainties in the world (Smuts, 1918: 71). He believed Europe's old multinational empires (i.e. especially Russia and Austria-Hungary) had been small 'Leagues of Nations', but war, revolution and the desire of subject nationalities to govern themselves had smashed them, leaving the continent fragmented politically. To avoid chaos, Smuts advocated creating an international organisation dedicated to 'the maintenance of good order and general peace'. As he put it, 'Europe requires a liquidator or trustee of the bankrupt estate, and only a body like the League could adequately perform that gigantic task' (Smuts, 1918: 27; Walters, 1952: 27). Smuts's South African heritage was also important because he went on to develop the idea of 'mandates' to regulate former colonies of the vanquished states [Doc. 7, p. 123].

In France, Léon Bourgeois echoed many of these ideas. Unlike British and American politicians, however, he thought a League of Nations should have a special armed force made up of units from all of its members and commanded by a special international general staff (Sharp, 1991: 47). It would be on hand to enforce peace, should all other measures fail. By 1918, then, one thing was clear: no statesman of any note could have avoided thinking about a League of Nations; but one name in particular will always be linked with it.

WOODROW WILSON AND THE PEACE SETTLEMENT

Wilson's war aims

President Woodrow Wilson played a major role in creating the League of Nations. According to his speeches, the USA had entered the First World War not just to defeat Germany, but to improve the world. Talking on 16 April 1917, he explained that 'There is not a single selfish element . . . in the cause we are fighting for. We are fighting for what we believe in and wish to be the rights of mankind and for the future peace and security of the world' (*Wilson elibrary*).

For him, there could be no return to diplomacy and international relations as they had been conducted prior to 1914. The balance of power had to give way to a 'community of power'. As he told the League to Enforce Peace on 27 May 1915, there had to be a:

> universal association of the nations to maintain the inviolate security of the highways of the seas for the common good and unhindered use of all nations of the world, and to prevent any war begun either contrary to treaty covenants or without warning and full submission of the causes to the opinion of the world – a virtual guarantee of territorial integrity and political independence.
>
> (Sharp, 1991: 44)

He believed achieving this vision was one of the great challenges of his day: 'Shall we or any other free people hesitate to accept this great duty? Dare we reject it and break the heart of the world?' (*Wilson elibrary*).

In his Fourteen Points speech of 8 January 1918 Wilson outlined the need for open diplomacy, freedom of navigation, free trade, disarmament, the progressive treatment of colonies, the evacuation of Russian territory, the restoration of Belgium, the return of Alsace-Lorraine to France, a re-adjustment of Italian borders, freedom for the subject peoples of Austria-Hungary (i.e. self-determination), evacuation of the Balkan states, the break-up of the Turkish Empire into smaller national units, an independent Poland and, finally, the creation of an association of states comparable to the League of Nations. He interpreted all these goals together as a war for morality, liberty and international justice.

Naturally plans such as those of the Phillimore Committee were sent to Wilson. They were also passed to his personal adviser Colonel Edward M. House, whom Wilson consulted extensively over the League. Initially Wilson had an open mind about the form such an organisation should take, so even if he usually said he was unimpressed by the materials coming out of London, he drew on their ideas anyway (Henig, 1973: 4). So when Colonel House drafted an American plan for a League of Nations in July 1918, he used the work of the Phillimore Committee as a template, although he added a distinctive moral rhetoric (*Aims, Methods and Activity*, 1935: 20).

The Paris conference

When statesmen met in Paris to start making peace in January 1919, creating a League of Nations was an integral part of their agenda. Lloyd George appointed Jan Smuts and Robert Cecil as representatives with a special interest in League affairs; Léon Bourgeois represented France; and Woodrow Wilson chaired the commission which eventually drew up the Covenant of the League of Nations. The group was based in the Hôtel de Crillon and started work on 25 January 1919. Two officials, Cecil J. Hurst (a Briton) and David Hunter Miller (an American), took the ideas of Cecil and Smuts, plus those of House and Wilson, and drafted a version of the Covenant which formed the basis of subsequent discussions (Henig, 1973: 3–4). Negotiations proved complicated and several different drafts of the Covenant emerged. Nonetheless, the commission managed to work quickly, and on 14 February 1919 Wilson presented a plan to the full peace conference. He did this with the famous words 'a living thing is born' (Sharp, 1991: 58–60). Even though Wilson returned to the USA shortly after this speech, discussion of the Covenant kept going for several more weeks, and the document was not finalised until the end of April 1919.

The finished product still owed something to the original Phillimore proposals, but it also reflected key disagreements which had occurred during discussions. For instance, some states, such as the USA, did not want to be *compelled* to take action against a state which broke the Covenant; that is, they did not want the agreement to *force* them to intervene in a conflict to guarantee the security of another state. As a result, Article 10 was diluted to stipulate that the Council could only *recommend* action be taken by the members. Furthermore, although Britain really did not want small states to belong to the Council, it was agreed that they should have four of the nine seats that were proposed. The trade-off for Britain was agreement that the Council's decisions must be unanimous. This made sure the views of the Great Powers would never be ignored, since in effect it gave each of them the power to veto Council decisions.

In other words, the Covenant of the League of Nations was a compromise between the competing demands of the various states at the peace conference.

A number of members were deeply disappointed (*The Times*, 20.4.1919). Belgium, for instance, wanted the head office of the League to be based in their country, not Switzerland. Japan wanted a clause committing the world to the principle of racial equality, but this was omitted because the Americans feared it would facilitate Japanese migration to the USA. Most important, however, French proposals that the League have an independent military force and a permanent committee monitoring armaments were also omitted (*The Times*, 6.9.1919). Such steps were thought to impinge too greatly on the sovereign rights of member states. On the other hand, discussion did lead to agreement on welfare clauses requiring that member states promote the work of the Red Cross, as well as take steps to combat the opium trade, people-trafficking and poor conditions of labour.

Finally the Covenant of the League of Nations was agreed in Paris on 28 April 1919. With this, it became an integral part of the Treaty of Versailles and was included in the other treaties ending the First World War.

OMISSIONS, BUT OPTIMISM NONETHELESS

Despite all the work that went into drafting the Covenant, the League of Nations began life with important gaps in its membership. Even though Wilson had worked hard to help produce the Covenant, and although the document foresaw the USA belonging to the Council, it did not join the League. In fact, the US Senate refused to ratify the Treaty of Versailles on three occasions between November 1919 and March 1920 (Stone, 1978: 2).

A protracted debate had taken place in the USA over League membership. Critics said it would limit America's sovereignty, that it would drag the country into Europe's unpleasant diplomatic machinations, that it would involve the USA in disputes all over the globe with which it had nothing to do, that it would breach the Monroe Doctrine and let foreign powers meddle in America's domestic affairs, and that it would inhibit America's ability to defend itself (*New York Times*, 20.2.1919, 3.6.1919). On the other hand, many Americans said the criticisms were exaggerated, that membership would signal that the USA was no longer a frontier society, that it was a big experiment they should be part of, and that while the rest of the world was looking to America for assistance, it was doing nothing helpful (*New York Times*, 7.3.1919, 27.6.1920) [**Doc. 8, p. 124**]. Unfortunately, the sceptics won the day, and the absence of such a powerful state damaged the League's ability to prevent international aggression.

Bolshevik Russia was absent too. Woodrow Wilson and other leading minds pushing for a League of Nations were hostile to communism. Wilson once described it as 'that ugly, poisonous thing' and authorised the deployment of troops to Siberia in July 1918 to fight against the Red Army (*Wilson elibrary*). Lenin regarded Wilson as a major counter-revolutionary force in the post-war world. Wilson had deliberately promoted his Fourteen Points as an alternative vision of international relations to that offered by Lenin, and he was not the only one to think along these lines (Armstrong *et al.*, 1996: 25–6). Jan Smuts believed bolshevism was 'as great a danger as war itself' and hoped the sort of humane ideals epitomised in the League could help insulate central and eastern Europe against it. For example, he thought that the benefits likely to accrue from disarmament (such as lower taxation for ordinary people) would help towards this end (Smuts, 1918: 11, 50–1). Given the hostility of the League's founding fathers to communism, it was hardly surprising that the Soviet Union did not join the organisation until 1934; but with all the international issues involving Russia in the 1920s – refugee movements, epidemics and famine – this was a major gap in the League's membership.

Germany was excluded from the League of Nations until 1926. It was a defeated power and the Treaty of Versailles maintained its responsibility for causing the First World War; hence Germany could not join the organisation until it proved itself ready to participate constructively in the international community. Clearly, then, the League of Nations began life as part of a treaty identifying Germany as an outsider. It also meant that, at the outset, a key European power was absent from Geneva. How could European, indeed world, affairs be addressed properly without Germany's presence?

Turkey was another defeated state which was absent from the League until July 1932. In its case, the absence also highlights the difficult relationship the League had with the Muslim world. More practically, given that a number of mandate territories had once been part of the Ottoman Empire, the country's absence only added to the challenges faced by the organisation.

The absence of the USA, the Soviet Union, Germany and Turkey damaged the League's credibility, made it harder to co-ordinate responses to crises and restricted its financial resource base. It also threw disproportionate responsibility on to powerful states which actually were members, most notably Britain and France. All the same, the organisation still opened on a tide of optimism. Its offices initially were located in London and began to be occupied as early as summer 1919. Later they were moved to Geneva where the organisation bought the National Hotel. The first Council meeting was opened by Léon Bourgeois and took place on 16 January 1920 in Paris (in the Clock Room of the Quai d'Orsay), while the first Assembly meeting began on 15 November 1920 in Geneva. The latter event was attended by 42 original member states. If this was a revolution in international relations, obviously it was incomplete, but something significant was happening nonetheless.

CONCLUSION

So how new was the League of Nations really? Was it a major breach with the past and its barbarous practices, or a crowning achievement perfecting prior developments? (*Aims, Methods and Activity*, 1935: 9).

President Wilson believed the League broke the mould, being the first modern attempt to prevent the outbreak of war by the application of open diplomacy (*New York Times*, 2.12.1921). A contemporary commentator felt that old labels just did not fit an organisation like this. It was not like a traditional state and did not involve the pursuit of relations between states in a traditional way. In a world where you were allied to everyone, it was like being allied to no one – or perhaps, better said, *against* no one (and for the first time no one was allied against you) (Zimmern, 1936: 278). Another commentator agreed that something fundamental had changed: international relations had outgrown all previous methods of conducting them, and for the first time there was a permanent mechanism for their regulation (Mowrer, 1931: 362). League employee Arthur Sweetser believed 'the effort to unite all nations, in all continents, into a single permanent agency of peace and co-operation was without any precedent in human history' (Sweetser, 1943b: 150).

Comparable views can be found in the historical literature. Authors have argued that the idea of an inclusive international front against aggression was new, adding that this very newness was extremely daunting (Northedge, 1988: 88; Armstrong *et al.*, 1996: 32). More recently, Annique Ginneken maintained that the League was 'an absolute novelty in the history of international relations. An organisation on such a scale, covering all fields of international co-operation, never existed before' (Ginneken, 2006: 1). So the list of what was novel about the League of Nations is a long one: it aspired to universal membership; it brought together very many different functions indeed under one roof; it sought to organise international relations comprehensively; it paid due attention to smaller states, tried to build an international system on something other than naked power, and afforded tremendous importance to international public opinion – the points are almost interminable.

And yet, as much material in this chapter has shown, the League of Nations was connected to the past. Some politicians and commentators of the day thought the organisation was trying to realise a unity of mankind which had been recognised for a very long time (*The Times*, 11.10.1918; Zilliacus, 1929: 2). Jan Smuts agreed that this was something history had always been heading towards (Smuts, 1918: 9–10). Yet, if it was said to be an experiment that had been on the drawing board for centuries, others also saw it as the culmination of trends growing specifically out of the nineteenth century (Walters, 1952: 2; Mowrer, 1931: 361).

But there are also questions about the true novelty of some of its practical arrangements. It has been pointed out that no matter how new the League claimed to be, what actually happened within its framework too often amounted to the pursuit of 'old diplomacy' rather than something more path-breaking and idealistic (Sharp, 1991: 62). This reflects the fact that the League of Nations remained a collection of sovereign states on which it had to rely to get things done. Furthermore, whatever its aspiration, the League's membership never was universal. On top of this, the composition of the Council and its emphasis on unanimous decisions still weighted the organisation towards the traditional Great Powers of Europe and their requirements.

There is a compromise position: that the League is best understood as something bridging the past and the future of international relations. It did have roots in the past and sometimes fell prey to the fallibilities of the political world in which it was formed. Nonetheless, it is impossible to read the words of Woodrow Wilson, Robert Cecil or Jan Smuts and ignore the fact that it was born of an idealism grasping after something better than existed at the time. This should help us understand why the League has been described as a culmination of some established political practices and a radical departure from others (Armstrong et al., 1996: 7). But, wherever the precise balance of interpretation is placed, Robert Cecil was right to call it 'a great experiment' – and in January 1920 that experiment was about to start in earnest (Cecil, 1941).

3

A Promising Start? Disputes, Borders and National Minorities in the 1920s

INTRODUCTION: THE SPIRIT OF THE AGE

The 1920s are sometimes referred to as the 'Golden Years', and compared with the 1930s they were a decade of relative normality. The term is not completely positive, however, because it can suggest that the period was based on circumstances which were only temporary. When these circumstances changed, everything might fall apart. This can provoke us to wonder whether ultimately the League would be master of its own destiny or controlled by powerful forces beyond its control. Nonetheless, if the League was to show signs of success in organising the peace of the world, the circumstances of the 1920s were not all bad. After four years of war, in some quarters at least there were indications of a desire for international reconciliation.

Outside the League of Nations, there were progressive developments in international relations. The Locarno Treaties of October 1925 saw Germany's post-war borders with France recognised as inviolable, hence addressing possible tensions over Alsace-Lorraine. Three years later, France's foreign minister, Aristide Briand, and America's secretary of state, Frank Kellogg, produced a pact which renounced war as an instrument of policy. In time, it was signed by 62 states. Inside the League there were positive developments too. Its membership increased significantly: Albania, Austria, Bulgaria, Costa Rica, Finland and Luxembourg joined in December 1920; Estonia, Latvia and Lithuania in September 1921; Hungary in September 1922; Abyssinia (today Ethiopia) and Ireland in September 1923; and the Dominican Republic in September 1924. Although Costa Rica withdrew in January 1925 and Brazil in June 1926 (perhaps reflecting a feeling that the League was predominantly concerned with Europe rather than the rest of the world), Germany joined in September 1926 (Ginneken, 2006: 217–18).

In addition, the League of Nations set to work quickly. For example, in accordance with the Treaty of Versailles, it established international administrations in areas which had the potential to become the subject of disputes.

Its presence in the Saar was scheduled to last fifteen years (when a plebiscite would determine whether the region passed to Germany or France), and it supervised the Free City of Danzig (today Gdańsk). In January 1922, the Assembly elected nine judges and their deputies to sit in the Permanent Court of International Justice in The Hague. They would rule on any international legal issues brought to the League. The idea that a family of nations dedicated to peace really was under construction gained credibility from the frequent attendance of the foreign ministers of Britain, France and, later, Germany at Assembly and Council meetings (Brierly, 1960: 486). So, if there were signs in the 1920s which gave some cause for optimism, how did the League fare when it began addressing the most pressing international disputes of the day?

SETTLING DISPUTES PEACEFULLY IN THE 1920s

The Åland Islands

For all the positive characteristics of the 1920s, the League still dealt with thirty disputes between states in the first ten years of its life. Although a few were handled by the Permanent Court, most were dealt with by the Council (*League of Nations*, 1930: 25). The first involved the inhabitants of the Åland Islands, which showed how the problems of a national minority could be internationalised very quickly, producing tension even between neighbours who were usually friendly.

There are about 300 of these islands lying between Finland and Sweden. In the early 1920s, 95 per cent of the 25,000 inhabitants were ethnic Swedes, but the islands did not belong to Sweden, which in 1809 had ceded them to Russia, and ownership passed on to Finland when it gained independence in 1917. The situation did not please the Swedish inhabitants of the Ålands, who felt the collapse of the Russian Empire should lead to a reappraisal of their position. They believed they would not be able to maintain their Swedish identity in a Finnish state. As two leading islanders put it in a letter to Secretary General Drummond, dated 22 July 1920: 'the Finnish race suffocates the Swedish mind, and no law can give us protection against this' (Bendiner, 1975: 173).

In February 1918 the islanders sent a petition signed by 7,000 people to the Swedish government, asking for union with it. Next, the island's governing body, the Landsting, wrote to the Principal Allied Powers with the same message; they even attended the Paris peace conference and presented a petition to the same end. The Finnish government did pass a law on 7 May

1920 granting the Ålanders extensive autonomy, but when the islanders kept up the campaign to secede, Finnish authorities arrested two of their number for high treason (Barros, 1968: 240).

In June 1920 Great Britain referred the case to the Council of the League of Nations. Under Article 11 of the Covenant, it was deemed an affair which 'threatens to disturb the good understanding between nations upon which peace depends'. As the Council investigated the issue, Sweden proposed that the islanders be allowed to hold a referendum on which country they wished to join. By contrast, Finland argued this was a domestic matter of no interest to the League. Helsinki added that, in any case, the autonomy law allowed the islanders to live freely and that the Ålands were vital to the security of the Finnish state [**Doc. 9, p. 125**].

The Council tackled the case in detail. There were investigative reports and deliberative committee sessions which went through the claims and counter-claims with a fine toothcomb. Two leading Åland islanders were called upon to address the Council on 23 June 1921, where they outlined their concerns about the danger of Swedish communities losing their traditions under Finnish government (*LONOJ*, September 1921).

In the end, however, the Council solved the issue in line with one of its own reports. The view predominated that to separate the islands from Finland would be to 'destroy order and stability within states and to inaugurate anarchy in international life' (Kellor, 1924: 291). This was because, in the first instance, if the Ålands were transferred from Finnish to Swedish sovereignty, other Swedish communities in Finland might try to follow their lead – and indeed other national minority groups settled in sensitive border regions around Europe might be encouraged to seek comparable goals for themselves. Letting the Ålanders secede would risk opening a Pandora's box of nationalist aspirations and produce pressures to start redrawing Europe's borders.

At the same time, the League's report and the British representative to the Council (H.A.L. Fisher) maintained that the autonomy of the islanders had to be extended. Swedish customs had to be underpinned more firmly still, mother-tongue language had to be guaranteed in schools, indigenous groups had to be guaranteed access to property on the islands, the right of local people to elect representative district administrations had to be safeguarded, the island's Governor had to be properly approved by the islanders, and all of these measures had to be guaranteed by the League of Nations itself. Later it was also agreed the islands should be neutralised militarily.

The application of autonomy was important. Political figures such as Woodrow Wilson and Jan Smuts had talked of the need for national groups to receive 'self-determination' and the idea justified the break-up of old empires into smaller nation states (*Wilson elibrary*, 6.4.1918; Smuts, 1918: 15). As *The Times* (18.5.1921) reported, however, the Åland case presented an

A Promising Start? Disputes, Borders and National Minorities in the 1920s

41

interesting study in how far self-determination could be taken. Of course there were critical voices. Hjalmar Branting, Sweden's representative at the relevant Council sessions, felt the decision could not strengthen the security of the Baltic region for the long term, while political scientist Frances Kellor believed the happiness of the islands' inhabitants had been sacrificed to geo-strategy (*LONOJ*, June 1921; Kellor, 1924: 297). But the views were misplaced. Technically, Finland had maintained its borders (so no precedent for ripping up the peace settlement was created); meanwhile the islanders could pursue their traditionally Swedish lives with so little interference from Helsinki that they were Finnish citizens only as a matter of formality. In other words, it was a balanced settlement which recognised the practical political needs of the Finnish state (not to say Europe as a whole), but responded to the requirements of ordinary people. In time, the point was realised and commentators began expressing optimism about the solution (Sederholm, 1920: 58). But could all international disputes of the period be dealt with as well?

The Corfu incident

The League's role in the confrontation between Italy and Greece which led to the Corfu incident has been quite widely criticised. The story starts with a diplomatic body that existed for several years in parallel to the League. The **Conference of Ambassadors** was based in Paris to supervise the completion of issues not resolved by the peace treaties. In August 1923, acting on its behalf, Italy's General Tellini was in Janina drawing the border between Albania and Greece. Unfortunately he was murdered, most likely by bandits. Although the culprits were never caught, reports were flashed to Mussolini blaming the Greek government. The Duce demanded restitution and, to guarantee it would be given, on 31 August he authorised the occupation of the Greek island of Corfu (Barros, 1965: 74–9).

On 1 September, the Greek foreign minister, Nikolaos Politis, brought the affair to the Council of the League of Nations on the grounds that the occupation of Corfu constituted a 'rupture' endangering peace as outlined in Articles 12 and 15 of the Covenant. Although Italy maintained the occupation was not an act of war, Robert Cecil (representing Britain on the Council) disputed the argument strongly and demanded assurances that no more acts of violence would be committed between the two countries (Barros, 1965: 94–5). Actually, Cecil favoured a hard line over Corfu. At one point he had Articles 10, 12 and 15 read to the Council session with Italy and Greece present. He wanted to underline the gravity of the situation. Cecil favoured imposing sanctions on Italy and even wanted a naval display by British and French warships off the coast of Corfu.

Conference of Ambassadors: A temporary organisation sitting in Paris in the early 1920s and consisting of ambassadors from France, Britain, Italy, Japan and the USA. It was created by the Supreme Council in the wake of the First World War and addressed especially undecided matters arising out of the peace treaties.

In the event, no such steps were taken. The British government did not share Cecil's views: it was loath to damage trade with Italy, and the Royal Navy was already over-extended in the Mediterranean. Meanwhile France did not want to criticise the Italian occupation too strongly because, at the time, French troops were occupying Germany's Ruhr to guarantee the payment of reparations. Consequently the Council settled for sending a commission of inquiry to the Albanian-Greek frontier to investigate Tellini's death. Arriving on 17 September and making its report just five days later, the commission discovered little to support any accusation of complicity by Greek authorities; neither could it find evidence suggesting that Greece had failed to investigate the affair properly [Doc. 10, p. 127].

On 25 September 1923 the Conference of Ambassadors met to consider the report. In this forum, Italian pressure led to an award of 50 million Italian lire to be paid by Greece as compensation for the killing. With this agreed, on 27 September, Italy began evacuating Corfu.

The Corfu incident had been a relatively minor event in European history, but it was not without significance. Robert Cecil was concerned that a state (Italy) had been able to get away with an act of war, and his opinion was shared by others. It also threatened to create the impression that League decisions were less likely to reflect considerations of strict justice than the desires of the Great Powers. Britain and France had not wanted to intervene, and so Italy was left to impose its will on a much smaller Greek state. Furthermore, the fact that the League had little to do with the final settlement suggested to some that the organisation was marginal compared to other available diplomatic channels, in this case the Conference of Ambassadors.

Even so, the whole affair was far from an unmitigated disaster for the League. First, there was a matter of principle. When Greece felt it was not getting fair treatment from the Conference of Ambassadors, it had been able to turn to an alternative forum for a hearing (Barros, 1965: 301). As such, discussion in the Council provided a good means for venting a perceived injustice, giving Politis the satisfaction of presenting a case he believed true and making life a bit more awkward for Mussolini. The intervention of Robert Cecil underlined the importance of peace to statesmen at a time of crisis, and the commission of inquiry left a record of what had most likely sparked the incident. Lastly and most obviously, with the gaze of the world upon them, Italy and Greece did not go to war, nor did Italy stay on Corfu very long. So, even if the Corfu incident was not a success for the League, neither was it simply a failure.

The Greco-Bulgarian confrontation

League intervention in the Greco-Bulgarian confrontation was more creditable. The affair began with a border incident sparked by a game of cards between soldiers. It occurred in the Demir Kapou region of the Greco-Bulgarian border on 19 October 1925. Two Greek border guards were killed, one under a white flag. An exchange of fire followed, causing Greek guards to retreat from their posts. News of the events reached Athens the next day, becoming exaggerated in transmission in a way that made it appear Bulgaria seemed to be launching an invasion. Consequently, the Greek government ordered an attack on Bulgaria. The trouble had flared in a particularly sensitive border zone since Greek refugees from Asia Minor were being settled nearby. Greece wanted these people to feel secure, and so it continued to pressure Bulgaria militarily even when the latter withdrew its troops from the region.

On 23 October the affair was communicated to Secretary General Drummond by Bulgaria's foreign minister, Christo Kalfoff. He said Greek troops had advanced into his country, while Bulgarian forces had been ordered to offer no resistance (Barros, 1970: 23). Drummond notified the President of the Council, Aristide Briand, who telegraphed both sides immediately telling them to cease hostilities and withdraw their troops to their side of the border (Bendiner, 1975: 219). Both sides held their positions and Briand invoked Article 11 of the Covenant to bring the matter before the Council on 26 October. He also issued a reminder to Greece and Bulgaria that under Article 12, members of the League should not resort to war.

When the Council met, its demand was unequivocal: within 24 hours both sides had to order their troops to withdraw, and within 60 hours they had to be completely within their own borders. British, French and Italian military attachés were sent to the location to verify compliance. They moved quickly and arrived on 28 October to find the Greek withdrawal already underway (*League of Nations*, 1930: 33).

When the Council met on 28 October, Bulgaria's representative, Bogdan Marfoff, reported that all Bulgarian troops had been ordered to cease military operations; the Greek representative, Alexandros Carapanos, stated the same, adding that Greek troops had been ordered to evacuate Bulgarian territory too. One day later, the evacuation was complete; two day later Bulgarian border guards were back at their posts as usual and the affair was over. So although at one point the British Foreign Office had feared the start of a major conflict in the Balkans (maybe drawing in Yugoslavia and Turkey), this had been avoided (Barros, 1970: 84).

It was only left to assess blame and possible compensation. A commission under British diplomat Horace Rumbold went to the area for three days [**Doc. 11, p. 129**]. It found that although invading Greek troops had barely damaged houses, they had taken crops and cattle as they retreated. On 14 December 1925, compensation worth 30 million Bulgarian levas was awarded by the Council, and Greece was given two months to pay. It actually did this in two instalments ending on 1 March 1926.

So, the approach of the League to this crisis had been simple. The first priority was to stop all hostilities, and only then did it investigate the reasons for what had happened. The strategy clearly paid dividends, and as a result the British representative to the Council, Austen Chamberlain, noted that while such border incidents had sparked wars in the past, this time things had turned out differently (Barros, 1970: 68–70).

One commentator referred to the 'complete success of the League on this occasion' (Brierly, 1960: 486). The success, however, was built on a helpful constellation of circumstances. Greece and Bulgaria were not well positioned for the pursuit of a military campaign: the former was struggling to cope with an influx of at least a million refugees from Turkey, while the latter was largely demilitarised and had domestic political difficulties. Neither country was tied closely to a Great Power likely to take up its cause in the Council. For once, in fact, all the powers were determined to prevent war for fear of where it might lead (Barros, 1970: 118–19). These realities promoted the peaceful outcome.

Balance of the disputes

The League mediated the Åland and Greco-Bulgarian disputes successfully. Although the Corfu incident was more problematic, a comment made in 1930 still applies: the League might not have solved every issue referred to it, but the publicity it brought to a dispute helped calm difficult situations (*League of Nations*, 1930: 27). So if the League's early record over disputes was quite positive, how did it fare in dealing with an issue that could well generate international difficulties: the drawing of borders?

ASSIGNING TERRITORIES AND DRAWING BORDERS

Across central and eastern Europe, the peace settlement established new states out of the old empires, but all of the borders were not settled at once. It was inevitable that such open questions would cause tension between states, and that the League would become involved in the difficulties.

Vilnius

With the Russo-Polish war raging, the Treaty of Moscow was signed between Lithuania and Soviet Russia on 12 July 1920. It recognised the city of Vilnius and its surrounding region as part of a sovereign Lithuanian state. The region had been occupied by Polish troops only shortly beforehand, and its population was a complicated mixture of Poles, Jews and Lithuanians, but this did not prevent the Lithuanian state designating Vilnius its capital. The Treaty of Versailles, however, had left much about Lithuania's borders – particularly with Poland – unspecified, and in September 1920 Poland brought the border issue to the attention of the Council of the League of Nations. Consequently, the League sent a commission to look at the question. It drew up a provisional border, which both states agreed at Suwalki on 30 September 1920, leaving the city of Vilnius and its immediate surroundings within Lithuania.

At this point, in early October 1920, Poland's General Lucjan Żeligowski and his troops took matters into their own hands. According to a Polish version of events, Żeligowski's troops were largely drawn from the population around Vilnius and wanted the region to be part of Poland (*The Times*, 12.10.1920). As a result, Żeligowski was forced to resign from the Polish army and marched on Vilnius, which he entered on 9 October. Thereafter he set up an independent central Lithuanian government. Naturally there was scepticism about this version of events, and it was also reported that no one in the region 'for a moment doubts that this coup is secretly supported by the Polish Government' (*The Times*, 13.10.1920). Although Lithuania was not yet a member, it referred the issue to the League of Nations under Articles 12 and 17 of the Covenant and in due course it was debated by the League's Assembly (Lloyd, 1995: 165). As events unfolded, Polish representatives did their best to maintain that Żeligowski was a rebel while nonetheless profiting from his actions – for instance suggesting that his troops should only withdraw once the region's future was agreed generally. Robert Cecil's moral compass pointed him in a different direction. Just two days after an international commission had outlined a border, Żeligowski had acted and, for Cecil, that was 'something impossible to defend' (*New York Times*, 25.9.1921).

The League considered its response. There was talk of sending an international police force, but the plan dissolved when the Swiss government refused to allow some units to transit its territory (Dell, 1941: 41). There were proposals to hold a plebiscite for the region, but Lithuania objected that the presence of so many Polish troops would distort the outcome. There was also concern that the plebiscite question would be phrased in such a way that it scared Jewish inhabitants into voting for Poland.

The League's final effort to solve the problem was a report presented to the Council by Belgian representative Paul Hymans on 21 September 1921. It recommended that the Lithuanian and Polish languages both be granted official status in Lithuania; that all 'racial' minorities in the country should have equal rights to education, religion, language and association; and that steps be taken to enable Lithuania and Poland to co-ordinate their foreign, economic and defence policies. The report went on to say that the Vilnius region should be established as an autonomous canton on the Swiss model within the Lithuanian state, being run by a diet made up of delegates numerically representative of the different nationality groups present (*LONOJ*, November 1921). The plan was a nice balancing act, but both sides rejected it. With that, the League felt it had exhausted all possible solutions open to it. In January 1922, the Council made a statement admitting defeat and calling on both sides to maintain the peace that had been in place since the League began its involvement (*LONOJ*, February 1921). So the occupation of Vilnius was allowed to stand and the fiction of Żeligowski establishing an independent state fell away. In March 1923 the Conference of Ambassadors recognised Vilnius as part of Poland (Lloyd, 1995: 165).

Some contemporary commentators were outraged at the Polish annexation of Vilnius. Frances Kellor maintained that Poland's leader, Josef Piłsudski must have known about Żeligowski's actions and that, as a result, the Council should have invoked Article 16 of the Covenant, opening the way to sanctions. Instead, thanks to a strong relationship between Poland and France, no such thing was done and a country was allowed to profit from aggression (Kellor, 1924: 252–63).

It is impossible to deny that Poland benefited from Żeligowski's actions and that the outcome did not help the League's standing in the world. In mitigation of the League's position, however, it had been left a difficult issue by the framers of the peace treaty, it responded once again with innovative thinking (even if this time it was rejected), and the spotlight which the Council shone on Vilnius at least helped ensure there was no full-scale war.

Memel (today Klaipėda)

Vilnius was not the only territorial problem affecting Lithuania; there was also Memel (Klaipėda), a port located on the Baltic coast at the mouth of the Neman River. Before the First World War it had been part of eastern Prussia (i.e. Germany), but the peace treaty said it should have an international administration until its future was decided. Although the majority of the city's 30,000 inhabitants were German, Lithuanians lived in the surrounding countryside and, overall, the region's 140,000 inhabitants were split equally between the two nationalities. It was generally expected that Memel would be placed under Lithuanian sovereignty, but the complexity of providing a final decision was increased by the fact that the Neman and the port were used to transport wood from what was now Polish territory. Hence Warsaw also had an interest in what would happen.

By the start of 1923, no final decision had been reached, but then, in early January, reports began to circulate that Lithuanian soldiers disguised in civilian clothes were advancing on Memel (*The Times*, 12.1.1923). The

Lithuanian government denied sponsoring this (a position which was generally disbelieved), but with only 200 French troops inside the city to protect its international status, Memel was taken over within days (*The Times*, 17.1.1923). Things happened so quickly that on 16 February 1923 the Conference of Ambassadors recognised that the city was part of Lithuania, although Poland's right to trade via the port and river were to be safeguarded.

Polish-Lithuanian relations were still tense owing to the Vilnius dispute, and agreement over Memel proved hard to reach. Consequently, the Conference of Ambassadors handed over the affair to the Council of the League in December 1923. The League set up a commission which visited Memel, Kaunas (the Lithuanian capital at the time) and Warsaw before reporting in March 1924. It re-affirmed Lithuanian sovereignty over Memel but, echoing the Åland agreement, stipulated the need to respect 'the traditional rights and culture' of Memel's diverse inhabitants. Consequently, the region was to be guaranteed substantial autonomy within Lithuania, having its own diet and governor. Polish concerns over the port and river were also addressed. Although Poland was denied a hand in managing the port, a three-man harbour board was to be set up consisting of representatives of Lithuania, Memel and the League's own transport organisation. It was to ensure that all goods would transit freely and efficiently. Free movement on the river was also guaranteed (*LONOJ*, March, April 1924).

In other words, although once again direct action had led to territory being annexed, the League of Nations managed to create a balanced solution. Although relations between Lithuania and Poland were soured by Vilnius, the Council and its commission met the main concerns of both parties, and still tried to keep an eye on the requirements of ordinary citizens (Steiner, 2005: 356). This is why even commentators who are generally critical of the League say that, in this case, it did 'extremely well' (Kellor, 1924: 281).

Upper Silesia

Upper Silesia was a heavily industrialised mining area which had belonged to the German Empire before the First World War. Apart from economic resources (the most important elements of which formed a rough triangle at the heart of the region), it had a complicated population structure in which two million people were split into two-third Poles and one-third Germans (Ginneken, 2006: 193). After 1918, both Germany and Poland wanted the territory in order to capitalise on its economic riches, and to provide a national home for their co-nationals. Unfortunately, the highly complicated distribution of economic resources and peoples made it quite impossible to draw a simple line on a map that would divide the province neatly into areas satisfactory to Germany and Poland alike.

Initially the region was put under international administration until Article 88 of the Treaty of Versailles could be enacted and a plebiscite held to decide Upper Silesia's fate. The vote took place in a mood of high drama, with emotional nationalist campaigns held on both sides and a turn-out of 97.5 per cent. Of 1,186,342 votes cast, 59.6 per cent were in favour of Upper Silesia staying German. The figures meant that roughly 200,000 ethnic Poles must have voted for Germany! (Tooley, 1997: 237) Dealing specifically with the industrial triangle, 54.2 per cent voted for rule by Weimar. The outcome was complicated and Polish complaints were shrill, saying that German industrialists had pressured Polish workers unfairly to vote for Germany. Then, in May 1921, a Polish insurrection occurred in the province. Clearly the **Supreme Council** (established during the Paris Peace Conference) faced tough decisions over how to deal with the situation, and in August 1921 it passed the affair over to the Council of the League of Nations. This established a committee of experts to draw a frontier for the troubled land.

Supreme Council: This was set up at the Paris Peace Conference and comprised the leaders of the main Allied Powers – USA, France, Britain and Italy. It was the ultimate body deciding international political questions immediately after the First World War.

The commission's report was issued in May 1922 and, running to 606 Articles, it was highly complicated (Steiner, 2005: 357). Germany got two-thirds of the territory, but Poland was granted the lion's share of the economic resources (Tooley, 1997: 258). Even so, things were sometimes 'given a twist' because economic resources could cross borders. So, for instance, water supplies sometimes were in a different country to the locations they served. Likewise the air intake shaft for a coal mine might be located in Germany while the exhaust shaft was in Poland (Kellor, 1924: 168–9). In terms of national population distributions, the picture was just as complicated, since Polish Upper Silesia became home to 282,000 Poles, but also 218,400 Germans; meanwhile the German part of the province contained 489,200 Germans and 197,300 Poles (Dell, 1941: 50).

Upper Silesia clearly had the potential to become a time bomb ticking at the heart of Polish-German relations, so the League's commission made further recommendations. Steps were taken to guarantee the rights of national minorities throughout the region and a joint German-Polish commission was established to supervise cross-border co-operation for fifteen years. In the event, these arrangements 'worked fairly well' (Ginneken, 2006: 193). Even a critic of the League, Robert Dell, admitted that 'on the whole the League of Nations can count the settlement of the Upper Silesian question as a success' (Dell, 1941: 50); and while national tensions remained very much in play in Upper Silesia for years to come, still the region prospered (Steiner, 2005: 357).

Mosul

In 1924, a border problem emerged not in central and eastern Europe, but in the Middle East. It concerned the region known as Mosul and became a novel challenge, as the press recognised: 'Never before has a frontier controversy between a European and an Asiatic Power been submitted to the judgement of an international tribunal' (*The Times*, 8.8.1925).

The oil-rich territory had formerly been part of the Ottoman Empire and stretched to the south and east of the territory into what is today Iraq. Following the Lausanne Treaty (1923), the exact status of the region was undecided. Britain had been given mandatory power over Iraq (see Chapter 5) and London was supposed to negotiate with Ankara to determine its border with Turkey. Unfortunately, no decision was reached and in August 1924 Britain referred the matter to the League of Nations. It came before the Council that September. Once again a commission was set up which held talks in London and Ankara, and visited Mosul itself.

The work of the commission was so difficult that some speculated it had the hardest task yet handed out by the League (*The Times*, 9.7.25). Emotions ran high when the commissioners took evidence in the region [**Doc. 12, p. 131**]. Pro-Turkish spokesmen sometimes were beaten up, while Christian leaders (representing 120,000 people) wrote to the Pope and other major religious leaders begging to be saved from Turkish rule. Kurdish groups set up local defence associations in case their region was handed to Ankara (*The Times*, 24.2.1925).

The commission issued its report in August 1925 and the affair went to the Council early the next month. The mountains to the north of Mosul were identified as Turkey's strategic frontier and it was stated that economically the region to the south of these looked towards Baghdad. The commission believed most people did not want return to Turkish rule, and that Kurds especially saw themselves as distinct from Turks. Consequently, the commission recommended that Mosul be given to Iraq, at least so long as Britain maintained mandatory control over the country. It also stated that Kurdish national groups should be guaranteed extensive rights of self-government and the Kurdish language accorded official status (*The Times*, 8.8.1925; *LONOJ*, October 1925).

The Council's decision was not welcomed by either Turkey or Britain: the former did not want to lose the land, and the latter was not keen on remaining in Iraq longer than necessary. Still, the two sides accepted the recommendations and, together with a representative from Baghdad, signed the Treaty of Ankara on 5 June 1926 which recognised Mosul as part of Iraq. So although questions to do with the Kurdish nation remained very much alive (and still are today), in 1925 the settlement by the League of Nations was probably as reasonable as could have been expected at the time.

The balance of border problems

It is hard to avoid the conclusion that the League dealt reasonably well with the border problems discussed here. The settlements for Memel, Upper Silesia and Mosul all were recognised as at least moderate successes in the face of difficult circumstances. And if aggression was rewarded in the case of Vilnius, at least the crisis did not escalate to the point of war.

NATIONAL MINORITIES: TRYING TO REMOVE A CAUSE OF WAR

The problem

One theme above all has run through this chapter. The Åland problem concerned Swedes living in Finland; Vilnius was a problem because it was inhabited by Poles and Lithuanians (Jews, too, for that matter); in Upper Silesia, Poles and Germans could not be separated easily; Memel was a mixture of Germans and Lithuanians; and Mosul was home to Turks, Arabs and Kurds. So how should such territories be managed?

No matter that Woodrow Wilson and others had promoted national self-determination, and no matter that old empires had been broken up into smaller nation states, the complicated distribution of national groups (especially in central and eastern Europe) made it impossible for all members of every national group to live in 'their own' nation state. That is to say, not all Germans could live in Germany, not all Poles could live in Poland, and so on. In fact, it was not even possible for all national groups to have their own nation state; so, for instance, there were Ukrainians living in eastern Poland but there was no independent 'home' Ukrainian state. The existence of national minorities, first, opened the possibility of tensions within a state between different groups if, for instance, the minority felt it was being treated unfairly; and, secondly, there was the risk that a domestic problem could be internationalised if a minority had co-nationals living in a 'home' nation state which might take up their cause. If national groups such as Swedes and Finns could be drawn into an international argument about the Åland Islands, how much more dangerous could other situations become?

Relations between majority and minority peoples were particularly challenging after the First World War and may have been the single most important security issue facing Europe. At least 14 different states were inhabited by at least 14 different kinds of national minority groups. Estimates said there were between 20 and 40 million members of national minorities – with 10 million living in Poland alone (Jankowsky, 1945: 111; *Sitzungsbericht*, 1931: 11). Furthermore, the relationship between majority and minority peoples could be difficult. The dissolution of old empires into new nation states meant that formerly subject peoples (such as Poles, Czechs, Lithuanians, Latvians and Estonians) were now running countries which had minorities consisting of former élite groups (such as Germans and Russians). There was a temptation for the new state-building majorities to settle old scores with the new minorities, while the latter often resented deeply their loss of status and affluence.

The basic idea

Although the nineteenth century had seen some attempts to protect national minorities the League of Nations made a more concerted effort to do so. This has been described as 'one of the most difficult and delicate tasks' which fell to it (*League of Nations*, 1930: 357). The League had to strike a difficult balance: on the one hand it had to protect vulnerable people but, on the other, it had to remember it was made up of sovereign states and could not interfere too extensively in members' domestic affairs. It was feared that if the organisation tried to intervene too much on behalf of national minorities, states would object with increasing determination and the work would become progressively more difficult. There was even the danger that League involvement would increase resentment towards minorities and make their position worse than ever. Clearly a tightrope would have to be walked, and this is why minorities issues fell to the Council rather than the Assembly. It was hoped that the relatively small executive body would be able to deal with such sensitive issues more discreetly than a large debating chamber (Kershaw, 1929: 166).

To make matters more difficult still, the Great Powers did not want their national minorities to be supervised by the League. Consequently the peace treaties did not establish a universal international system of protection. Rather, in line with principles applied by the Congress of Berlin (1878), it addressed the requirements of people living in Europe's new and enlarged states. Although on the whole these were the areas most likely to be problematic, the states concerned did not like being singled out in this way. As a result, in 1922 the Assembly expressed the hope that states not covered by minorities agreements nonetheless would treat their minorities according to the expected standards (*League of Nations*, 1930: 359).

The new legal basis for the regulation of minorities began with Article 92 of the Treaty of Versailles. It specified that Poland would reach an agreement with the principal Allied Powers to protect its racial, linguistic and religious minorities (Azcarate, 1945: 92–3). Thereafter comparable clauses were included in the treaties of St. Germain, Neuilly, Trianon and Lausanne. Poland and the Allied Powers concluded a minorities treaty on 28 June 1919, and other agreements followed between the Allied Powers and Czechoslovakia, Greece, Romania and Yugoslavia. Guarantees for minorities were also contained in declarations made before the Council of the League by Albania, Estonia, Finland, Latvia and Lithuania; they were also included in conventions concerning Upper Silesia and Memel (Aun, 1951: 25–6; *League of Nations*, 1930: 358–9). Minorities were guaranteed equality before the law, full civil and political rights, and the use of mother-tongue language in primary schools and the legal system (Robinson *et al.*, 1943: 37–8). These were the foundations of a system of national minorities protection that stretched from the Baltic to the Aegean Sea, and its implementation fell to the League.

It was a formidable task, made more difficult because the peacemakers did not explain how the obligations were to be monitored and enforced (Fink, 2004: 267). Hence it was uncertain what the League should do if a state breached its obligations towards a minority (Fink, 2004: 271–3). In this light, we can begin to understand why, in practice, the League became more of a conciliator and lobbyist over the treatment of minorities than a policeman threatening prosecution and punishment.

The system of protection

The Council assumed responsibility for minorities in 1920. The mechanics of the system it was supposed to apply were updated in 1921, 1923, 1925 and 1930 – a fact which highlights how difficult the job was to define. A minorities office was established with about nine staff headed by the Norwegian diplomat, Erik Colban (1876–1956). The group supported the Council in its work with minorities, for instance obtaining information from the groups themselves and from the states in which they lived. Colban and his colleagues met with representatives of the minorities and travelled to areas of interest to see what was happening there. They had to make protection procedures work 'on the ground', at the same time promoting the authority of the League and gaining the confidence of the states concerned (Fink, 2004: 275).

The system was roughly as follows. A protected minority could write a petition of complaint to the Council – and roughly 350 were sent in during the first ten years of the League's existence (*League of Nations*, 1930: 373). The petition was forwarded to the minorities section to decide if it was 'receivable', for example to make sure it was neither anonymous nor couched in violent language. If it was receivable (and about half were), the petition was sent back to the Council where members were given a copy and one was forwarded to the government against whom allegations were being made. If the Council felt the petition contained a substantive issue, then a 'Committee of Three' was formed to investigate it. This consisted of the President of the Council plus two other members; it sat in private, did not keep minutes of its meetings and most of its deliberations were not passed on to all of the interested parties – not even to the original petitioners. The Committee pursued the issues raised with the state concerned until it felt as much of a satisfactory outcome as possible had been achieved. In very rare cases, the treatment of minorities was referred to the Permanent Court of International Justice (Claude, 1955: 23–4; *League of Nations*, 1930: 367–8). In fact, the Council received all manner of petitions from highly diverse groups, from Muslims in Greece to Jews in Hungary, from Poles in Silesia to ethnic Germans in the Baltic States, and dealt with them in a way which the Assembly in 1922 defined as 'benevolent and informal' (Scheuermann, 2000).

Many negotiations between League and states happened off the record and were carried out by Colban, or else were informed by his knowledge and that of his staff. Over time, Colban devised his own way of dealing with frequently cited states such as Poland and Romania. He would make on-site visits to discuss what was happening with the very local government officials accused of transgressing the rights of minorities (Fink, 2004: 280). With such an informal system in operation, there were widely differing results from case to case. So while the Council encouraged some countries to improve their treatment of minorities (for instance Greece and Romania), others (such as Poland and Czechoslovakia) did their best to circumvent the system (Steiner, 2005: 364; Fink, 2004: 281). Unfortunately, as far as the latter cases were concerned, there were few serious sanctions the League could threaten.

Disappointments of the national minorities

The League's protection system was not supposed to create a situation akin to a courtroom in which a state stood accused of crimes; it was supposed to facilitate conciliation and improvements for the future. The minorities themselves, however, had hoped for something more certain (Claude, 1955: 25). They disliked the secrecy of the system and were affronted that they might not even hear what had been done in response to their petitions. They were unhappy that the system was not universal, since (for instance) Italy's poor treatment of the Germans in South Tyrol was beyond investigation, as were the experiences of Polish workers in the Ruhr and Catalans in Spain. Very simply, since Italy, Germany and Spain had not signed general minorities treaties, the League could not address these issues. Also, the minorities wanted the creation of a Permanent Minorities Commission to supervise their concerns authoritatively across the year, not *ad hoc* committees set up whenever a petition demanded it.

The minorities needed a firmer kind of representation in the League of Nations. The organisation was a gathering of state representatives, and members of national minorities were scarcely present at all. It was all very well for Colban to meet national minority leaders occasionally, but it was not like actually participating in Assembly debates and Council discussions. Probably the Åland case was the only time representatives of a national minority sat at the Council's table. Feelings of alienation were compounded when statesmen such as Austen Chamberlain made misguided comments to the effect that ultimately minorities should be merged into majority populations. The whole point of the minorities' activism was to maintain their distinctive identities (Jankowsky, 1945: 130).

Finally, it should be noted that many national minorities did not simply want individual rights to be guaranteed, they wanted collective rights. That is to say, they did not just want to send their children to a mother-tongue school (for instance), they wanted their whole national group to be recognised as a legal entity within a given state. Some minorities actually achieved this status. Estonia passed a Cultural Autonomy Law in February 1925 which allowed its minorities to create cultural parliaments, to run their own educational and cultural lives, even to raise their own cultural taxes: but this was the exception rather than the rule (Hiden and Smith, 2006; Housden, 2000). In fact, even in Estonia the German minority still was highly dissatisfied by, amongst other things, land reform which saw their traditional estates requisitioned by the government. As a result, Baltic Germans petitioned the Council complaining about their treatment.

A balanced view of the League and national minorities

When national minorities criticised the League of Nations, they were expressing disappointment in a body which should have been an ally. After all, the interests of minorities and the League coincided considerably. Both wanted to keep the peace: the League because this was its basic purpose and the minorities because, in the event of war, they were likely to be the first to suffer. So why was the League of Nations' treatment of minorities not a clearer success?

As Carole Fink says, the Council was 'wary' of using its investigative powers against sovereign states, the states were 'suspicious' of what the League might do, and the minorities felt 'excluded' throughout the process (Fink, 2004: 277). These responses were characteristic of a time lacking in goodwill between majorities and minorities. The Swiss politician and representative to the League of Nations, Giuseppe Motta, once said that, for the world to be at peace, 'Majorities must be just and generous and minorities must be loyal' (Robinson *et al.*, 1943: 99). Unfortunately, all concerned had not yet learned that truth and did not have the confidence to take it seriously.

Admittedly, Aristide Briand was right that the League of Nations could never become 'indifferent' to the 'sacred cause' of national minorities, and its work marked an important step forward in the management of what could be a source of tension between states (*League of Nations*, 1930: 378). It was a success that no wars broke out over minorities issues during the 1920s. Furthermore, it was quite right that minorities protection should have been internationalised rather than left to the states immediately concerned, since the League had more chance of providing an objective voice on an issue that could involve tremendous emotions. That the organisation construed its job in terms of conciliation rather than prosecution was probably reasonable too, since many high-profile and controversial cases appearing in the Permanent Court of International Justice could have had a negative impact on relations between minorities and majorities across Europe.

And yet the Council took the confidentiality of its work too far. A system which did not even inform the original petitioners of what was done about their complaints was not acceptable. If nothing else, the League should have done more to publicise its successes in the field of minorities protection, in order to win over the hearts and minds of all those who were unsure about the project and to give confidence to those whom it was supposed to be protecting. The judgement of Robert Cecil is about right: in his memoirs he concluded that 'the minority work of the League has been beneficial and that the treatment of the minorities within its scope has been better than that of those outside it' (Cecil, 1941: 120). But still he felt the League could have done better.

CONCLUSION

Were the 1920s some kind of 'golden' period in which temporary success was assured for an organisation such as the League of Nations? The idea goes too far. In the wake of the First World War, this was a challenging, problem-strewn environment. In the words of Elmer Bendiner, it was a 'hard time for heroes' (Bendiner, 1975: 161). Central and eastern Europe had been transformed into a complex of small, new states. In some cases, such as in the borderlands between Poland and Russia, fighting was still going on when the League began to sit. There were borders that had not been finalised by the peace settlement, and the goodwill of interested parties could not easily be assumed. Time and again the League was called on to manage the situation, and the difficulty of the job should not be underestimated. So, although it has been said that the League dealt with the 'small change' of international affairs, even if this were true, there was an awful lot of small change around at the time (Northedge, 1988: 72; Steiner, 2005: 355).

The 1920s were better years than the 1930s, but they were still a minefield of problems with few simple solutions. This is why *The Times* could say in 1923 that 'Europe is on the verge of several possible disturbances . . . Diplomacy, like other old-established institutions, is on its trial' (*The Times*, 17.1.1923).

In this environment, the League of Nations pursued careful work. Time and again it had to strike difficult balances – not least between the demands of geo-strategy, separate states and ordinary people. It approached its challenges with diligence, innovation and imagination, in the process often hinting at the limits of a world organised on the basis of sovereign states. This was clear as it advocated autonomy for Ålanders and Kurds, organised the international supervision of Memel harbour, and attempted to promote the rights of national minorities. All of these measures showed that states could not be allowed to act however they chose even within their own borders.

Was this a promising start for the League of Nations? Robert Dell thought not. Seeing Poland occupy Vilnius, Lithuania seize Memel, and Italy invade Corfu (albeit temporarily), he quoted Tennyson: 'Unchecked aggression broadened down from precedent to precedent' (Dell, 1941: 25). He thought these cases sowed the seeds of the League's eventual collapse. But such a conclusion ignores the full scope of the League's work. It does not give credit for the organisation's undoubted successes (e.g. the Ålands and the Greco-Bulgarian incident), for its more equivocal successes (e.g. Upper Silesia and Mosul), or even for the silver linings when it struggled. For instance, concerning national minorities, at least the Council and Minorities Section maintained a record of treatment of these people as a source of pressure on potential persecutors. In the context of the time, the overall picture warrants a conclusion that the League made a promising start, thanks to the careful work of its staff.

4

International Humanitarian Action: Refugees and Security

INTRODUCTION

From the outset, the League of Nations was not just involved in high politics; it played an important part in international humanitarian projects too. Nowadays it is easy to think of these operations as offering welfare rather than security. The likes of Oxfam, the United Nations High Commission for Refugees (UNHCR) and the Red Cross can be viewed as caring for needy people after security has already broken down. They seem to become active only after the outbreak of war, famine or some other catastrophe; they do not seem to prevent disasters in the first place; but this way of thinking is incomplete. The League of Nations began to show how international humanitarian and social co-operation could encourage peace through the successful management of issues which, if left untreated, had the potential to destabilise international relations, even to the point of war. Its work managing refugees and other people displaced from their homes was particularly important in this connection (Northedge, 1988: 166).

True, refugee questions were hardly new. People had been driven from their homes by disasters since ancient times; but the scale of the problem as experienced by Europe in the wake of the First World War was colossal. Millions upon millions of people were set in motion and just about every country on the continent felt the effects in one way or another. This is why the inter-war period has been called 'the era of refugees' (Skran, 1995: 14, 31).

Of course, multiple causes stood behind what was happening. The to-ing and fro-ing of the eastern front had led the Russian Empire to evacuate population groups to the Russian interior where later they were left destitute. The Russian Revolution, followed by the country's civil war, caused hundreds of thousands more to try to flee the country. Meanwhile, in Anatolia, tensions between Muslim and Christian associated with, first, the 1914–18 war, and then the conflict between Greece and Turkey, caused almost two million people to leave their homes for good. Then famine in the Ukraine (1921–23) made still more people homeless. All of this happened ten years before Hitler's anti-Semitic policies unleashed a fresh wave of refugees across Europe.

If the League of Nations aspired to establish co-operation between states as a habit which would help insulate the world from the threat of war in the future, common work over so many refugees was a good way to go about it. Article 25 of the Covenant mandated action 'in mitigation of suffering throughout the world' and without doubt there was a humanitarian imperative to help these people. So when states banded together to secure the lives of refugees, they could be confident that they were addressing an urgent humanitarian cause while promoting the long-term security of the world.

Of course, the movement of so many people clearly constituted a security threat in its own right. In a world still fragile after more than four years of war, such a massive burden of humanity could disrupt political and economic systems within states and provoke tension between neighbours. The situation called for a distinctly international response, and as T.F. Johnson (Nansen's deputy) once put it, if the problems associated with refugees did not fall to the League of Nations, to whom should they fall? (Johnson, 1938: 11).

Who else was either competent or able to address such international catastrophes? The League was an international organisation, and as a rule both causes of, and solutions to, refugees problems were international. Often refugees had been put to flight not simply by domestic actions, but by events such as wars, which involved several different states. As they crossed borders, refugee movements had consequences for a number of countries. What is more, the sheer numerical scale of the refugees, the demand for immediate humanitarian relief, the danger of epidemic diseases, the need to find employment, a population often lacking official papers such as passports, and groups of overwrought people displaced into sensitive border regions, could only be dealt with by some kind of international effort. Generally the problems outstripped the capacities of even established charities such as the Red Cross – especially if they were acting in isolation.

Governments working together were the only agents in a position to create long-term responses. Finances had to be raised from every corner of the globe (including rich countries often far removed from the site of the trouble) and the work of international charities (such as Save the Children, Near East Relief and the American Red Cross) had to be co-ordinated. This is why the issues posed by refugees have been said to show the 'inter-connectedness' of the world (Skran, 1995: 65). By their very nature, they cried out for international co-operation: they demanded to be addressed by the League of Nations.

With all this said, the League's work with refugees faced its share of difficulties. Given that it was an organisation of states, and that some of these were responsible for creating refugee movements in the first place, it followed that relations between the organisation's political institutions and the refugee office could be tense; but there were other limitations too. In the 1920s, refugees were conceptualised as a temporary problem, and so the refugee office was supposed to be temporary also – a situation which unfortunately damaged its authority. Neither was it supposed to be universal. Its remit never covered *all* groups of refugees around the globe, but was restricted geographically according to the location of any given crisis. Hence, for instance, it dealt with displaced Russian, Greek, Armenian, Assyrian and German refugees, but not (say) African refugees. Its financial foundations were always flimsy, since states typically were slow to donate funds and, in any case, the High Commissioner for Refugees was not supposed to undertake extensive relief initiatives himself, only to facilitate the ongoing work of voluntary and government agencies. As might be expected under the circumstances, the League lacked a grand strategy for growing its refugee services. Instead of having a clear-sighted plan for developing the work over the years, it responded in *ad hoc* fashion to problems as they emerged.

This work had quite a complicated organisational history within the League. Its story began with a phase between 1920 and 1922, when Fridtjof Nansen was High Commissioner, repatriating prisoners of war; but his work in that capacity overlapped with the period 1921 to 1924 during which he was also High Commissioner for Russian Refugees (Plate 4). In these early years, the dominant concern of refugee work was, if at all possible, to get people back home. When the option no longer looked viable, the emphasis switched to finding long-term employment for refugees, and so the refugee office (now under Nansen's former deputy T.F. Johnson) was moved from its old home in the League's Secretariat to the International Labour Office. At the same time, there were independent specialist bodies dealing with Greek, Bulgarian and Armenian refugees. Particularly after Nansen's death in 1930, the refugee office (now named after him), was given a number of different organisational 'homes', but the main feature of the period was the creation of a High Commissioner for Refugees coming from Germany, a post which lasted from 1933 until the start of the Second World War.

The League's refugee staff always faced institutional challenges and their position within the organisation was complicated. Nonetheless, the scale of the refugee problems encountered in the 1920s, the necessity for action, and the dynamic character of the staff involved meant that these were very important years as the first serious attempts were made to deal 'systematically, and along international lines' with people forced to flee from their homes (Macartney, 1930: 5).

TAKING SOLDIERS HOME, 1920–22

The League of Nations' engagement with refugees started with former prisoners of war (POWs). At the end of the First World War, roughly 1.5 million

POWs were on the territory of the former Russian Empire. About 10 per cent came from Germany and 88 per cent from Austria-Hungary. According to Red Cross reports, they were spread all over the place: 120,000 were in southern Russia, 30,000 in Turkestan, 90,000 in western Siberia, 35,000 in eastern Siberia and 11,000 on the Siberian coast (Housden, 2007: 64). Although the Soviet government declared all POWs free in 1919, the statement had little meaning for people like these. They were stranded in remote regions, lacked access to good transport facilities and, given the disruption in Russia at the time, had very little chance of making their own way home. In effect, they were rendered refugees.

The plight of these people, many of whom had been captured as long ago as 1915–16, was exacerbated by desperate living conditions. Ordinary soldiers existed in overcrowded barracks that could be little more than holes in the ground. Food was minimal, clothing was scarce, camp officials were corrupt and there was the persistent threat of disease, whether typhus or cholera. It was estimated that roughly half of the POWs held in Russia died, while many more had their health damaged permanently (Housden, 2007: 64). All of this was supplemented by the threat of being forced to work in a Soviet munitions factory or even to fight for Bolshevik or anti-Bolshevik forces during the Russian civil war. Emotions ran high in central Europe at this time. In early 1920, a British peace activist attended a public meeting in Vienna town hall which was addressed by former POWs just back from Russia. The hall was 'crowded to suffocation' with people 'in a state of intense emotion' [**Doc. 13, p. 133**]. For millions of Europeans with family members still in Russia, the war was not yet over – even though weapons had been silent for over a year.

At the same time, Russian POWs were unable to return home from camps in Germany. Not only did they become involved in both left- and right-wing political uprisings after the war ended, but by the start of 1920 they were so homesick that there were rumours that they planned to leave their barracks *en masse* and start walking home. No one welcomed the prospect of hundreds of thousands of penniless Russians simply hiking across Germany and the lands to its east. By this point everyone was agreed it was time for the Russian POWs to be returned to their motherland in organised fashion.

On 7 February 1920, the Supreme Economic Council managing the peace asked that the League of Nations take steps to repatriate POWs from Soviet territory. A month later, the General Council of the League of Red Cross Societies reinforced the request by calling for 'immediate action . . . in the name of humanity' (Housden, 2007: 65). The Council of the League of Nations duly accepted responsibility for the issue on the basis of Article 25 of the Covenant which mandated action in 'mitigation of suffering'. In April, the Council turned to Norway's most famous son, Fridtjof Nansen, to lead the project. Although well known as a polar explorer and scientist, Nansen had travelled around Siberia just before the First World War and so had a clearer idea than most about the difficulties involved in organising transport systems across the vast region (Nansen, 1916).

Nansen's acceptance of the job was well timed because German authorities, anxious to return their fellow countrymen home and to remove troublesome Russians, were in the final stages of establishing a repatriation route across the Baltic Sea. Four German ships, each with a capacity of 650 men, were identified to run between Narva (Estonia) and Stettin (then Germany, but now Szczecin, Poland). With POWs finally being brought out of the Russian interior by train and allowed to cross the border into neighbouring Estonia, the first among them embarked on a repatriation ship at Narva on 14 May 1920. Meanwhile, Nansen set up a small secretariat of largely British officials in London and began collecting funds from interested governments. The British Treasury agreed to contribute £227,000, with additional revenue coming from countries that included France, Denmark and Holland. At the same time, Nansen's staff drew on British government expertise to locate shipping and identify routes which would allow the initial German venture to be expanded. Over the next few years, although their system certainly creaked and groaned from time to time, they created something which proved remarkably successful.

In due course, further shipping connections were established across the Baltic. Stettin was connected to Koivusaari (Finland), Ino (Finland) and Riga (Latvia) – but the most important crossing remained via Narva [**Doc. 14, p. 133**]. The town's old Swedish fortress became the focal point for a genuinely international humanitarian effort as aid agencies ran a tented village to assist transiting former soldiers. The place was extremely busy. Designed to accommodate 600 people, in September 1920 it had 3,700; but Nansen's system never collapsed. And as soon as central Europeans disembarked at Stettin, Russians boarded the ships in their place – sometimes waving Bolshevik flags and singing communist anthems as they went. The sense of mission that accompanied the repatriation paid dividends; while Nansen had hoped 60,000 people would be returned home before Christmas, 100,000 had been by September 1920. At this time, 10,000 POWs per month were crossing the Baltic.

As he managed the project, Nansen discovered that several repatriation routes would not work properly. POWs could not be transported by train through Poland, first, because of proximity to the site of the Russo-Polish War and, secondly, due to international sensitivity over the newly created Polish Corridor (i.e. the former German lands given to the new Polish state at Versailles which separated East Prussia from the rest of Germany). Some POWs were transported between Europe and Russia's far eastern port of

Vladivostok, but this proved more difficult than expected. Distance and shipping costs were not the main stumbling blocks here; the difficulties revolved around the presence of anti-Bolshevik military units around Vladivostok and the cost of transporting thousands of people from the Russian interior by rail to the far eastern port. Consequently, only 6,851 POWs were brought out of Vladivostok and only 2,753 returned through it. Russia also had several ports on the Black Sea, and some POWs transited Novorossiysk. Once again, however, transport problems between the port and the Russian interior, plus the lack of reliable information about the number of people waiting for League ships, meant that only 12,191 central European POWs were brought out of the port and no Russian POWs returned through it.

When Nansen made his final report to the Council of the League of Nations in September 1922 he deployed an impressive set of statistics: 427,886 POWs drawn from 26 different national groups had been returned home thanks to the League of Nations. Of these, 406,091 had travelled through the Baltic, mostly via Narva, where they had been assisted in the international camp before getting on a German steamer organised by British maritime experts under the auspices of a Norwegian High Commissioner. And all of this cost, on balance, less that £1 per POW. It was no wonder that the Council responded to Nansen's report as follows:

> If there were any compensation for the evils of war, it was that war gave rise to great virtue. Dr. Nansen had been the embodiment of the great virtues of courage and charity. The work of repatriation was one of the greatest achievements of the League of Nations, and Dr. Nansen had most worthily executed it.
>
> (*LONOJ*, November 1922)

The operation had thrived because Nansen delivered benefits that were internationally recognised and because he had managed to secure a remarkable degree of international co-operation. In addition, he ran the project on a shoestring budget. The success ensured Nansen would receive more work from the League of Nations.

FLIGHT AND REPATRIATION: RUSSIAN REFUGEES, 1920–25

Since it was agreed generally that the POWs desperately needed repatriating, this first project was largely uncontroversial. The treatment of refugees who fled revolution and subsequent civil war in Russia, however, posed more difficult political problems. In fact, even before all of the POWs were returned home, Russian refugees had started moving in numbers that caused a stir. In 1920, there were about 1.5 million Russian refugees spread across Europe, most being destitute and unable to earn a living. It was hardly surprising that, from an early point, relief organisations such as the Red Cross, Save the Children and the American Relief Administration were offering them what support they could.

The collapse of anti-Bolshevik, or 'White', forces in the civil war in 1920 was followed by a mass exodus of people which highlighted the level of crisis afflicting Russia. In March 1920, General Denikin's troops fled from the Black Sea ports of Odessa and Novorossiysk. Eight months later General Wrangel departed the Crimea, taking 135,000 followers with him (Macartney, 1930: 13). The latter evacuation produced the remarkable sight of 75 ships full of refugees heading towards the Bosphorus and Constantinople (today Istanbul). These upheavals caused 130,000 refugees to land in Turkey (with 24,000 on Gallipoli). At the same time about 50,000 made their way to Yugoslavia, 31,500 to Greece and 30,000 to Bulgaria. The refugees tried to help themselves. Nansen recognised they showed 'determination and enterprise', for instance creating an All-Cossack Agricultural Union to form farming settlements in Turkey and beyond (Macartney, 1930: 9). But the scale of the problem outstripped their capabilities.

In February 1921, the International Committee of the Red Cross (ICRC) called on the League of Nations to establish a post of High Commissioner for Russian Refugees. The ICRC thought the job should involve co-ordinating immediate relief, finding refugees work, defining their legal position and repatriating them (*League of Nations*, 1930: 268). Initially, however, the Secretary General, Eric Drummond, was reluctant to get involved because he did not feel his organisation could accept the 'moral obligation' of dealing with the refugees (Housden, 2010). Nonetheless, Britain and France were already deeply engaged in supporting these people financially (having already assisted Denikin's and Wrangel's armies in Russia), and the longer time went on, the more desperate they became to hand on the problem to someone else (Skran, 1995: 89). Furthermore, in spring 1921 the Red Cross sent its own commissioner, General Thomson, to report on refugees in Turkey and the Balkans. The mixture of practical pressure from Britain and France plus the desperate picture painted by Thomson led the League to offer Nansen the post of High Commissioner in June.

He took up the position in August with a mandate to co-ordinate existing relief efforts for refugees rather than the expectation of delivering relief directly through the League of Nations, which would have required a massive budget. To facilitate co-ordination, during August and September two conferences were held involving Nansen, his staff and the main charities assisting the refugees. In the meantime, Constantinople (which has been called the 'dumping ground' for White Russians) and its surroundings emerged as a critical test for the new High Commissioner (Skran, 1995: 38).

Initially General Wrangel had wanted to keep his troops as military formations and organised a camp on Gallipoli accordingly, but by summer 1921 his resources were running low and he was badly in need of outside assistance **[Doc. 15, p. 134]** (Plate 5). Constantinople's existing problems were compounded by news in early autumn that both the French government and the American Red Cross planned to cease their relief efforts there, leaving 15,000 refugees without any means of subsistence. An absolute crisis was averted only by the work of the director of the Imperial Ottoman Bank and the Constantinople Relief Fund for Russian Refugees which managed to get rations from the British army to feed 11,500 people daily (Housden, 2010).

Lacking the budget to provide direct relief to refugees, Nansen had to rely on other strategies. So he negotiated the dispersal of refugees away from Constantinople. With his assistance, large numbers of former White Russian troops were taken in by other states, especially by Bulgaria and Yugoslavia. Typically, they formed work gangs on roads and railways, but in Yugoslavia they were also used to establish military units and border guard formations. Czechoslovakia took groups of students to attend university there. Hungary accepted several thousand people to help collect the harvest. Others were taken in by France to work in the motor industry. The result of all this activity was that, by July 1923, 20,000 refugees had been evacuated from Constantinople to 44 different countries and consequently the threatening situation had been dealt with.

An important step in this process had involved the provision of identity documents to refugees – so-called 'Nansen passports'. Many refugees lacked official papers and it was not clear how they should be dealt with. The lack of documents was important because without them the refugees could not cross borders to find work or homes. In July 1922, however, 16 governments had accepted the 'Nansen passports' – the documents issued by his office which included photographs and personal details of the refugees concerned (Macartney, 1930: 28). By 1929, 50 governments fully recognised them (Skran, 1995: 105). It was thanks to these documents that refugees were able to move away from Constantinople.

But in the early 1920s, most people agreed that the best way to deal with Russian refugees was via repatriation. To quote Nansen from September 1922:

> in the long run, there can be no final satisfactory solution to the problem created by the presence of such a large number as one and a half million [Russian] refugees in Europe except by the repatriation of, at any rate, the greater part of them.
>
> (*LONOJ*, Appendix 401: November 1922)

Both the American Relief Administration and the Red Cross agreed that Nansen should contact the Soviet government with a view to returning refugees to their homeland.

Not everyone was enthusiastic. At the Third Assembly held in September 1922, several representatives spoke out passionately against forcing Russians to return to territories now controlled by the Bolsheviks (Skran, 1995: 152). Later Nansen emphasised that he was only contemplating *voluntary* repatriation; he certainly had no intention of forcing anyone to return to Russia against their wishes. Some White Russian émigré groups, however, disliked the idea of repatriation altogether. They did not want manpower to return to a Soviet empire and maintained that any former White Russian soldier going home was likely to be executed on arrival. They also argued that Nansen was working too closely with the Soviet government to be a reliable representative of refugee interests (*The Times*, letter from Nabokov: 11.2.1922). At the same time, the Soviet government was suspicious that former refugees returning home might stir up trouble against the regime and its revolutionary social order.

Immense problems stood in the way of Nansen repatriating Russian refugees. Nonetheless, as he went about his job he must have taken heart from the fact that many rank-and-file White soldiers certainly wanted to go home. Following an amnesty for White soldiers declared by the Soviet Central Executive Committee in November 1921, during 1922 refugees made their own way back to southern Russia, hundreds at a time. It was appropriate, therefore, that in the autumn of that year, an agreement was finally struck between Nansen and the Soviet government permitting repatriation to the Cossack lands of Don, Kuban and Terek.

When the repatriation system was set up, it involved refugees assembling at the Black Sea port of Varna (Bulgaria) where, first, they declared they were returning home voluntarily and, second, they underwent a security check by Soviet officials. Next, they sailed to Novorossiysk where they had another security interview before setting off for home. Especially notable about this repatriation project was the fact that Nansen had two representatives in Russia, a Briton called John Gorvin and a Swiss citizen called Simonett. The two men observed the Soviet security interviews in Novorossiysk and toured the regions to which the refugees were repatriated, checking that they were treated decently [**Doc. 16, p. 135**]. As a result of this system, 771 refugees were returned home in January 1923, 810 in February, 797 in April and 1,062 in May (Reynolds, 1949: 234).

The care Nansen took to ensure the welfare of the refugees upon return to Russia defines this event as the first *modern* repatriation of refugees from civil conflict. As he said to the Council of the League in March 1924: 'Of the refugees repatriated with the assistance of the High Commission, no cases of unfavourable discrimination have come to the notice of the representatives of the High Commission either direct or through delegates of the foreign relief societies still working in Russia' (*LONOJ*, April 1924). The system actually worked – at least for a short time. Unfortunately it fell apart completely in June 1923 when the Bulgarian government accused Soviet officials working on its territory of spying. This debacle put a stop to repatriation as a means to deal with Russian refugees, since the Soviet government entered into no more comparable agreements. This meant that refugee issues now had to be seen in terms of transferring people from overcrowded centres (such as Constantinople) to lands where they could find employment; and this is why, at the start of January 1925, the refugee bureau was taken away from Nansen and was re-constituted in the International Labour Office.

But none of this should detract from all that Nansen achieved. In addition to the story of Constantinople, he intervened in Romania and Poland to prevent thousands of refugees being sent forcibly back to Russia and without any official papers – a situation that would have landed them in jeopardy (Skran, 1995: 235–6). And Nansen wanted to do much more for Russians. In particular he wanted to tackle the consequences of the Russian famine (1921–23) which displaced millions from their homes in the south of the country. He painted a particularly heart-rending picture of the catastrophe in a keynote speech delivered to the Assembly in September 1922 (Johnson, 1938: 222). Once again he was entering difficult political territory, because many competing voices hoped the disaster might cause the collapse of communism. Hence, during the Assembly debate, representatives from Yugoslavia spoke out against him. For Nansen, however, 20 million people could not be allowed to die just to destroy a political system (Reynolds, 1949: 229). In the end, Nansen personally became involved in relieving the Russian famine, but he had to work directly with charities such as the Red Cross, not via the League of Nations and its governments.

EXCHANGING POPULATIONS: GREECE AND TURKEY

Not only did the Russian refugee disaster overlap with the POW project, it was concurrent with major population upheavals in Greece and Turkey. Given the location of Constantinople at the point where Europe and Asia Minor join, the city was affected further by these additional major events.

What happened between Greece and Turkey was the culmination of events stretching back decades. During the Balkan wars of 1912–13, Greece had increased her size considerably, but in the process gained an increasingly mixed population, including Muslim Turks in Western Thrace. Even so, the country did not encompass all Greek communities and, most notably, large numbers of ethnic Greeks still lived in Turkey. The point was highlighted in the Treaty of Sèvres (August 1920) which recognised that Smyrna (located on Turkey's Aegean coast and at the time home to a Greek community of about 600,000 people – today it is called Izmir) should become part of Greece (Pentzopoulos, 2002: 29). In June 1921 war began between Greece and Turkey as the former tried to extend its borders to include as many of Anatolia's Greek communities as possible. By summer 1922, however, the tides of war were turning and August saw a major Greek defeat. Thereafter, Turkish troops swiftly took back Greek-occupied territory and in early September sacked Smyrna so savagely that between 12,000 and 30,000 Christians, mostly Greeks and Armenians, were killed (Pentzopoulos, 2002: 79; Skran, 1995: 43).

This Turkish victory, and its apparent brutality, acted as a signal for Greek and Armenian communities to flee Turkish territory. Hundreds of thousands began to move at once (Plate 6). This was quickly noticed by Colonel Proctor who now acted as Nansen's official representative in Constantinople (at the time controlled by Allied High Commissioners, not the Turkish government). On 16 September 1922 Proctor wired the Council requesting permission to start helping the refugees from Anatolia arriving at Constantinople. Two days later, the Council granted the request and the Assembly went on to authorise that Nansen open negotiations with Greece and Turkey over the crisis (Pentzopoulos, 2002: 62). In October, Nansen travelled to Constantinople. One evening he went out from the city and described what he saw:

> When at night we came on top of a hill, I thought I saw a whole city before me with its thousands of lights – it was their [the refugees'] camps spread out over the plain, camp-fire by camp-fire, and there they were sleeping on the ground without shelter of any kind . . . They do not know where they are going and will find no shelter when they come.
>
> (Clark, 2006: 48)

As a young journalist, Ernest Hemingway also witnessed the refugees leaving Turkey. He saw miles and miles of carts pulled by cows and oxen, followed by dead-tired people bringing all their worldly possessions with them (Clark, 2006: 48).

Nansen's organisation was soon assisting people. It helped 156,000 leave Asia Minor, tackled food shortages on the islands of Chios and Samos, and gave £5,000 to the Epidemics Commission (see Chapter 5) to combat disease among the refugees. Some help was also given to the Muslim equivalent of the Red Cross, the Red Crescent, because Turkish refugees had also started moving out of Greece. But apart from these humanitarian initiatives, Nansen undertook political and diplomatic moves as well (Macartney, 1930: 85).

As the Assembly had recommended, from the time he reached Constantinople Nansen held discussions with the Greek and Turkish governments. Out of these came an idea which today sounds appalling – enforced population exchanges. Who exactly was responsible for this is a matter of some debate, since all parties subsequently disowned the approach. Nansen played a part, but a League of Nations document suggests that initially he thought the exchange would be voluntary, not compulsory (i.e. people were to 'emigrate freely'). At the time, he also observed that given the size of population movements already under way, if they were not regulated officially somehow, the result could be disaster in all the states affected (*LONOJ*, January 1923). In Athens, Premier Eleftherios Venizelos accepted that there was no alternative to enforced population exchanges, not least because 800,000 Greek refugees were heading for his country – which had a population of only about 4.5 million. Where could he put these people if not in the houses of ethnic Turks who should make the reverse journey? Meanwhile in Ankara, the Turkish government seems to have assumed that any agreement over refugees would be on the basis of a large-scale and compulsory re-sorting of populations. Finally, although British statesman Lord Curzon described the exchange as 'thoroughly bad and vicious', the Allied High Commissioners for Constantinople also endorsed the idea of an exchange on 15 October (Pentzopoulos, 2002: 63).

So enforced population exchange became a commonly agreed policy among the politicians in autumn 1922, and the thinking was not unique. Already the Treaty of Neuilly (1919) had made provision for population exchanges between Greece and Bulgaria, and now the Greek-Turkish problem became the subject of an international agreement (Pentzopoulos, 2002: 18). The Lausanne Conference opened in November 1922 and the negotiations it hosted led, on 30 January 1923, to the signing of a convention allowing the compulsory exchange of Christians living in Turkey and Muslims in Greece. The only exceptions were Greeks in Constantinople and Muslims in Western Thrace (Pentzopoulos, 2002: 12; *LONOJ*, annex 565: November 1923). The agreement increased the numbers of refugees moving between the two countries, and in the end roughly 1.4 million Greeks left Turkey while 400,000 Turks were forced out of Greece. These were massive numbers, which led to the question of what was to be done with so many uprooted people.

Rightly or wrongly, it was assumed that Turkey did not face such major problems with her incoming refugees. It was believed they could be settled in properties vacated by the much more numerous Greeks (Macartney, 1930: 85–6; *LONOJ*, January 1923). But how could Greece accommodate such a massive addition to her modest population? Nansen's colleague, Colonel Proctor, began important practical work. In October 1922 he started settling 10,000 Greek refugees in Western Thrace in homes vacated by Turks fleeing east. Proctor worked so efficiently that by April 1923 they had been settled in eleven villages and were already becoming self-sufficient by farming maize and tobacco (Clark, 2006: 149; Nansen, 1976: 22). In truth, this was a deceptively easy experiment, because most of Proctor's refugees had only travelled from Eastern Thrace, were farmers and had brought livestock and tools with them (Macartney, 1930: 90). Nonetheless, Proctor's successful venture pointed towards a strategy which the League took up with enthusiasm.

By early 1923, Greece was awash with refugees. They made up 40 per cent of the population of Athens, 25 per cent of Piraeus and 48 per cent of the Aegean islands (Clark, 2006: 151). Through the League of Nations, US statesman Henry Morgenthau became involved in managing these people. When he looked at this sea of humanity, he did not just see a problem. Building on what Proctor had achieved already, Morgenthau saw an opportunity. As he put it:

> the refugees themselves are an additional asset. They bring you fresh manpower to develop your resources of lands and materials. For example, the Turks who are being removed from Macedonia are evacuating more than 40,000 houses and farms. The refugees will cultivate these farms more efficiently, and wholly for the benefit of Greece.
>
> (Clark, 2006: 157)

To deal with Greece's problems, in September 1923 the Council approved the establishment of a Refugee Settlement Commission. Initially it was chaired by Morgenthau and, with the League's backing, by December 1924 it had raised a loan worth £12.3 million from banks in London, New York and Athens to facilitate the settlement of refugees in new homes and to make them productive components of the Greek economy. The Refugee Settlement Commission's work was assisted further by the agreement of the Greek government to make available 500,000 hectares of land for new homes. This was to come mainly from the property of Turks who had left Western Thrace and Macedonia, plus land reclaimed from swampy districts.

The Refugee Settlement Commission promoted rural settlement especially, spending roughly three-quarters of its budget in this way. Over the next three years, as well as taking over Turkish houses, it supervised the construction of 40,000 new homes in the countryside and, together with the Greek government, provided 145,051 cattle and horses plus 99,940 goats for new farms. Stockbreeding refugees received 20 sheep per family. Tools, seed crops and fodder were all provided too. Model farms were established to teach the refugees good practices and health centres were created to help them avoid illnesses such as malaria. By December 1930, 570,156 refugees had been settled in agricultural areas of Greece (Pentzopoulos, 2002: 105). It is hardly surprising that the rural settlement project has been called 'a success so remarkable as to border on the prodigious', but there was urban settlement too (Macartney, 1930: 99–102, 107). Suburbs were built in town after town and by the end of 1929 almost 30,000 new town houses had been constructed in 125 urban quarters (Pentzopoulos, 2002: 113). Refugees housed there were employed in some of the public works schemes supported by the government, for example building roads, canalising rivers and draining marshes.

The Refugee Settlement Commission handed over its work to the Greek government in 1930. The changes it had helped manage left an indelible mark on the country. In terms of demography, with so many Muslim Turks leaving the country, the percentage of ethnic Greeks rose steeply – from 42 to 88 per cent in Macedonia and from 17 to 62 per cent in Western Thrace (Pentzopoulos, 2002: 134–5). But apart from this ethnic homogenisation of the country, the Greek economy benefited. Eyewitness accounts describe rural landscapes which used to be barren springing to life in a matter of years. Apart from providing manpower to till the land and for public works, the refugees brought new industries with them, such as carpet manufacture, as well as financial and trading skills which benefited the country. For these economic reasons (and regardless of whether the refugees would have agreed at the time), the 'Hellenic disaster' has been called a 'blessing in disguise' for Greece (Pentzopoulos, 2002: 115). That its heritage could be looked on so positively was, in large measure, thanks to the work of the League of Nations.

THE ARMENIANS: SUFFERING WITHOUT A NATION STATE

The League of Nations became involved in other resettlement schemes. One was instituted for Bulgaria in 1926 to help 26,000 families evacuated from Greece as a result of the Treaty of Neuilly (1919) (Macartney, 1930: 117–20). Far more complicated, however, was the effort of the League, and particularly of Nansen, to assist Armenian refugees.

At the same time as Greek refugees moved out of Turkey, 300,000 Armenians did the same (*League of Nations*, 1930: 271). Armenians had a tortuous history in the Ottoman Empire. The infamous atrocities suffered during the First World War are well known, but as a Christian people, they experienced further persecution following the collapse of the Greek army in 1922. So they fled. But the parallels with the Greek case were not exact because, while Greek refugees could cross a border into a state they could regard as 'theirs', this was not so easy for Armenians. An independent Armenia had existed only briefly after the First World War and in early 1922 it was absorbed by Soviet Russia to form a Soviet Socialist Republic. So what was to happen to the 45,000 Armenian refugees who fled to Greece? When the Greek government, weighed down with its own problems, wanted 9,000 Armenians to be removed quickly, where were they supposed to go? (Nansen, 1976: 23).

In September 1923 Armenian refugees themselves proposed to the League of Nations that 50,000 of their number be assisted to move to desert land near Yerevan in the Armenian S.S.R. (Nansen, 1976: 5; Macartney, 1930: 56). They asked the organisation to raise £1 million to help fund the project and, in September 1924, the League's Assembly invited the International Labour Organisation and Nansen to investigate the idea's viability. In 1925 a committee of experts led by Nansen visited Yerevan and the surrounding area. It found the project was feasible if suitable investment was made to irrigate some of Armenia's deserts. In fact, Nansen felt 15,000 people could be settled relatively quickly (*LONOJ*, annex 804: October 1925). In September 1925 the Assembly sent back another commission which found the project 'technically sound and commercially possible' (Macartney, 1930: 61). Unfortunately, the plans came to nothing, the nub of the problem being that any loan supporting the project would have to be guaranteed by a Soviet bank. Although Nansen argued long and hard that the money involved only amounted to the cost of a single battleship, western financiers refused to accept the arrangement (Reynolds, 1949: 262–4). Consequently, over the next four years the project fizzled out.

More successful was the treatment of 90,000 Armenians who fled to Syria and Lebanon – 40,000 of whom made their home in camps in Aleppo, Alexandretta and Beirut (*League of Nations*, 1930: 276). In 1925, a report by English Quakers drew attention to the dire conditions in which these peoples were living: only 10 per cent had regular jobs, and 40 per cent had no jobs at all (Skran, 1995: 177). Other eyewitnesses related how refugees near Beirut lived in hovels made out of rough boards and sacking. At Alexandretta the population was ravaged by malaria. The situation in Aleppo became especially serious in 1925 when a spate of anti-refugee riots broke out, leading those people to be moved to Beirut (Macartney, 1930: 67).

With the refugee office now led by Nansen's former deputy, T.F. Johnson, and located in the International Labour Office, a special committee was set up in November 1926 to deal with Armenian refugees. Thereafter Johnson toured Lebanon and Syria to see for himself how people were living. The International Labour Office decided to treat the matter urgently and drew up a plan to settle 20,000 of the most needy refugees. France, which was the mandatory power in the region, donated £25,000 which permitted the project to start swiftly. As a result, within two years 8,000 refugees had been settled in urban and rural areas (Plate 7).

The project went on for another ten years. Although more funding came from France and philarmenian charities, a system of revolving funds proved vital to keeping things going. Loans were made to help establish refugees and were paid back when the recipients could afford to do so. The returned money was then lent again to a fresh set of refugees who required settlement. As a result, by 1938, 36,000 Armenian refugees had been settled in towns and 1,100 in agricultural colonies. The settlement project not only brought better conditions of life for the refugees, who moved away from malaria-infested areas, but benefited the Syrian and Lebanese population as a whole, since the improved sanitation and water supplies required by the new settlements offered general advantages (Skran, 1995: 181–2).

REFUGEES IN THE 1930S

As the Armenian case shows, the issue of refugees remained highly topical during the 1930s. The League's engagement with it, however, suffered an 'irreparable loss' in May 1930 when Nansen died (McDonald, 1944: 211). His charismatic and forceful personality did much to keep refugees on the League's agenda, even if (as in the case of settlement around Yerevan) solutions could be hard to find. It was fitting, therefore, that during the 1930s, the section dealing with refugees was called the 'Nansen Office'.

During this decade, Hitler's government of Germany led to a fresh wave of refugees. Consequently, in October 1933 James McDonald was appointed High Commissioner for Refugees coming from Germany – a post which caused him much frustration. The new Secretary General, Joseph Avenol, wanted the refugee office located outside Geneva and reporting to a special governing body, not the Council of the League – an arrangement which damaged its status. Furthermore, McDonald became convinced that the only way to deal with refugees was to influence the domestic policies of the countries causing the movements in the first place. He really wanted pressure put on the Third Reich to cease its anti-Semitism. Unfortunately his advice was not acted upon, and so McDonald put his convictions into a lengthy letter of resignation sent on 27 December 1935 [**Doc. 17, p. 136**].

McDonald's efforts were not entirely wasted. The League still was responsible for protecting some 600,000 refugees in total, and between 1933 and 1935 the High Commission assisted roughly 60,000 people to establish themselves (McDonald, 1944: 215–20). This was done mainly through the application of private rather than government funding, which helped 25,000 people find homes around Europe, while 27,000 migrated to Palestine and 9,000 to the USA (Skran, 1995: 200).

The High Commission was re-founded in 1936 under Sir Neill Malcolm and again two years later under Herbert Emerson. By this point, however, refugee issues were being ignored relative to Europe's deteriorating general security situation. As the Évian Conference of July 1938 showed, states became increasingly wary of engagement with international problems that could be avoided. Hence, when statesmen met at the French spa town to discuss Europe's refugees, only the Dominican Republic offered to take in settlers. Although Neill Malcolm blamed a poor economic environment for the lack of generosity, by this time the European powers were more concerned with preparations for war (Skran, 1995: 214).

CONCLUSION

Not everyone was impressed by the League's achievements with refugees. Robert Dell maintained that even if it did good work like this, it was not enough to justify the organisation's existence (Dell, 1941: 24). His argument was contradicted by League officials, for whom the organisation's humanitarian projects were an inescapable obligation.

It is true that the League of Nations was not perfect: Nansen's repatriation of Cossacks to southern Russia did not achieve its potential; perhaps he should not have been party to an agreement that justified the uprooting of almost two million people in Greece and Turkey; homeless Armenians were not settled around Yerevan; and during the 1930s more might have been done to combat Germany's anti-Semitism. But, even with all this said, it is impossible to deny that a vast amount was achieved. Over 400,000 prisoners of war were repatriated, crisis was avoided in Constantinople, hundreds of thousands of Greeks were settled, tens of thousands of Armenians were given homes in Syria and Lebanon, and even in the difficult circumstances of the 1930s, efforts were made to find homes for those fleeing Germany. And the achievements in the 1920s were all the greater, given both the massive numbers involved and the fact that crises overlapped. There was more than enough here to justify the work of the High Commission, particularly given that it seldom received more than 1 per cent of the League's budget (Johnson, 1938: 207).

The documentation left by Nansen and his team tells an exciting story. Whether it is Gorvin's reports from the Cossack lands, Nansen's tale of visiting Yerevan or Johnson's description of Armenian camps in Lebanon, there is a sense of men exploring new worlds. This was humanitarianism as adventure. But not only were they pioneers in a geographical sense, they were explorers in terms of policy too. With central and eastern Europe as a laboratory for their endeavours, they were trying for the first time to develop proper international systems to address staggering tragedies. In the process, they were helping to organise the peace of the world. Their humanitarian activities defused situations which could have threatened the security of vulnerable regions directly. Thousands of destitute Russians trekking across central and eastern Europe could have provoked a crisis in 1920, while Wrangel's private military camps on Gallipoli were a potential source of trouble. But more simply still, the swamping of places such as Constantinople and Greece by so many desperate people clearly called for major work to prevent social and economic collapse.

On the other hand, there was a more general aim of increasing understanding and co-operation between nations. When Nansen repatriated prisoners of war, he undertook a global mission in which many states had a direct interest. The same could be said of the Russian refugee work. Many states were affected directly, and many more were required both to help fund the solution to the problem and to provide homes for the unfortunates. Through these projects, Nansen was not only promoting humanitarianism in world affairs, but also contributing to the formation a world community of states (Sweetser, 1943a: 71).

It has been said that the League's failures over refugees were due to timid governments, while its successes were thanks to a few brave men (McDonald, 1944: 208). With his achievements of the 1920s, Nansen showed what could be done with courage, a driven personality and unassailable moral purpose. Certainly the systems he helped create, and the priorities he championed, contributed to a sea change which left refugees in a much better situation after the First World War than they had been before it. In the process, Nansen laid the basis for a refugee regime which can be recognised today in the UNHCR. Many of its ongoing strategies, including repatriation and relocation to a new country, were pioneered in the 1920s. In fact, the idea that refugees are a special class of people who deserve the international community's generosity dates to this period. It is not by chance that this organisation still gives out annually a Nansen Refugee Award to individuals who have done outstanding work assisting refugees. Nansen's story, then, is a history which has particular resonance today.

5

Removing the Causes of War: Social and Economic Projects

INTRODUCTION

In addition to its work with refugees, the League of Nations undertook social and economic reforms which became elaborate and comprehensive. Compared with the arbitration of disputes between states, this work has been described as an 'afterthought' inspired by Jan Smuts's *The League of Nations: A Practical Suggestion* (Brierly, 1960: 478). The rationale behind it was simple. On the one hand, it was to improve the lot of ordinary people – something that was good in its own right and which might stimulate popular support for the work of the League. On the other hand, it was to eradicate the conditions likely to provoke social unrest, destabilise governments and create tension between states. There is no doubt that the project was linked, in part, to the anti-communism of men like Smuts, but this was not the whole story. The social reforms were broad and the reformers were building on a strong tradition of earlier activity (see Chapter 2).

Several articles of the Covenant were relevant. Article 22 promised the 'well-being and development' of peoples living in former German and Turkish colonies; Article 23 dealt with conditions of labour, people-trafficking, the drugs trade and disease; Article 25 promised to improve the health of the world **[Doc. 4, p. 118]**. Increasingly, the work based on these clauses has been regarded as admirable. Zara Steiner has applauded the League's 'painstaking progress' (Steiner, 2005: 371). Even if its ventures were not always high-profile, usually they were careful, considered and determined – all of which was necessary in dealing with entrenched problems requiring national, inter-national and even global solutions. The League's work necessitated experts to come together from around the world to form technical committees investigating challenges through research and deliberation. They had to liaise with the Secretariat, Council or Assembly to execute the resulting recommendations – perhaps to inaugurate an international convention designed to combat the problem at issue.

All manner of local difficulties were encountered in the League's social and economic projects and its staff were sent around the globe to witness the problems at first hand. When it came to dealing with servitude and slavery, for instance, someone had to penetrate close-knit Turkish communities in search of Armenian women, while others ventured into Liberia's tropical interior. The skill and dedication individuals brought to such tasks meant the League amassed valuable knowledge about numerous issues. Their efforts added up to something that was substantial and original.

Furthermore, tackling the major scourges of mankind might remove potential causes of war. Rather than a world threatened with instability arising from epidemics or economic collapse, the aim was to build healthy, prosperous societies in which citizens were at peace with themselves and each other. People satisfied with their lives were unlikely to support warlike policies; with social stability, politics could be more thoughtful and constructive; with potential causes of war removed, states were less likely to confront one another. Gilbert Murray summarised this aim: 'No man can prosper in another's ruin' (Northedge, 1988: 168). This was why the social and economic agenda of the League of Nations mattered so much.

CURING THE WORLD

The First World War and its aftermath turned disease into more of an international matter than ever. Four years of conflict had ruined public health systems, marching armies had carried infections with them, and new states were barely able to control movements of sick people across their frontiers. The privations of war left populations in desperate conditions, not least lacking the nutrition necessary to fight off bacteria and viruses. Consequently, disease threatened Europe in an unprecedented way. Given the terms of the Covenant, the League had to act.

It was hoped that the League's engagement would be straightforward. An International Office of Public Health had been established in Paris in 1909 to collect information about the spread of disease. By 1919, it was supported by 31 countries, so initially it seemed logical to use this as a seedbed for a health organization for the League (Walters, 1952: 181). Unfortunately the USA objected to the incorporation of the Paris organization into the League, and while discussions were going on about how to establish a health institution in Geneva, events generated a momentum of their own.

Typhus

Central and eastern Europe was facing a typhus epidemic. The disease is carried by fleas, can produce a mortality rate of between 10 and 50 per cent, thrives

Plate 1 Sir Eric Drummond (front, middle) with some of his staff, early 1920s.

Photo: UNOG Library, League of Nations Archives

Plate 2 Members of the opium committee, early 1920s. Dame Rachel Crowdy is on the left.

Plate 3 Palais Wilson, formerly Hotel National – the first home of the League of Nations in Geneva.

Photo: UNOG Library, League of Nations Archives

Plate 4 Fridtjof Nansen, High Commissioner for Russian Refugees.

Plate 5 Some of Wrangel's soldiers encamped on Galliopoli, c.1921.

Photo: UNOG Library, League of Nations Archives

Plate 6 Refugees trying to leave Constantinople, October 1922.

Photo: National Media Museum/SSPL

Plate 7 An Armenian refugee camp in Syria, 1929.

Photo: UNOG Library, League of Nations Archives

Plate 8 Haile Selassie delivering his speech to the Assembly, 30 June 1936.

Photo: UNOG Library, League of Nations Archives

in cold conditions and preys on people who are already weak. It had been rare in Europe before 1914 and probably was introduced by Russian troops during the offensives of 1914–15. The upheavals in Serbia led to 150,000 cases of typhus, while the retreat of Russian troops in 1916 (associated with the evacuation of civilians from Poland and the Baltic area to central Russia) caused another outbreak of 154,000 cases (Housden, 2009: 22–5).

According to Russian statistics, in 1919 there were 2,229,071 typhus cases in European Russia, rising to 2,649,816 in 1920. League of Nations staff later reckoned that a truer incidence was actually 25 million, i.e. 20–25 per cent of Russia's western population being affected by typhus in this two-year period. The epidemic was more significant than ever because populations were in such a state of flux. About 600,000 prisoners of war were returning home to Poland from Russia, supplemented by a similar number of those who had been evacuated to the Russian interior in 1916. In all, 3 million people swamped Polish quarantine stations in the east between November 1918 and February 1922 – and many had come from, or travelled through, infected parts of Russia.

For some of this time war raged between Poland and Russia, and eastern Poland (especially eastern Galicia) was devastated by typhus [**Doc. 18, p. 137**]. During the war, as many as 200,000 refugees entered Poland without any kind of supervision and in 1919 there were over 230,000 cases of typhus in the region; between 1918 and 1922 there were about 4 million (*New York Times*, 27.6.1920; Balinska, 1998: 43). Disease on this scale soon threatened nearby countries such as Lithuania and Latvia. Western European governments became concerned that, if Poland's health services broke down, the disease would spread further afield still.

Reports from Red Cross organisations active in central and eastern Europe were passed to the League of Nations. They described a situation so serious that voluntary bodies could not master it; only governments could hope to do so. Thus, in April 1920, the League established an Epidemics Commission staffed by a number of people who would become important in the League, including Dame Rachel Crowdy (who headed the League's Section for Social Affairs and Opium), Dr Norman White (the Epidemic Commission's medical commissioner) and Ludwik Rajchman (an influential Polish expert on epidemics who went on to head the League's health organisation). They organised a meeting in Warsaw in March 1922 which was attended by 27 states (including the Soviet Union and Soviet Ukraine), to plan how to combat the epidemic.

True, the League's response could not be as extensive as some had hoped because member governments only contributed 5 per cent of the £2 million of funding which was requested. While states feared typhus, they would not pay to prevent it spreading. On the other hand, with Poland spending 1.5 per cent of its national revenue on disease prevention, sundry international contributions to the humanitarian effort, and the League facilitating the assistance of key medical experts, a major health campaign was mounted. In the first instance, a sanitary cordon was set up between Poland and Russia consisting of 152 medical facilities in the border region (Balinska, 1995: 92). In time, however, Rajchman became convinced that this alone would not stop the disease. It had to be tackled where it originated. So, in September 1921, he and Norman White travelled to Russia to negotiate with Soviet authorities how best to deal with evacuees and refugees travelling through typhus regions. This trip helped pave the way for an eventual sanitary agreement between the Soviet Union and Poland (1923).

Typhus died down during 1923, but the medical work left a lasting legacy. Further sanitary agreements were made between other European countries, for instance Poland and the Baltic States. Investigations were made into the control of diseases in ports on the Baltic and North Seas. Enquiries followed into sanitary practices in the Mediterranean, Red Sea and Far East. Moreover, the typhus epidemic had shown the importance of medical information. During 1921, the League had set up an Epidemiological Intelligence Service to provide information about infectious diseases in Eastern Europe (Manderson, 1995: 113). This initiative grew as Russia began contributing her statistics and then, in 1923, monthly and annual reports began to appear. The system became a worldwide venture when, at Japan's request, an office was opened in Singapore dealing with the Far East. Eventually, over 160 ports contributed regular reports (*Aims, Methods and Activity*, 1935: 150).

In other words, the League started off concerned with typhus in eastern Europe, but went on to look at infectious diseases globally; and this work was recognised as a contribution to peace. It was understood that so long as epidemics raged in eastern Europe, the region could not be rebuilt. As Brazil's representative to the League, Gastoa da Cunha, said in 1920: 'health and wealth, prosperity and peace, are closely bound up with one another' (*LONOJ*, June 1920).

Malaria and much more

In May 1923 the League finally established a Health Committee, and soon health ministries from all over the world were collaborating in its work (Dubin, 1995: 63). Medical institutions and specialists gave their expertise to support its projects, while the Rockefeller Foundation (an American charity) provided generous financial support. One of the first diseases to be tackled by this new international body was malaria.

Malaria affects millions of people even today, but while it is now largely a tropical disease, in the 1920s it affected parts of Europe and Russia too. It is caused by a parasite which can be introduced into a person's bloodstream by a mosquito carrying traces of infected blood picked up when it fed on someone who was already carrying the disease. The unusual system of transmission makes malaria an interesting disease to fight. Should you try to combat the parasites inside infected individuals? Should you destroy the mosquitoes or their larvae? Or is it best to deal with human behaviour, adapting how we live to combat the disease?

The Health Committee created a Malaria Commission in 1924. That year it carried out a research tour of Europe which took in Yugoslavia, Greece, Bulgaria, Romania, Russia and Italy. Apart from noting that war and refugee movements had caused a surge in the disease, the commission recognised the importance of social factors in its transmission. Primitive housing, poor harvests (leading to bad nutrition), and lack of knowledge about malaria all helped it spread. Lack of prosperity made it difficult for states to purchase the amount of medicine (quinine) required to treat all infected citizens. Weather played a part too, since drought could reduce rivers to a series of ponds in which mosquitoes bred. Lastly, at a time when many states were only in the process of setting up effective public health services, the report claimed there were too few medical staff to fight the disease properly (Malaria Commission, 1924). From 1926, therefore, the Commission began to organise malaria training courses in Hamburg, London and Paris, as well as practical sessions in Italy, Spain and Yugoslavia. In 1928 an institute for the study of malaria was opened in Rome and the commission took steps to promote anti-malaria projects in Yugoslavia, Albania, Corsica and Bulgaria (*League of Nations*, 1930: 247).

Another research tour took place in 1925. The commission visited Palestine to observe a project tackling malaria through the destruction of mosquito larvae. The resulting report detailed how the British administration had approached the disease effectively since the First World War. Cisterns in urban areas had been oiled so that mosquitoes could not lay eggs in them, water sources had been closed for the same purpose, steps had been taken to stop larvae being laid in springs, swamps had been drained and water courses canalised to ensure that water either flowed steadily or else dried out completely (Malaria Commission, 1925). There had even been a Health Week in 1924 during which the fight against malaria was publicised, and public health officials travelled around villages treating sufferers with quinine.

On the negative side, some commissioners doubted whether Palestine's anti-malaria success could be replicated in other areas. The Volga, Romania and Bulgaria had soils and vegetation that made canalisation much more difficult, while the water supply system in Bombay (Mumbai) was more complicated than that of Jerusalem (so that all of its cisterns could not so easily be oiled); but even so, the League's report showed how an effective anti-malaria programme could be run under a certain set of conditions.

Later work on malaria saw comparisons made between different drugs used in its treatment (Malaria Commission, 1937). In other words, over the years, the League of Nations managed a sustained and thoughtful investigation of a disease that could damage and destabilise whole communities; and its work did not stop there. The Health Committee investigated diseases such as syphilis, tuberculosis, sleeping sickness, leprosy, rabies, plague and smallpox. It responded to requests from countries including Greece, Yugoslavia and China for assistance in constructing public health systems. It also supported work to standardise medications around the globe. All in all, it did tremendous work in promoting the health of the world and, in the process, underpinned the prospects for peace.

THE DRUGS TRADE

Globalisation and the drugs trade

Addiction to narcotic drugs is a different kind of challenge to public health, and the League's response at the time was called 'the most important branch' of its 'social work' (*League of Nations*, 1930: 299; *Aims, Methods and Activity*, 1935: 175). Opium and its derivatives (including morphine, heroin and codeine) were the main targets, but cocaine was important too. Particularly active in the fight against drugs was the head of the Secretariat's Section for Social Affairs and Opium until 1930, Dame Rachel Crowdy (Plate 2). She was a qualified pharmacist and had participated in the British Red Cross during the First World War (Spaull, 1924; Northcroft, 1926). As a result, she understood the benefits such drugs could confer, but the problems they brought too.

The main aim of the League's opium committee was to restrict the production, manufacture and distribution of narcotic drugs to the amounts required for scientific and medical purposes. It was to acquire information about the scale and methods of the illegal drugs trade so that appropriate responses could be worked out, including more efficient policing and plans for the alternative development of opium-growing regions [**Doc. 19, p. 138** and **Doc. 20, p. 140**]. International issues were involved here, since the production, manufacture and consumption of narcotic drugs could each happen in different countries. Furthermore, the international transport system made use of underhand practices to ensure that shipments of opium from Persia (now Iran) to Vladivostok were diverted to China (where opium smoking was a major problem). At the time, the challenge of opium was becoming so great that no state could hope to address it alone (*Aims, Methods and Activity*, 1935: 176). It only took a single state to flout the efforts of any number of others to regulate the drugs trade, and everything could be subverted at a stroke. Hence the 'chain' of states policing drugs, could only be as strong as its 'weakest link' (Renborg, 1947: 4). And the consequences of weak links were startling indeed. In Egypt half a million people in a population of 14 million became opium addicts in just ten years (Greaves, 1931: 222; *League of Nations*, 1930: 310).

Institutional responses

Concerted attempts to deal with narcotic drugs had begun with the international conferences of 1909 and 1912. Opium was also mentioned in the Treaty of Versailles. In addition to its place in the Covenant, Article 295 of the treaty specified that signatories agreed to the 1912 opium convention.

As the League got underway, the First Assembly set up an Advisory Committee on Traffic in Opium and Other Dangerous Drugs. It comprised representatives of centrally concerned countries (e.g. India, Thailand and China) plus four European states (Britain, France, Portugal and the Netherlands). In line with the Treaty of Versailles, it was commissioned to realise the 1912 convention – in other words, it had to restrict the drugs trade to what was legitimately necessary and compile information about global drugs traffic (Ginneken, 2006: 142; Mowrer, 1931: 486). Conferences followed in 1924 and 1925, the former yielding a commitment to stamp out opium smoking and the latter a pledge to reduce production of raw opium and cocoa leaves. Although some states initially opted out of these proceedings on the grounds that they were not sufficiently ambitious, 41 countries attended the events and a new convention was drawn up (Willoughby, 1976: 441–5).

The 1925 convention sought to control drugs manufacture, established supervision of imports and exports through the use of certificates and licences, and called for regular reports about the workings of the drugs trade. Although only 13 states signed the convention at once, by 1930 the number had risen to 37. These efforts were consolidated by the creation of a Central Opium Board in 1928 to collate, examine and criticise the information being sent to the League by member states about the drugs trade. The idea, of course, was to build up a full picture of what was going on, in order to identify where the system was leaking narcotics for illegal purposes. These initiatives were supplemented in 1929 by an enquiry into opium smoking in the Far East, and new conventions followed. In 1931 there was agreement over a Convention for Limiting the Manufacture and Regulating the Distribution of Narcotic Drugs, which again aimed to restrict production to scientific and medical requirements.

Behind these benchmark events, the League's interest in narcotic drugs changed over time. The organisation started out concerned with the smoking of prepared opium in the Far East, but gradually extended its interest to the abuse, illegal manufacture and supply of narcotic drugs (including morphine, cocaine and heroin) which could have been used for medicine or science. Since efforts to control established medical facilities more closely only led to the proliferation of covert drugs-making factories, the League had to revise its tactics. Some also thought that the drugs problem became worse as the 1920s progressed. The later years of the decade saw large quantities of raw and prepared opium seized in Hong Kong, the Dutch East Indies, Malaya, the Philippines and Australia, while cocaine streamed into India and Burma, and various kinds of drugs were smuggled into the USA and Canada. Japanese and Chinese shipping was said to be carrying much of the contraband opium, while drugs firms in Switzerland, France, Germany and Japan were suspected of supplying narcotics illegally (*League of Nations*, 1930: 301–10).

As the illegal drugs trade developed, the League responded by assuming wider powers – a development that has been likened to an 'international government' which attempted to control how this enterprise functioned across the globe (Sweetser, 1943b: 65; *Aims, Methods and Activity*, 1935: 179–80). League experts estimated the amount of drugs to be manufactured for legitimate purposes and supervised their production and distribution as reported by governments. If a state breached a convention, the experts could recommend an embargo on pharmaceutical trading with the offending country. This system brought about a 50 per cent reduction in official morphine production between 1929 and 1932, and there were also reductions in heroin and cocaine production. It was also credited with reducing the number of addicts in the USA from 100,000 to 50,000 (Sweetser, 1943b: 65–6; Renborg, 1947: 9–10).

SALVAGING HUMANS AND PREVENTING PEOPLE-TRAFFICKING

The League of Nations also took up the cause of individuals whose human rights were flouted. Early on, the organisation became interested in the plight of Armenians in Turkey, who had been subjected to atrocious treatment during the First World War. Many were force-marched to the Syrian desert, but some Armenian women and children were taken into Turkish households where they lived in variable circumstances. The League of Nations tried to help these unfortunates. For instance, a Danish peace activist, Karen Jeppe, worked in association with the League to provide a sanctuary for Armenian women and children who escaped Turkish households (Spaull, 1924: 59–61). A special committee consisting of Jeppe, W.E. Kennedy and Emma Cushman (an American) worked with Armenian women and children in Turkey and reported to the Second Assembly that 90,000 had been rescued

– although adding that a similar number were believed still to be living in harems and orphanages (*League of Nations*, 1930: 279).

The increasing mechanisation of transport through rail and steamships, however, meant that most people who had fallen under the thrall of others probably would not remain incarcerated somewhere like a Turkish harem. Now, more than ever, they could be moved around (or 'trafficked') for purposes of exploitation, and this trafficking could be international – with women and girls being enticed in one state, then moved to a new country where (a long way from home and feeling more vulnerable than ever) they were ensnared and exploited. At the time, this trade often was referred to as 'white slavery', the idea being that white women were particular targets of procurers attempting to supply brothels – often in countries where people had darker skin. There had been an international congress discussing people-trafficking before the First World War, and the issue was mentioned in Article 23 of the Covenant.

Debate in the First Assembly led to a conference in 1921 which was attended by over 30 states and produced the Convention for the Suppression of the Traffic in Women and Children. This raised the age at which a woman could consent to being trafficked from 20 to 21 years. Governments were expected to provide information about how they were implementing the convention within their borders, and an Advisory Committee on the Traffic in Women and Children was to analyse this information (Castendyck, 1944).

The League also conducted special investigations into people-trafficking. The first took place between 1924 and 1926, and was funded by the American Social Hygiene Bureau. It looked at people-trafficking in Europe, the Mediterranean and America and found that hundreds of girls (many aged between 14 and 16) were being moved around for purposes of prostitution. The report suggested that the victims actually consisted of four rather different kinds of people. First, there were regular prostitutes moving to new locations to earn better pay; second, there were part-time prostitutes looking for more money; third, cabaret workers whose contracts turned out to be deceptive; and, last, completely innocent young women who were trapped by unscrupulous procurers. The investigation found that girls were taken from Austria, France, Germany, Greece, Hungary, Italy, Poland, Romania, Spain and Turkey to South and Central America (particularly Argentina, Brazil, Mexico, Panama and Uruguay), although there were also routes to Egypt and North Africa which went through Alexandria. The traffickers used forged documents to facilitate the movement of these women, but were prepared to use bribery, smuggling or any other technique to pass the women from one country to the next (*League of Nations*, 1930: 291–4).

This investigation was so successful that in 1929 the Tenth Assembly instigated something similar in the Far East, with the American Bureau of Social Hygiene this time contributing $125,000. The commission visited cities in the Near, Middle and Far East which had 17,000 prostitutes registered in them. Many were Chinese in origin – Chinese prostitutes were found in any territory from British India eastwards – and had been recruited from the lowest social classes. Their impoverished background suggested that all of the Chinese prostitutes found abroad had, in fact, been trafficked. The report felt their social status, coupled with youth and traditional expectations of obedience to parental authority, left the girls particularly vulnerable to exploitation. As for the procurers, they fell into two categories: brothel keepers and those who recruited and transported the girls in order to sell them to anyone willing to pay [**Doc. 21, p. 142**].

The girls were traded at very young ages. Once owned by a brothel keeper, however, their lives could go in a number of directions: those who showed ability to sing and entertain could be sold on as entertainers; less able girls could be sold for domestic service; others could be sold into forced marriage or concubinage. So this left only a portion of the girls likely to end up working in brothels. Some Chinese ports took special measures to curb people-trafficking, a special voluntary organisation searched ships at Shanghai, while at Swatow, women and children were not allowed to board ships on their own.

Given that China was exporting girls who were turned into prostitutes, it was perhaps ironic that Russian women were brought into China to follow the same profession. Ethnic Russians, for instance, would be told wonderful tales of life in Chinese cities such as Beijing or Shanghai. Then they would be trafficked to such a destination where, completely at the mercy of the trafficker, they would be forced to work in a brothel (*Summary of the Report to the Council*, 1934).

All of these findings led the League's experts to ask whether the existence of licensed brothels was helping to sustain people trafficking. There was a feeling that these establishments kept alive a demand for sex workers and so encouraged traffickers to supply young women. Hence the Far East inquiry recommended that licensed brothels should be closed down. When a League-sponsored investigation into brothels was published in 1934, it found that prostitution could be dealt with more effectively once brothels were closed (*Committee on Traffic in Women and Children*, 1934). In all of these ways, therefore, the League of Nations provided extensive information about the state of people-trafficking and the sex trade in the world, and so contributed to a new style of policing based on international co-operation.

ABOLISHING SLAVERY AND ITS KINDRED FORMS

Linked to people-trafficking was the issue of slavery, an issue that had been addressed internationally well before the First World War and which was mentioned in Article 23 of the Covenant. It was put on the League of Nations' agenda thanks to a speech by Sir Arthur Street-Maitland to the Assembly in 1922 which outlined the continued existence of the institution, especially in Abyssinia (Ethiopia). In response, in 1924 the Council set up an Advisory Committee of Experts on Slavery.

The League's interest soon yielded practical results. In January 1925 it emerged that slavery still existed in the Hukawng Valley in Burma. Closer inspection proved that roughly a third of the area's 10,000 people were enslaved. It was proposed that the slaves be ransomed against a payment of 80 rupees each and that a British officer subsequently should visit the valley each year to assess the progress of the emancipation (*Memorandum Regarding Slavery*, 1925).

Meanwhile, the Advisory Committee's work stimulated the Assembly to draw up the Convention on Slavery, Servitude, Forced Labour and Similar Institutions (1926). It defined slavery very widely, as 'the status or condition of a person over whom any or all of the powers attaching to the right of ownership are exercised'. It sought to abolish the slave trade, including 'all acts involved in the capture, acquisition or disposal of a person with intent to reduce him to slavery', all acts aiming at the sale or exchange of a human being and 'every act of trade or transport in slaves'. The Convention out-lawed the acquisition of girls 'by purchase disguised as payment of dowry', the adoption of children with a view to enslaving them and enslavement as payment of a debt. Compulsory labour was included too (Bales, 2005: 43–4; 2004: 275–6). By the end of 1929, the Convention had been ratified by 30 governments (*League of Nations*, 1930: 287). The League's interest in slavery encouraged Nepal (1926) and the rest of Burma (1928) to eradicate the institution, as did Jordan and Persia (Iran) in 1929.

Abyssinia and Liberia proved particular focuses for the League's anti-slavery work. A report of 1931 noted that although slavery was still permitted in some of the Arab lands to the north of the Red Sea, it also occurred in Abyssinia even though the government had been trying to tackle the problem for some time (*Slavery*, 1932; *The Times*, 7.4.1932). To help end the practice, the report proposed steps to turn popular culture against slavery and recom-mended that local clergy be enlisted to this end. Furthermore, the Abyssinian and Somali coasts had to be supervised to make sure that slaves were not transported across the Red Sea to the Arabian peninsula. The report added that individual Arab states should be admitted to the League only after they abolished slavery [**Doc. 22, p. 143**].

Even more major investigations of slavery took place in Liberia, which had been created in the early nineteenth century as a refuge for freed slaves. In 1929, concern about the continued existence of slavery there, however, led the Liberian government to request that the League investigate. A com-mittee was established under British slavery expert Dr Cuthbert Christy and travelled to Liberia to take evidence (*Report of the International Commission*, 1930). The final report found the allegations to be true. There was evidence of domestic slavery, the pawning of human beings, forced transportation of native workers to the Spanish island of Fernando Po and forced labour on road construction (with many of the workers little more than children). To make matters worse, senior members of the government were implicated in the practices, as were government frontier forces. The report implicated Vice-President Yancey and recommended that the five regional governors of Liberia all had to be replaced [**Doc. 23, p. 144**].

Christy's work led the USA to send a protest to the Liberian government just before the president, vice-president and a number of senior government officials resigned. New laws were adopted prohibiting the abuses outlined in the report and Liberia requested that the League assist in the necessary reform process (Walters, 1952: 569). In time a rift developed between Liberia and the League over these reforms, but nonetheless the organisation had focused an international gaze on some horrible practices inside the country (*The Times*, 12.1.1931, 17.3.1932).

BEYOND IMPERIALISM: MANDATES

The system

While Liberia was a republic, many African territories either were, or had been until recently, colonies. This caused a practical problem at the end of the First World War: what was to be done with the colonies of the defeated powers? The fifth of Woodrow Wilson's Fourteen Points had specified that the needs of native populations had to be paramount when it came to settling colonial questions, and the enactment of this point produced an innovation in international law (Anker, 1945: 7). The solution began to emerge in Jan Smuts's book *The League of Nations: A Practical Suggestion* and took the form of a 'halfway house' between a territory being a colony and fully independent [**Doc. 8, p. 124**]. It was proposed that lands formerly controlled by Turkey and Germany would be supervised by members of the victorious powers (mandatories) until they were ready for complete independence. To ensure that they were administered in the best interests of the native inhabitants (as opposed to being exploited for the benefit of colonial powers), a mechanism would be put in place permitting League officials to supervise what was happening inside these 'mandate' territories.

Mandates were established in Article 22 of the Covenant. It maintained that the progressive government of former Turkish and German colonies with people 'not yet able to stand by themselves under the strenuous conditions of the modern world' amounted to a 'sacred trust of civilisation', adding that 'the tutelage of such peoples should be entrusted' to advanced nations which would look after the 'well-being and development' of native inhabitants.

The idea was supposed to guarantee justice, welfare and progress for native populations. The system was supposed to outlaw slavery and forced labour, while stringent controls were imposed on the supply of alcohol and armaments. But it was recognised that different territories displayed different levels of development, and thus there were to be three different kinds of mandate. 'Category A' mandates were well-developed territories close to independent statehood. These would receive administrative supervision promoting self-government through 'advice and assistance'. 'Category B' mandates required a greater degree of administrative intervention to ensure, for instance, public order, personal freedom and the equality of individuals. The least developed of the categories, 'C', had to be run according to the laws of the mandatory, as if it were a portion of its own territory (*League of Nations*, 1930: 335; Henig, 1973: 13; Greaves, 1931: 172). The mandates were confirmed in three main phases. 'C' mandates were assigned on 17 December 1920 and included South West Africa (to South Africa), German New Guinea (to Australia) and Samoa (to New Zealand). 'B' mandates were confirmed on 20 July 1922 for lands including Rwanda (to Belgium), Cameroons and Togoland (both to France and Britain), and Tanganyika (to Britain). 'A' mandates were assigned on 24 July and included the former Ottoman lands of Syria and Lebanon to be supervised by France; later a British mandate was instituted over Iraq (Anker, 1945: 20).

A Permanent Mandates Commission was set up in February 1921, thereafter meeting twice a year to monitor how the territories were run. Staffed by an international set of ten officials, including most famously Lord Lugard who had been the British governor of Nigeria, each year the Commission collected reports from the mandatory states. It could call senior mandate administrators for interview and receive petitions from native inhabitants.The Commission considered annually how the system was working in a meeting with a representative of the mandatory's state. It then forwarded its report to the Council of the League and published its deliberations – together with supporting materials such as any petition of complaint from native inhabitants.

Discussing mandates

Controversy surrounds the mandates system. This reflects the fact that judgements on colonialism have long been caught between its twin possibilities of civilisation and exploitation (Likhovski, 2006: 7). The mandates system has been called by one critic 'the most elaborate fig leaf ever devised to conceal naked imperial expansion on the part of the victorious nations after the First

World War' (Dumbuya, 1995: vii). France opposed the whole system as a 'serious disruption to the imperial structure' (Callahan, 2008: 104). In Tanganyika British rule did little to promote independence for Africans and instead strengthened Britain's control and 'enhanced the interests of the British Empire in Africa' (Dumbuya, 1995: ix). So, when a new legislative council was established in 1926, no Africans were permitted to sit on it (Dumbuya, 1995: 137). Furthermore, there was often a basic lack of understanding of the mandated regions. Despite the careful work of the Mosul Commission, the construction of Iraq has been described as a senseless sticking together of three very different provinces (i.e. Mosul, Baghdad and Basra). Lebanon has been called similarly artificial (Firro, 2003: 9). Opportunism also played a part when it came to deciding which territories became mandates and which did not. Hence, even though Armenia fulfilled all of the criteria to have been accepted as a mandate, the difficulty of projecting international power into the region militated against the step (Gzoyan, 2009).

For all these negative points, however, there were positives too. The mandates system was novel and certainly spoke of more idealism than simply annexing the territories. The plan for international supervision to benefit the native inhabitants indicated a basic optimism which should not be ignored (Archive 5.1). Ginneken maintains that the publicity attendant on the system did, on balance, make mandatories consider the needs of natives, and the annual publication of petitions of complaint meant it was not easy to ignore their demands [**Doc. 24, p. 145**]. For instance, Geneva's scrutiny encouraged Britain to promote a tolerant religious policy in Tanganyika (Callahan, 2008: 190). Likewise Ginneken argues that the ability of individuals to petition the commission directly contributed significantly to the growing appreciation of human rights internationally. So she concludes that the 'achievements of the Mandates Commission are still regarded as examples of the successes of the League' (Ginneken, 2006: 22, 127). Furthermore, the mandates system did deliver independence: Iraq became a fully-fledged state in 1932. Perhaps understandably, then, William Rappard (a former director of the mandates section) maintained that although the system was not beyond criticism, it was still a progressive solution to the problem of German and Turkish colonies (Callahan, 2008: 191).

ECONOMICS OF PEACE: SOCIAL JUSTICE AND INTERNATIONAL STABILITY

Economics stands behind many of the points raised in this chapter. The quest for economic gain drove the drugs trade and people-trafficking, it was a reason for slavery and helps explain why European states built up world empires (i.e. the trend which the mandates system was supposed to react against). Economics could be associated both with tensions between different groups within states, and between states as jostling for pride of place in the world. It was inevitable, therefore, that the League of Nations address domestic and international economic issues as it organised the peace of the world.

The International Labour Organisation

The International Labour Organisation (ILO) was established in Part 13 of the Treaty of Versailles which maintained that existing conditions of labour involved such 'injustice, hardship and privation' for large numbers of people that peace was jeopardised. Long-term tranquillity had to be founded on 'social justice' – the conditions under which people worked had to be fair, equitable and not injurious to health. The issues involved included hours of work, regulation of the labour supply with a view to preventing unemployment and the protection of women, children and the elderly. In addition, the ILO was supposed to promote the welfare of workers by ensuring their rights of association and access to education. For reasons of 'justice and humanity', it followed that states should co-operate to create a generally decent approach to work. They had to establish good common standards of living and conditions of work, plus protection against 'sweated' labour (Noel Baker, 1926: 78). To pursue such ends, the ILO first met in conference in Washington in October 1919, that is, even before the League of Nations came into existence formally. Its constitution declared that 'all human beings, irrespective of race, creed or sex, have the right to pursue both their material well-being and their spiritual development in conditions of freedom and dignity, of economic security and equal opportunity' (Guigui, 1972: 1).

Albert Thomas, a French Socialist who had spent years understanding how workers and governments approached economic issues, was appointed director of the ILO in January 1920. He was also thoroughly committed to lessening tensions between states and to the idea of the League of Nations (Alcock, 1971: 49–50). He presided over a new kind of organisation and, consequently, often found himself engaged in pioneering work (Shotwell, 1934: xx). The ILO was established as an autonomous institution within the League of Nations which, rather than being controlled by the Council or Assembly, had its own governing body, its own annual conference (with delegates drawn not only from governments, but also from employers' and workers' organisations) and its own office. Furthermore, it sent representatives to sit on various League committees (such as the Permanent Mandates Commission) with a view to commenting on labour issues when they arose.

The ILO could also make recommendations to national governments about labour affairs. These took the form of conventions which could be agreed by the ILO's annual conference. Here, proposals were drawn up by ILO staff after discussion with national governments. They were debated, and if the conference decided to adopt one as a convention with a two-thirds vote, members had to present it for discussion by their national parliaments within the next year. In other words, even though a national parliament might decide not to agree the convention, there was an opportunity to debate publicly the issues involved. Conventions passed by the conference dealt with topics such as length of the working day, night work by women and children, labour conditions at sea, international co-operation over unemployment, the prevention of accidents and control of white lead paint. Although much of this was technical, the work of the ILO had positive impacts around the world. The organisation's efforts to regulate child labour, for instance, led to children only working eight hours per day in the Persian carpet industry, to their seats having back rests, and to their rooms being properly ventilated (Goodrich, 1944: 91–3; Noel Baker, 1926: 83–6). By the time war broke out in 1939 the ILO's conference had agreed 67 conventions which had been subject to 887 national acts of ratification. In other words, little by little, an international network of progressive labour legislation and regulation had begun to emerge (Goodrich, 1944: 94; Clavin, 2007: 347).

Economic and financial work

In addition to matters of social justice and welfare, the fact that national economies were becoming increasingly interrelated meant that sooner or later steps would have to be taken to regulate the international economy. Furthermore, the difficult economic environment which followed the First World War, plus the economic turmoil in central Europe as a result of the demise of empires, made it impossible for the League of Nations to ignore economics. As a result, an Economic and Financial Section was founded within the Secretariat (Clavin, 2007: 339).

Austria presented the first major economic problem for the League. Prior to the First World War, Vienna, a city of two million people, was the hub of a massive, multinational empire. After the war, however, Austria-Hungary had been dissolved and Vienna's hinterland was reduced to a small, largely agricultural area. What were all of its manual and intellectual workers supposed to do? Similar problems were experienced in other formerly imperial cities. It should be no surprise, therefore, that from 1919 onwards ordinary Austrians began suffering great economic distress. This led the Principal Powers to request that the League investigate a scheme of economic reconstruction for the country, which it did by sending a representative there for a month in spring 1921. Action did not become urgent, however, until the next year. With inflation at 3,000 per cent per annum, in September 1922 Austria's chancellor, Ignatz Seipel, came to Geneva pleading for support. Thereafter things moved quickly. Dr Zimmerman, previously Lord Mayor of Amsterdam, became a commissioner supervising the economic reconstruction of the country; £26 million was raised for the project, and a reform programme was agreed between the League and the Austrian parliament. The League's involvement helped restore confidence to the country, ensured that budgets were balanced, that currencies were stabilised and that economic reconstruction was at least begun. As a result, by July 1926 the project was brought to a close. The success of the venture has been described as a 'practical achievement' which showed the League had 'real authority and efficiency' (*League of Nations*, 1930: 188; Noel Baker, 1926: 102–3; Clavin, 2007: 340).

A similar scheme, complete with another international commissioner (Jeremiah Smith, an American banker), was instituted to assist Hungary between 1924 and 1926. This saw £10 million raised in loans and proved successful even more quickly than the Austrian case. Furthermore, Greece received substantial economic assistance, not least via an international loan worth £14 million arranged by the League's commissioner, to help it deal with refugees. Bulgaria received assistance to help with refugees too, while between 1926 and 1928 Estonia required a foreign loan organised by the League worth £1.35 million to help reform the banking system (Hiden, 2006–07). On top of all this, the League set up an Economic Intelligence Service to provide information about the international economy, backed two World Economic Conferences in 1927 and 1933, and employed a variety of the leading economic minds to provide 'state of the art' advice (Clavin, 2007: 340). Even though, of course, the League could not ward off the Great Depression which closed the 1920s, time and again historical evaluations of its work in the field of economics have been positive (Clavin, 2007: 340; Mowrer, 1931: 508; Greaves, 1931: 78–9; Noel Baker, 1926: 108–12).

CONCLUSION: ORGANISING PEACE AND REMOVING THE CAUSES OF WAR

In all the areas discussed in this chapter, the League of Nations was doing something significant and new. It was adopting genuinely international approaches to address social and economic issues of the day, the scope of which lay beyond any individual state. It did so in the conviction that a more prosperous, healthy society in which people did not exploit and enslave each other, or traffic either people or drugs, would be more at ease with itself, more stable and so more peaceful. When we add the information in this chapter to the work the League did with national minorities and refugees, we can appreciate that it was not an organisation simply dedicated to solving conflicts between states as they arose; it was also trying to organise society in such a way that the possibility of war would be marginalised – it was trying to organise peace.

Economic envy and exploitation, social instability, vice and injustice: all of these things were to be bridled, so regulating friction between individuals and states alike. In their place were to be put 'channels of international co-operation' which could draw on nationally disinterested, expert points of view derived from the League's specialist work (Greaves, 1931: vii). The value of this work was underlined by the fact that participation in many of these areas came from states which were not formally members of the League of Nations. So, from the USA, Henry Morgenthau worked with Greek refugees, Emma Cushman with Armenian women, the American Social Hygiene Bureau funded research into people-trafficking, and Jeremiah Smith helped reconstruct the Hungarian economy. The observation underlines that where it was possible to identify issues of clear general concern, it was possible to build a phalanx of common cause. Such work helped states develop confidence in the League of Nations and underpinned the idea that it had a valid role to play in international life (Steiner, 2005: 368).

The scope and success of the social and economic work of the League took people by surprise. As Walters says, it made 'an immense contribution to human welfare' and became 'a necessary element in the complex life of the modern world' (Walters, 1952: 176). Consequently, during the 1930s, League of Nations staff came to see the organisation's social and economic contributions as ever more central to what it had to offer. This is why, in early 1939, Secretary General Avenol proposed that the League should develop its technical capabilities extensively (Barros, 1969: 191). It was also reflected in the Bruce Report which recommended the creation of a Central Committee for Economic and Social Questions and foresaw pride of place being given to projects in this area (see the next chapter) (Barros, 1969: 195; Ghébali, 1970).

As it worked, the League wove together an elaborate system of international civil servants, governmental bodies, voluntary organisations and world experts to provide knowledge and insight which could underpin international security; and the values it epitomised are still evident today. The ILO still exists as a specialised UN agency, the World Health Organisation (WHO) has taken up the League's health work, while UNESCO promotes (amongst other things) education and human rights. Following in the League's footsteps, the UN has created a host of conventions and protocols designed to underpin humane conditions around the globe. They deal with slavery (1956), people trafficking (2000), the drugs trade (1988) and fair labour conditions. Building on the work of the League, the values they enshrine are constituent parts of peace as we understand it today.

6

The League Betrayed: Collective Security in the 1930s and Disarmament

INTRODUCTION

It was relatively straightforward to identify themes for international collaboration in social and economic areas. The participants often had clear problems that needed to be solved and the shared benefits of co-operation could be obvious. But social and economic initiatives were only parts of the League's mission. So, while its experts were addressing these areas, the League was still trying to arbitrate international disputes and attempting to get the world to disarm. In both these areas, especially as the 1920s gave way to the 1930s, common causes proved increasingly difficult – if not impossible – to define.

The League of Nations was supposed to maintain the peace of the world by organising collective action on the part of its members to prevent war, and it had a number of ways to deal with disputes as they arose: it could publicise inappropriate behaviour via the Council and Assembly (so subjecting a potential aggressor to popular moral pressure); the Council could arbitrate a settlement; a legal case could be handed over to the Permanent Court; and pressure could be exerted on an aggressor through economic sanctions and even the threat of military force. In addition, the League's founders had believed that fewer weapons in the world would make aggression less likely. Consequently, they wanted all states to disarm to the minimum level necessary for their security.

At first sight, the League's agenda for collective security was attractive: 'No weapons, no war'; 'deliberation not conflict'; and 'international pressure to restrain rogue behaviour'. Over the years, however, challenging questions were posed about these principles. Regarding disarmament: was everybody ready to take the necessary steps or, ultimately, did too many people still regard large numbers of national armaments as a source of security rather than insecurity? And when it came to international disputes, the record of the 1920s showed successes, but over Vilnius, Corfu and Memel there had been difficulties too. Which side of the balance would be decisive when fresh disputes arose? What would happen if the demands of collective action in the face of a really significant aggressor conflicted with the national interests of influential member states? How many politicians would make genuine sacrifices to benefit a victim of aggression which might be located on a different continent? And regarding collective security itself: would powerful states put their faith in something so new when a serious crisis appeared on the horizon, or would they revert to traditional policies of independent diplomacy, balance of power politics and rearmament? All of these issues, and more, came to the fore as the League of Nations pursued disarmament, tried to bring peace to Manchuria and endeavoured to stop the conquest of Abyssinia (Ethiopia).

DISARMAMENT: AN IMPOSSIBLE QUEST?

The men who framed the Covenant of the League of Nations understood that enormous resources could be redirected into progressive social projects if they were no longer used to create armaments; but their commitment to disarmament was more idealistic than this. They believed firmly that Europe's armaments race in itself had provided a major cause of war in 1914. Competition and suspicion between different states, national military establishments and armaments firms had generated psychological conditions which encouraged governments to choose war over other methods of con-flict resolution [**Doc. 25, p. 146**]. This was why Article 8 of the Covenant specified that 'the maintenance of peace requires the reduction of national armaments to the lowest point consistent with national safety and the enforce-ment by common action of international obligations'. It is why one League of Nations publication described disarmament as the 'touchstone of the more general work of organising peace' (*League of Nations*, 1930: 49).

While the idea of reducing armaments to promote world peace was simple enough, its practice proved altogether different. As soon as would-be disarmers began discussing the practical form disarmament should take, they encountered a whole series of difficulties. Was it possible to differentiate offensive from defensive weapons? Could the value of one kind of weapon be balanced against that of another – maybe a tank against some kind of ship? And once disarmament was agreed, how was implementation to be verified? Furthermore, it soon became apparent that disarmament was difficult to deal with as a stand-alone issue in isolation from wider notions of security. Rather than assume that security would grow out of the destruction of weapons (as the authors of the Covenant had done), statesmen in the 1920s began to argue that steps should be taken to provide security *before* armaments were destroyed. This was particularly the case in France.

Which comes first: disarmament or security?

In spite of these complexities, the Covenant demanded disarmament, so on 19 May 1920 the Council established a Permanent Advisory Committee consisting of military men. The body pursued its work in a very technical way and, when it failed to make rapid progress, in September the Assembly authorised the creation of an additional Temporary Mixed Commission. This had a wider membership and began meeting in 1921.

Initially, there were some hopeful signs for disarmament, particularly out-side the framework of the League. Most notably, from November 1921 until February 1922, the five leading naval powers met at Washington to negotiate limits to their warships according to ratios. Inspired by their success, later in 1922 a member of the Temporary Mixed Commission, Lord Esher, tried to apply the technique to land armaments. Counting in units of 30,000 soldiers, he proposed that Britain should have three units, Italy four, France six, and so on (Archive 6.1). Although one historian has judged Esher's proposal 'the most realistic British paper on land disarmament in the inter-war years', it failed to replicate the success achieved at Washington (Towle, 1993: 135). Apart from the fact that his plan had some obvious gaps (such as omitting colonial troops), it was generally accused of simplicity and arbitrariness – it was too 'sketchy' and suffering from 'mechanical crudities' (Yearwood, 2009: 223–4). It was rejected in short order.

Discussion of Esher's proposal, however, provoked the realisation that it was difficult to deal with disarmament in isolation from the wider political context of security – that is, it showed states were unwilling to put their weapons to one side unless there was a trustworthy international security system in place to compensate for what they were losing. In particular, France was not ready to forgo its massive army so long as there was the slightest chance of another invasion by Germany. The League took steps to try to deal with these concerns. In 1923, following an initiative of Robert Cecil, a Draft Treaty of Mutual Assistance was drawn up which was supposed to go hand-in-hand with disarmament. The document envisaged a strengthened system of collective security, including regional pacts, which would enable the Council to provide rapid military assistance to any victim of an attack which was party to the League's disarmament agreements.

Although the Draft Treaty was popular with small states which had power-ful neighbours, Britain in particular refused to sign up. Ramsay MacDonald said it would have committed his country to over-extensive obligations to other states (Towle, 1993: 138). Undeterred, in 1924 the League drew up another document designed to guarantee security to states willing to disarm. The Protocol for the Pacific Settlement of International Disputes (or 'Geneva Protocol') pledged every signatory not only to participate in disarmament, but to renounce war in favour of a peaceful settlement of quarrels. Legal disputes were to be handed over to the Permanent Court, while political disputes would be arbitrated by the Council. Unfortunately, although many League members supported the Protocol, once again Britain did not. Its officials and statesmen were both suspicious of compulsory arbitration and thought the system likely to draw them into disputes – especially in eastern Europe (Walters, 1952: 284; Steiner, 2005: 381). So this initiative also fell by the wayside.

For all of this lack of progress within the framework of the League, elsewhere promising developments still occurred. The Locarno accords of October 1925 guaranteed the existing position of Germany's western borders. Moreover, like the Geneva Protocol, the accords stipulated that the signatories (Britain, France, Germany, Belgium and Italy, supplemented by Czechoslovakia and Poland) would opt for arbitration via the League should international disputes arise. Understandably, the provisions were scheduled to come into effect when Germany joined the League, which happened on 10 September 1926. This also meant, incidentally, that a link existed between Locarno and the League's disarmament project, because Germany (having been largely disarmed under the terms of the Treaty of Versailles) would push for general disarmament once it joined the organisation. The cause of peace in international relations received a further boost three years later when, in August 1928, US secretary of state Frank Kellogg and French foreign minister Aristide Briand created their famous pact in Paris. It renounced war as an instrument of policy, maintained that disputes should be settled in peaceful ways and was soon signed by 64 states, including Britain. The drawback, however, was that the Kellogg–Briand Pact included no way of enforcing the sentiments it expressed. Hence the document was of much greater symbolic than practical importance.

The Disarmament Conference

Locarno and the Kellogg–Briand Pact were drawn up outside the League of Nations, but still gave heart to everyone dedicated to the pursuit of disarmament. That is to say, if the general security environment was improving through greater understanding between Germany and her neighbours (especially those to the west), and if so many states were prepared to renounce war as a means of policy, then perhaps a context was forming that might permit disarmament one day. It was also true that disarmament remained very popular with many sections of the public, particularly in Britain (Towle, 1993: 150).

Enduring hopes of negotiating disarmament successfully were reflected in the League's establishment of the Preparatory Disarmament Commission on 12 December 1925. This was to lay the foundations for a massive international disarmament conference. The commission first met in May 1926, but the scale of its task soon became apparent. In the first place it was given a horrendous set of questions to answer: How were armaments to be defined? Can military war-strength be limited or only peace-strength? How does civil aviation relate to military aviation? Should warships be limited by total numbers or by numbers per class? And how can stocks of materiel be limited? With discussions constantly bogged down in technicalities and participants usually placing their national interests first, the commission proceeded extremely slowly and left many problems in abeyance. In fact, the commission proved quite incapable of settling a number of key differences – most notably between France and Britain over the former's desire to maintain a massive military superiority over Germany. When, in December 1930, the draft convention for the disarmament conference was finally produced, it had a number of flaws. At key points the document just left gaps, refusing even to suggest the actual military strengths that different countries might be allowed (*Report of the Preparatory Commission*, 1931: e.g. p. 89).

In Geneva on 2 February 1932, when 59 states finally gathered for the World Disarmament Conference, the delegates ignored the League's prior work, presented new ideas and shamelessly pushed their particular national security conceptions and agendas (Kitching, 1999, 2003). Russia advocated the abolition of all weapons; Britain suggested eradicating offensive weapons; and Germany demanded equality with those states which had not been forced to cut armaments by the post-war peace treaties (Northedge, 1988: 122–7). The French Minister of War, André Tardieu, presented security-based proposals (including the ideas that the League should control the world's most powerful weapons and have an independent international police force) which deflected the meeting from its area of primary focus: getting rid of weapons per se (McKercher, 1992: 184; Walters, 1952: 502).

Given the chaos of ideas, it was predictable that the conference would only make slow progress, and perhaps it was also understandable that German patience began to fray. At this point the relatively moderate Heinrich Brüning was still Reich Chancellor, but the German delegation withdrew temporarily from the conference in July 1932 on the grounds that their demand for full equality with other states was not being addressed. When the German delegation returned in February 1933, it was under a new national leader – Adolf Hitler – and it soon became evident that the World Disarmament Conference had missed its chance. Hitler had his own way of looking at international relations and withdrew Germany from the League in October 1933. Quickly, he budgeted for increased armaments spending and reintroduced conscription in March 1935. It was simply impossible for European states to ignore the new reality Hitler represented. Hence, although the disarmament conference continued until June 1934, it was in a hopeless position since no one would dare disarm so long as Hitler was in Berlin.

Discussing disarmament

Some commentators have suggested that the League should not have invested so much time and effort in disarmament. To do this, but produce no positive results, damaged its prestige severely (Northedge, 1988: 116). A possible alternative would have been to focus, in the first instance, on promoting wider international security arrangements with a view to creating an international mood of peace, trust and confidence. Once this was established, states might have been better prepared to take the next logical step and consider disarming. This way of looking at things was proposed by Salvador de Madariaga who, for a period, led the disarmament section of the League's Secretariat. Writing in the late 1920s, he maintained that before disarmament could become a realistic prospect, the prevailing spirit of international rivalry had to be replaced by one of co-operation. He even thought that before any state would get rid of weapons, a 'well-organized World Community' had to be created (Madariaga, 1929: 60–2). So soon after the First World War, he realised this was a long way from reality since Europe was experiencing all manner of cleavages, not least between the victors and vanquished of the war. Under the circumstances, states looked on each other with suspicion and were unwilling to give up whatever advantages they had. The time was not yet conducive to the concessions and compromises required to make a successful, extensive and durable disarmament agreement [**Doc. 26, p. 147**]. As it turned out, even before delegates began assembling at the World Disarmament Conference, serious questions had begun to be raised about the commitment of the League's members not just to disarmament, but to making the very system of collective security work; and the test case was Manchuria.

MANCHURIA: A TURNING POINT FOR COLLECTIVE SECURITY?

The beginning

For all the difficulties faced by the disarmament process, on 10 September 1931 Robert Cecil still spoke to the Assembly as follows:

> I do not think that there is any prospect of any war. I know . . . how rash it is to prophesy as to the future of international affairs; but, nevertheless, I do not believe that there is anyone in this room who will contradict me when I say that there has scarcely ever been a period in the world's history when war seemed less likely than it does at the present.
>
> (Thorne, 1972: 4)

Barely a week later, on 18 September, at roughly 10.30 at night a bomb exploded on the South Manchuria Railway. It was not a big explosion, because soon afterwards a train passed by the spot without incident, but it had happened on a portion of Chinese territory occupied by Japan's Kwantung Army. The Japanese had a perfect right to be there, thanks to the 1905 Treaty of Portsmouth which permitted them to guard a zone around the railway. Immediately following the explosion, members of the Kwantung Army moved quickly to occupy the whole town of Mukden, ostensibly to guarantee order. There was, however, more to these events than met the eye. Although relations between China and Japan had been improving since the late 1920s, elements within the Japanese military were at odds with the trend. By 1931 commanders of the Kwantung Army were becoming increasingly irritated by a number of unresolved problems about their position in China and so, by staging an explosion in Mukden, they had acted autonomously to provoke a crisis from which they hoped to benefit (Thorne, 1972: 3–4; Nish, 1977: 176–7). And, as would quickly become apparent, the Kwantung Army had far greater ambitions than merely to bolster its position in the railway zone.

The League becomes involved

China wasted no time in raising the issue in the League of Nations. Within days it brought it to the attention of the Council, invoking Article 11 of the Covenant which said that 'war or threat of war' was of concern to all members of the League and that the Council could be informed of circumstances which might 'disturb international peace' and 'good understanding between nations'. Unfortunately, this did little to restrain the Kwantung Army. When the Council addressed the matter in mid-October 1931, Japanese troops had begun assaulting Chinchow, an administrative centre well outside the railway zone. On 24 October, the Council members apart from Japan itself (which held a permanent seat on the Council) demanded that Japanese troops withdraw to the railway zone by 16 November.

This was actually quite a complicated situation. Japanese troops had a right to be in Manchuria, just not as extensively as they actually were. There had been no declaration of war, and the Japanese representative in Geneva gave assurances that they had no ambitions in the region, expressed goodwill towards the League and said that Japanese troops would be withdrawn when the time was right. Furthermore, Tokyo had only tenuous control of the troops in Manchuria. Amidst these uncertainties Japanese aggression continued, with Chinchow falling in December 1931 and a key railway junction being seized at Harbin in February 1932. More dramatic still, a new Japanese assault was made around Shanghai in January 1932, which aroused considerable concern among western European states with substantial business interests there. As a result, in January 1932, China once more invoked Article 11 of the Covenant, now supplemented by Article 15 which specified that in the event of a 'rupture' between members of the League, steps should be taken to investigate events. China also requested that the matter be handed to the Assembly for consideration.

The situation was further complicated because Britain regarded Japan as a longstanding friend who was underpinning capitalism in the Far East. In fact, Foreign Office memoranda stated that British policy in the region depended on a good relationship with Japan. Hence, it was hardly surprising that the foreign secretary, John Simon, told the British cabinet that Japan had genuine grievances against China which had to be addressed whether or not Japanese troops had been wrong to cross the border out of the railway zone (Steiner, 2005: 724–5). It was also true that, beyond the League, the USA did not favour steps against Japan which might force it into political isolation. Britain's influential position in the League coloured its response to the crisis.

But doing nothing was not an option for the League. There was no ignoring the fact that a large area of Chinese territory had been put under Japanese occupation illegally, and small states were particularly outraged. As a Finnish delegate told the Assembly in March 1932, the League had to prove what it was made of. Was it just a 'debating body', or was it 'a live force' offering 'a real guarantee' of security? (Thorne, 1972: 8) How were views as different as those of Britain and Finland to be reconciled?

The Lytton Commission

The Council's favoured course of action became clear on 10 December 1931. It was decided to constitute a commission of enquiry which would travel to the Far East and ascertain what exactly was going on in Manchuria. This was headed by Lord Lytton and unfortunately it took until the end of February for the group to make its journey east, time which Japan spent shoring up its position in China. By the start of March 1932 the Japanese zone of occupation had declared itself an independent state called 'Manchukuo'.

There is no doubt that Lytton took his job seriously. He travelled extensively, acquiring information in China and Japan alike – although it seems he was treated rather poorly by prime minister Uchida of Japan when they met (Nish, 1977: 186). Lytton's diligent approach produced a detailed report of Manchurian affairs, but it was not completed until September 1932. The final document went out of its way to provide balanced views of events, yet there was no disguising the fact that, in the end, Japanese actions were insupportable [**Doc. 27, p. 148**]. So, while the report concluded that the prior position of Manchuria was not satisfactory and that an international framework would have to be created for a full discussion of the future of the region, it also argued that most people living in Manchuria did not support the Manchukuo regime and saw themselves as Chinese, and that it would be necessary eventually to establish Manchuria as an autonomous part of the Chinese state (*Appeal by the Chinese Government*, 1932: ch. 9).

In Geneva, a Committee of Nineteen was set up to consider the Lytton report. Its findings confirmed the commission's views, stating that Japanese troops should withdraw to the railway zone and that Chinese sovereignty over Manchuria had to be recognised clearly. When the Assembly met on 24 February 1933, it too confirmed these points of view, by 42 votes to 1. As a result, a little over a month later, on 27 March 1933, Japan announced its intention to withdraw from the League of Nations. Ill-will between China and Japan was left to fester until Japan launched further hostilities in the summer of 1937.

Manchuria: a turning point for the League?

In the Manchuria case, therefore, the League of Nations was approached to provide assistance to a state which was the object of aggression, but it did not fulfil expectations. The difficulties so clearly on display, of course, only increased the pressure on the already troubled disarmament conference even before Germany left. Put simply, if the League had such trouble applying collective security procedures, how could any state agree to give up its weaponry? Furthermore, the whole experience of the Manchuria crisis underlined that a variety of serious problems really were inherent in the practice of collective security. It could be difficult to identify a clear-cut aggressor (especially when that party kept announcing its goodwill); Great Powers could be wary about how they dealt with other Great Powers (especially if they were friends to start with); and procedures could be long and drawn out (e.g. it took nine months for the Lytton Commission to be established and report). Moreover, the League's difficulty in dealing convincingly with Manchuria served to underline the Eurocentric nature of the organisation.

Manchuria was different to the other crises the League had faced. The scale of the aggression was greater and the consequences (the establishment of a new state and a Council member deciding to leave the organisation) were more significant. This is why the problem has been called 'the first major crisis of the League', and it led many to fear that the Council was 'not able or willing to apply the principles of the Covenant' (Ginneken, 2006: 17). In fact, the whole episode has been identified as pivotal. Manchuria has been called 'a turning point in the history of the League and of the world' (Walters, 1952: 466). At a time when the very foundations of the Covenant seemed under attack, the only result was a commission of inquiry, not sanctions or the threat of military action. The lack of more determined leadership was noted around the world. Small states had their confidence in the system shaken badly. Meanwhile, as Robert Cecil later observed, fascist dictators took heart as they dreamed of grand adventures (Cecil, 1941: 235–6).

THE ABYSSINIAN CRISIS

Background and beginnings

Like Japan, Italy was a member of the Council – and she had territorial ambitions too. In fact, if Japanese ambitions in Manchuria proved a 'turning point' for collective security, Italy's colonial ambitions in Africa sounded its death knell. The country had a long-standing interest in dominating Abyssinia (Ethiopia). In 1896, Italy had attempted an invasion, but failed. In the late 1920s, interest in Abyssinia came back on the agenda and a policy was pursued of exerting pressure on the country from the neighbouring colony of Italian Somaliland (Carocci, 1974: 77). Invasion plans began to be drawn up in 1932 and Mussolini's warlike intent became firmer the next year (Morgan, 1995: 140). The flashpoint came early in December 1934, at Wal-Wal, located in an undelimited border region between Italian Somaliland and Abyssinia's Ogaden province. Roughly 30 Italians and three times as many Abyssinians were killed in a skirmish and Mussolini began demanding compensation at once. Abyssinia responded by invoking a 1928 treaty between the countries allowing for the arbitration of disputes. Rome, however, refused to co-operate. Instead, Mussolini took a 'definite decision' for armed conflict in December 1934 and communicated it to his civilian and military leaders the same month. As he once put it, his empire could not 'be made in any other way' than through war (Morgan, 1995: 140–2).

With relations tense between Rome and Addis Ababa, Great Powers began trying to influence affairs. Their interventions occurred outside the framework of the League and collective security. They also showed a clear interest in building a balance of power against Hitler's Germany which, of course, was now outside the League and becoming an increasing source of concern at the heart of Europe. In short, notwithstanding what was happening in Abyssinia, Britain and France wanted to count on Italian friendship in the face any possible German threat. By comparison, guaranteeing the rights of Abyssinia and strictly enforcing the Covenant of the League of Nations appeared to be of secondary importance. Hence, on 7 January 1935 the French foreign minister, Pierre Laval, held talks with Mussolini in which he guaranteed Italy a strong position in Africa. Encouraged by this, barely a fortnight later, on 23 January 1935, Mussolini ordered preparations for war (Lamb, 1997: 116).

When Britain, France and Italy met at Stresa in April 1935, all the talk was of Germany, not Abyssinia. Furthermore, a couple of months later, in June 1935, Mussolini acquired a copy of a British memorandum (the Maffey Report) which stated quite simply: 'No vital British interests exist in Abyssinia or in adjoining countries sufficient to oblige His Majesty's Government to resist a conquest of Abyssinia by Italy' (Whittam, 1995: 111).

If these were the impressions received by Mussolini from French and British sources in diplomatic interactions conducted outside the scope of the League, what was he to make of any words uttered in Geneva? Where did all of this leave Abyssinia? And how could collective security deliver the required results when vitally important states were not respecting its obligations?

The League becomes involved in Abyssinia

In January 1935, Abyssinia appealed to the Council, based on Article 11 of the Covenant, concerning a situation threatening war. Two months later, on 16 March, it appealed to the Council on the basis of Article 15, which talked of a 'rupture' between states. It took until May, however, for Italy to agree to League-sponsored arbitration. Already hostile to such a procedure, and with Italian troops being sent to Italian Somaliland via the Suez Canal since February, Mussolini never took it seriously. When the arbitration finding finally emerged in September 1935, stating that neither side was to blame for the Wal-Wal incident, the procedure had been bypassed by events.

To make matters worse, at the same time as the League was trying to provide arbitration, Britain and France continued pursuing diplomatic contacts with Italy outside the framework of collective security – which underlined how little they were committed to a major confrontation over Africa. As early as May 1935, the British cabinet heard from foreign secretary Simon that Italy was planning military action in Abyssinia, most likely scheduled for October. The next month, in June 1935, in the foreign office Lord Vansittart (permanent under-secretary of state) penned arguments suggesting that Britain try to buy off Italian ambitions by giving her part of British Somaliland. He felt that an invasion of Abyssinia would lead Italy to leave the League and eventually seek an accommodation with Nazi Germany – a possibility to be avoided. British Minister for League Affairs, Anthony Eden, travelled to Rome to see Mussolini on 24 June and offered him territory from British Somaliland. The Italian replied that France was allowing him a completely free hand in Africa and displayed a map on which were marked whole areas of Abyssinia which he expected to subject to direct Italian control (Lamb, 1997: 120–8).

British responses to the accelerating crisis were complicated by the announcement on 27 June of the results of the 'Peace Ballot' which had been organised mainly by the League of Nations Union. Over ten million people agreed that statesmen should unite behind the Covenant to stop international aggression. Hence it was understandable when the new foreign secretary, Sir Samuel Hoare, went to Geneva on 10 September 1935 to state in public that Britain would back collective action to ward off international aggression. Unfortunately, on 2 September Hoare had already told Mussolini that there was no talk in the League either of closing the Suez Canal to Italian shipping (which would have made supplying Italian troops impossible and would have damaged the Italian economy) or of implementing military sanctions (Lamb, 1997: 127). Once again, this was hardly the sort of behaviour likely to deter a dictator from military adventure.

Italian troops finally crossed into Abyssinia on 3 October 1935. Within days, the Council denounced the resort to war and prepared to introduce economic sanctions. Emotions were running high during debates as Haitian delegate Alfred Nemours told the Assembly that 'Great or small, strong or weak, near or far, white or coloured, let us never forget that one day we may be somebody's Abyssinia' (Walters, 1952: 653). The first decision ever to impose economic sanctions according to Article 16 of the Covenant was taken by 50 representatives in the Assembly on 10 October, with only Italy, Albania, Hungary and Austria dissenting. The action, to be supervised by a specialist sanctions committee which first met on 11 October, involved steps to prevent the sale of armaments to Italy, to prohibit the supply of strategic war materials and to cut credit to the Italian government and Italian firms. By the end of the month, 50 states had announced their readiness to participate in the initiative (Walters, 1952: 663). The very fact that sanctions began to be applied by so many supporters, plus the fact that they soon started to hurt the Italian economy, can be counted a success for collective security – albeit one of limited importance.

Talk of collective action to turn the screw even tighter emerged in November 1935, and the issue was oil sanctions. This seemed a viable proposition since two of Italy's oil suppliers (Romania and the USSR) were agreeable to participation (Armstrong et al., 1996: 44). The step certainly would have hampered Mussolini's capacity to fight a long-term campaign in Abyssinia – a relevant point because his army increasingly was getting bogged down. In London, however, Samuel Hoare balked at such a development, telling cabinet that an oil embargo might spur Mussolini to a 'mad dog' act. It seems the dictator showed his displeasure at even talk of an oil embargo by moving troops to the French border. The implication was that if Italy suffered too seriously because of collective economic measures, the result would be war in the heart of Europe (Lamb, 1997: 142).

This was the context in which Britain and France once more showed a lack of commitment to collective security, this time through the disastrous Hoare–Laval plan. On 8 December 1935, Hoare met with Laval (now prime

Minister) to create a plan to satisfy Mussolini. It proposed allowing Italy to annex roughly 60,000 square miles of territory from Abyssinia in exchange for 3,000 square miles of land giving her an outlet to the sea. It was also suggested that the southern half of the country be identified as a zone of Italian economic domination. Initially, the plan was confidential but was leaked to the press within a few days. So soon after the Peace Ballot, reaction was especially strong in Britain where Hoare was forced to resign on 18 December. Laval fell from office the following month. This whole episode undermined further the credibility of collective opposition in Mussolini's eyes.

January 1936 saw the Italian dictator take steps to reinvigorate his flagging Abyssinian campaign. A new commander, Field Marshal Pietro Badoglio, was installed and a fresh campaign launched on 12 January. This time Italian troops made greater headway, not least because they began using mustard gas. At the same time in Geneva close attention was again given to the possibility of an oil embargo. An expert committee reported in February that this could have a real impact on Italy within just a few months, even allowing for the possibility that some oil would still be supplied by the USA (which was not a member of the League and so might not participate in sanctions) [**Doc. 28, p. 150**]. Although important figures, such as foreign minister Anthony Eden, favoured such an effort, France did not (Lamb, 1997: 156–63). At the start of April 1936, Eden also asked cabinet to consider closing the Suez Canal to Italian shipping to disrupt Mussolini's lines of communication, but prime minister Stanley Baldwin refused.

By this point, Europe was becoming more concerned with Hitler's challenge to the status quo. In March 1936 he had violated the Treaty of Versailles and remilitarised the Rhineland. Consequently, the Great Powers capable of exerting moral and practical leadership in the Council and Assembly remained largely paralysed as Abyssinia was overrun. Addis Ababa fell on 5 May 1936. Four days later, Mussolini declared himself Emperor of Abyssinia, revelling in the popular acclaim generated by the successful campaign. On 10 May Haile Selassie (the vanquished Emperor of Abyssinia) announced he would end the war, an event which led Guatemala to leave the League saying 'events have demonstrated the impossibility of putting into practice the high ideals aimed at when the League was founded' (Armstrong *et al.*, 1996: 46). Thereafter, things ended quickly. True, Haile Selassie travelled to Geneva to give a heartfelt oration to the Assembly on 30 June which managed to be dignified, outraged at the use of Italian chemical weapons and accusatory towards the Great Powers all at the same time [**Doc. 29, p. 150**] (Plate 8). But with the conflict so clearly over, League members had little stomach for maintaining sanctions. These were abandoned in July, leaving Italy to enjoy the fruits of aggression. In December 1937, Mussolini announced his country's withdrawal from the organisation.

Abyssinia: the consequences

This was the only occasion on which the League of Nations launched a full-scale collective security action. It went beyond investigation, negotiation and the passing of resolutions to realise practical coercion through economic sanctions. In the process, it posed a number of difficult questions for the Great Powers – Britain and France in particular. The basic problem, of course, was that membership of the League brought commitments to Abyssinia, but traditional diplomatic methods and the increasing anxiety over Hitler's Germany necessitated a working relationship with Italy. In fact Britain and France felt compelled to try to take account of the two conflicting positions and so ended up creating a foreign policy mess. In particular, when seen from the perspective of Rome, their vacillation between the pursuit of policy within the framework of the League and action independent of it can only have appeared irresolute, confused and weak – it certainly did not provide grounds for Mussolini to reconsider his territorial ambitions.

Unfortunately, even though the attempt to make collective security work had been half-hearted in important quarters, its practical deficiencies (no matter whose fault) could only serve as a hammer blow against its future application. It had not become accepted as a viable alternative to traditional Great Power diplomacy and hence states could not rely upon it in times of crisis. The system had not saved a League member from complete obliteration and so it was not to be trusted. It was doubly unfortunate, as one contemporary observer put it, that Britain had played a part in destroying collective security, because in so doing it was ushering in a return to 'the old system of international anarchy, the arms race, and Imperialism, which always has ended, and is bound to end, in war' (Vigilantes, 1938: 86). After the Abyssinia crisis, the League of Nations and collective security increasingly were sidelined from the pursuit of international security. They did not play a significant part in either the Munich crisis of 1938 or the drift to war in 1939.

EARLY MOVES TO REAPPRAISE COLLECTIVE SECURITY: ADDRESSING THE CAUSES OF WAR

The Abyssinian crisis proved catastrophic for the League of Nations. It was no small irony, therefore, that as this came to an end the Secretariat began moving into new, tailor-made accommodation – the still impressive Palais des Nations (see the cover image) which provides brilliant views of Lake Geneva and Mont Blanc. But a magnificent working environment could never conceal that the 1930s was a depressing time for League of Nations staff who could only watch so much progressive work fall apart. As war once more appeared on the horizon, soul-searching began within the organisation. Where had it managed to succeed and where had it proved fallible? What lessons should it learn if it were to survive in one form or another?

Particularly interesting are the published proceedings of an international conference on collective security held during 1934–35 (Bourquin, 1936). The editor himself noted that many preferred the phrase 'organisation of peace' to 'collective security', not least to highlight the aspiration of one day banishing armed violence from the world of politics (Bourquin, 1936: 10). But as contributor after contributor argued about the character of 'collective security', or 'the organisation of peace', Italian voices emerged as particularly challenging. At a time when their country was preparing to dispute the sovereignty of Abyssinia, they suggested that a universal security system was impossible. One critical Italian contributor, F. Coppola, maintained that security could only be built on the separate needs of individual states and required that each develop its own weapons purely according to its specific needs. He found it absurd to suggest that any given state could genuinely be interested in the security of another, and rejected the idea that it could ever make sense to go to war purely for the benefit of a third party. He also proposed that by encouraging numerous states to become embroiled in a conflict, collective security actually risked turning any local confrontation into a world war (Bourquin, 1936: 145–8).

Coppola provided an astute critique which certainly provoked other contributors. Bourquin himself contradicted Coppola by proposing that individual security had become bankrupt, since the sheer horror of war was now so great that only a collective response to its threat was appropriate (Bourquin, 1936: 445). Apparently more irritated still by the Italian, Gilbert Murray argued that all history had led up to the creation of the League of Nations, that the maintenance of peace was a vital national interest, and that war was incompatible with civilisation. On the other hand, Murray did admit that in their present form, League mechanisms for preventing war were imperfect and incomplete (Bourquin, 1936: 460–2).

There was, however, one point of common ground between Coppola and his critics. He held that the real key to security was to remove the causes of war from international life. H.R.G. Greaves agreed with this sentiment, reasoning that the peace treaties ending the First World War were now out of date. The expected moral regeneration of political life had not occurred; rather, the sources of tension between states had been augmented by increasing nationalism and capitalist economic rivalry. He thought it necessary not only to bolster the certainty that international law would be applied between states, but also to establish a central body to regulate the international economy (Bourquin, 1936: 137–44). A.B. Plaunt agreed that in future, if collective security were to work effectively, more would have to be done to address the economic causes of war (Bourquin, 1936: 193–5).

Given that the League had failed so clearly to mediate the key disputes of Manchuria and Abyssinia, but had experienced so much success in social, humanitarian and economic work, it was perhaps predictable that, in due course, the idea of establishing an enhanced organisation with super-state functions to address the causes of war would became popular inside the organisation. Important here was the work of a reform-minded committee chaired by the Australian Stanley Melbourne Bruce. Reporting in August 1939, the group identified the economic and social work of the League as particularly praiseworthy. Hence, it proposed that from now on the League should concern itself less with political affairs and more with these areas [**Doc. 30, p. 152**]. The committee recommended establishing a Central Committee for Economic and Social Questions to take the lead. Although the Bruce Report was not implemented on account of the start of war that September, nonetheless it is generally accepted that its insights helped pave the way for the elaborate social and economic work pursued by the United Nations (Bennett and Oliver, 2002: 43).

Of course there were still more frustrations. After all, there were limits beyond which the League could not spread its doctrine of humanitarianism. We have already seen McDonald's anger at the inability to stem the flow of refugees from Nazi Germany and he was far from the only League official to be frustrated at the limited tools available to tackle Hitler. In the mid-1930s, Sean Lester was the League's High Commissioner for Danzig (Gdańsk) and wrote reports making plain the undesirability of Nazism's activities there (Archive 6.2). Although protests by Jews from Upper Silesia to the League about persecution led the Third Reich to suspend anti-Semitic laws in that region for so long as the Treaty of Versailles gave the organisation administrative rights there, the sad fact remained that as soon as the League's interest terminated in 1937, the persecution began again [**Doc. 31, p. 153**]. Nonetheless, the realisation that social and economic work could bring long-term security benefits was correct, built well on Articles 23 and 25 of the Covenant, and pointed the way towards useful lines of thinking for the future [**Doc. 1, p. 116**].

CONCLUSION

It is easy to maintain that, in the end, the League and collective security failed. This is not quite correct, however. It is more accurate to say that collective security was not properly applied when it most needed to be: over Manchuria, when sanctions were not considered seriously; and over Italy, when they were implemented half-heartedly. We must also accept that collective security was let down badly, betrayed even, by the very states which should have been leading it most enthusiastically. After all, a system can only be as good as the elements comprising it. In this light, it was lamentable that two Council members (Japan and Italy) embarked on international aggression in clear contravention of the Covenant, but also that centrally important states such as Britain and France failed to live up to their obligations more fully. As an observer noted in the 1930s, too often they seemed willing to respect international obligations only insofar as their narrow national interests dictated (Vigilantes, 1938: 58–62). To have prevented war, the League would have required a better quality of Great Power commitment than was forthcoming. Likewise, the inability of the disarmament process to produce sufficient results was hardly the sole responsibility of officials sitting in Geneva. Foot-dragging over disarmament reflected a lack of readiness on the part of statesmen to move away from old ways of thinking. France in particular did not *want* to get rid of her massive army and its numerical superiority over Germany. How could disarmament thrive in the face this reality?

True, we can admit that the Secretary General who took over from Drummond in 1933 probably was 'the wrong man in the wrong place at the wrong time' (Barros, 1969: 18). Joseph Avenol (1879–1952) favoured right-wing politics and was overly sensitive to the German government, apparently hoping that it would one day return to the organisation. It is symptomatic of his lack of impact on the international scene in the 1930s that Avenol has not been mentioned by name before this point in the chapter – although we can also ask if Drummond could have used his position more effectively in respect of disarmament and Manchuria. Although Drummond's biographer describes him as a 'political animal', he was also a career civil servant who tried to wield influence subtly behind the scenes, certainly not through high-profile public interventions. Hence his manner of working has been characterised as 'tedious' and 'self-effacing', but certainly not 'dramatic' (Barros, 1979: 399). Perhaps we would have wished both Drummond and Avenol to have spoken out more obviously against the iniquities of the time, as did McDonald and Lester. This would have left a clearer record of struggle for the history books (Barros, 1969: 18). Unfortunately, in their different ways, they were not the men to do this.

But the League did not really fail in the 1930s, rather it was sidelined, as politicians chose increasingly to work beyond its corridors. The Covenant was not applied, its spirit was not honoured, and principles of universality were not taken seriously. For all the deficiencies of Drummond and Avenol, in order for collective security to have worked, there would have had to be a wider and more genuine appreciation by states that world peace was a national interest; a fundamental willingness to make sacrifices on its behalf;

solidarity around such an end (as indeed any collective system of security requires – even that of the UN); and a readiness on the part of the Great Powers to provide an appropriate moral lead. In other words, the statesmen of the day would have had to do full justice to the vision provided by the founders of the League.

Perhaps this was asking a great deal of Europe's democratic statesmen who had so recently experienced a world war and who found themselves confronted by crises in inaccessible places, world economic meltdown (1929–32) and ever more strident dictators in the heart of Europe. Under the circumstances, it would have taken distinct courage to put faith in new strategies such as collective security, sanctions and disarmament. But even with this said, one further observation is imperative: although statesmen turned away from collective security, they still did not avoid war. In other words, while collective security was bypassed, the more traditional diplomatic and security practices of the time certainly did fail to prevent September 1939.

Conclusion

Assessing the League of Nations

A PATH-BREAKING ORGANISATION

So how are we to assess the League of Nations now? The very creation of such an organisation has to be counted a success of a kind. It carried out so much good work that any other conclusion would not be apt. Admittedly, it did not always fulfil its potential, and sometimes its benefits were restricted to the statement of good ideas and intentions rather than their effective implementation, but as a rule it marked progress over the approaches to international relations which characterised the period before 1914. Notwithstanding its inability to prevent the outbreak of the Second World War, the League still had shown that a massive international organisation of governments could be formed and could make a difference to politicians and ordinary people alike. As Howard Sweetser, a spokesman for the League, put it a long time ago: 'The League's greatest success undoubtedly lay in . . . the creation of a complete system of international co-operation ramifying into practically every domain of international interest' (Sweetser, 1944: 7). Although it could not demand that statesmen always made use of its benefits, at least the League of Nations offered important options and opportunities to those who were inclined to seek them out.

The Council aspired to being the first world cabinet; the Assembly was the first international parliament; and the Secretariat was the first permanent international civil service supposed to administer peace. Together, these institutions became significant mechanisms for airing and investigating all manner of novel ideas and themes of common concern; and the very fact that the League promoted the flow of ideas and thoughts between governments about the issues of the day ought not to be undervalued. As US secretary of state Cordell Hull acknowledged: 'the League of Nations has been responsible for the development of mutual exchange and discussion of ideas and methods to a greater extent and in more fields of humanitarian and scientific endeavour than any other organisation in history' (Northedge, 1988: 190). As such, it was an important addition to the international scene.

CHANGING CONVICTIONS

Hitler's invasion of Poland hit League supporters hard. It showed graphically that their aims had not been achieved. Events in the international sphere had run out of control, and the League of Nations had been unable to apply a brake; should it have done better?

As noted in Chapter 6, the League would have been strengthened by a Secretary General more charismatic than either Drummond or Avenol. Even under such circumstances, however, the organisation would not have enjoyed plain sailing. It was new and, as such, offered untried ways of working. Consequently, no matter how remarkable its leader, it was unlikely to replace Great Power diplomacy at a stroke. There was simply too much weight of past practice for this to happen overnight. So, the sorts of changes the League of Nations was working towards have to be seen as part of a long process of change rather than rapid reforms to be completed in a decade or so. In this light, the League's advocates probably were at fault for expecting too much from their organisation too soon.

In this connection, the challenges faced by the League in remoulding political convictions in the inter-war period should not be underestimated. The values of liberalism, humanitarianism and internationalism were not the only ones abroad at the time. There was also nationalism, which sought to break up the global community into smaller, competitive components. There was a residue of imperialism, involving a refusal to accept all states and peoples as equal. Antidemocratic castes of mind were increasingly ascendant, fascism bringing with it respect for force of arms rather than the settlement of disputes by law or arbitration. In other words, it was not enough that the League of Nations had been created; this was just the start. In the inter-war world, it experienced a constant competition for the hearts and minds of statesmen and their peoples. Given the collective nature of the organisation, it followed that it required the commitment of the Great Powers to help reaffirm what it offered. Unfortunately, this commitment clearly faltered over disarmament, Manchuria and Abyssinia.

BALANCE

The idea that the League was involved in a process of change fits well with the notion that, for all its novelty, there was still something transitional about it. British diplomat Arthur Henderson put it like this:

> At present we are in the transition stage between the old individualistic diplomacy, under which each nation or group of nations played for its

own hand, and the post-war diplomacy of conciliation and co-operation. In the old days men and nations thought largely in terms of potential warfare, but under the new dispensation towards which we are striving they would, I hope, think in terms of permanent peace.

(Rappard, 1931: 115)

There was a gradual movement away from the acceptance of violence as a way of solving problems, from the appreciation of national interests to the valuing of global ones.

In a challenging environment, the League showed that, if they chose, it was feasible for states to work together to organise world affairs in all manner of ways; and despite the fact that its key members ultimately let down the League, nonetheless its imperfect existence still left a forceful impression. As was said long ago, 'few institutions in world history have made a greater appeal to man's imagination' (Hitchner, 1943: 176). After its existence, there was never any doubt that a similar organisation (albeit one which learned from its mistakes) would have to follow. As this short study has noted, elements of the UN such as the UNHCR, ILO, UNESCO, WHO and its socially progressive conventions all owe something to the League of Nations. And even if the Security Council functions in a way that is different to collective security, nonetheless the recent Human Security policy displays an undeniable echo of the League's wider agenda. Under the circumstances, it does not go too far to say that, once the League of Nations had been founded, things would never be the same again. The organisation established beyond doubt that there had to be a global body contributing permanently to the organisation of the peace of the world.

Part 2

DOCUMENTS

Document 1 HUMAN SECURITY

In 2003, the United Nations published an agenda supplementing security as viewed from the perspective of states: Human Security. *It addresses themes such as economics and security, security and people on the move, and the security implications of health. Its impassioned language has something in common with the way League of Nations supporters talked about the suffering of ordinary people as a result of war, famine and epidemics.*

Human security in its broadest sense embraces far more than the absence of violent conflict. It encompasses human rights, good governance, access to education and health care and ensuring that each individual has opportunities and choices to fulfil his or her own potential. Every step in this direction is also a step towards reducing poverty, achieving economic growth and preventing conflict. Freedom from want, freedom from fear and the freedom of future generations to inherit a healthy natural environment – these are the interrelated building blocks of human, and therefore national, security.

Source: Commission on Human Security, Final Report, UN, 2003. p. 4. http://www.humansecurity-chs.org/finalreport/index.html

Document 2 DIFFERENT WAYS TO PREVENT WARS

Having discussed the League and conflict resolution, Robert Cecil went on to consider the prevention of war in a wider sense. This extract shows his conviction that tackling social and economic problems had an important role to play. It inspires co-operation and trust between nations; it also develops public opinion such that war becomes much less likely.

In this sense the policy of the League is a policy to prevent war. So far, it is a negative policy; and a negative policy is not enough. The negative commandment 'Thou shall not kill' must be completed by the positive commandment 'Love one another'. Among nations it is not enough to prevent war. We must foster and encourage good-will between the nations of the world, and bring it into effective operation . . .

I remember well the first Assembly when the League began to have a real existence, and began to work for great causes. I remember when it began to consider what could be done to save the suffering populations of Armenia. It was not in any way the selfish interest of any nation represented there. It was a common altruistic object, and therefore it brought all the nations together, anxious to do their best. In the recent history of the League, and especially in its last Assembly, nothing has been more admirable than the joint effort made by so many nations to come to the assistance of Austria, not only because it was of value to this or that nation that Austria should not be allowed to fall into chaos, but because they felt the appeal of a nation in distress, and because they thought it was the duty of the League, as a League and as representing international opinion, to do its best to rescue a nation which was in dire straits and in danger of falling into the abyss . . .

There have been many other things in which the members of the League have worked together for common objects, recognizing the great truth that the nations are far more interested in common objects than they are affected by diverse hostilities. The opium question, the release of prisoners of war, the attack on the white slave traffic, and a large number of other activities which are not so well known but which represent valuable efforts of international co-operation, have made it possible for something like a spirit of international amity to exist; and no one who has attended the Assemblies at Geneva can fail to recognize that an atmosphere has been created there, in which international disputes lose their bitterness, and their solutions become possible without disaster or humiliation to either of the contestants.

What, then, is the conclusion? It is this. The League can work. It has proved that public opinion and international co-operation are and have been weapons against war, and that peace can be secured by their means . . .

Source: Robert Cecil, *The Moral Basis of the League of Nations*, London: Lindsey Press, 1923, pp. 34–8.

MANKIND IS ONCE MORE ON THE MOVE   **Document 3**

Jan Smuts's book was a significant attempt to popularise the idea of a League of Nations. At a number of points, the text highlights the author's understanding that security had an important social component.

For there is no doubt that mankind is once more on the move. The very foundations have been shaken and loosened, and things are again fluid. The tents have been struck, and the great caravan of humanity is once more on the march. Vast social and industrial changes are coming, perhaps upheavals which may, in their magnitude and effects, be comparable to war itself. A steadying, controlling, regulating influence will be required to give stability to progress, and to remove that wasteful friction which has dissipated so much social force in the past, and in this war more than ever before. These great functions could only be adequately fulfilled by the League of Nations. Responding to such vital needs and coming at such a unique opportunity in history, it may well be destined to mark a new era in the Government of

Man, and become to the peoples the guarantee of Peace, to the workers of all races the great International, and to all the embodiment and living expression of the moral and spiritual unity of the human race.

Source: J.C. Smuts, *The League of Nations: A Practical Suggestion*, London: Hodder & Stoughton, 1918. p. 71.

Document 4   THE COVENANT OF THE LEAGUE OF NATIONS

This is an essential but lengthy document which has been published elsewhere. It can be found easily in full on a number of websites, such as the following: www.avalon.law.yale.edu/20th_century/leagcov.asp; and www.archive.org/details/pariscovenantfor00leagiala. Here we are only reproducing the most important extracts.

Article 8
1. The Members of the League recognise that the maintenance of peace requires the reduction of national armaments to the lowest point consistent with national safety and the enforcement by common action of international obligations.

Article 10
The Members of the League undertake to respect and preserve as against external aggression the territorial integrity and existing political independence of all Members of the League . . .

Article 11
1. Any war or threat of war, whether immediately affecting any of the Members of the League or not, is hereby declared a matter of concern to the whole League, and the League shall take any action that may be deemed wise and effectual to safeguard the peace of nations. In case any such emergency should arise the Secretary General shall on the request of any Member of the League forthwith summon a meeting of the Council.
2. It is also declared to be the friendly right of each Member of the League to bring to the attention of the Assembly or of the Council any circumstance whatever affecting international relations which threatens to disturb international peace or the good understanding between nations upon which peace depends.

Article 12
1. The Members of the League agree that, if there should arise between them any dispute likely to lead to a rupture they will submit the matter either to

arbitration or judicial settlement or to enquiry by the Council, and they agree in no case to resort to war until three months after the award by the arbitrators or the judicial decision, or the report by the Council . . .

Article 15

1. If there should arise between Members of the League any dispute likely to lead to a rupture, which is not submitted to arbitration or judicial settlement in accordance with Article 13, the Members of the League agree that they will submit the matter to the Council . . .

3. The Council shall endeavour to effect a settlement of the dispute, and if such efforts are successful, a statement shall be made public giving such facts and explanations regarding the dispute and the terms of settlement thereof as the Council may deem appropriate . . .

Article 16

1. Should any Member of the League resort to war in disregard of its covenants . . . it shall ipso facto be deemed to have committed an act of war against all other Members of the League, which hereby undertake immediately to subject it to the severance of all trade or financial relations, the prohibition of all intercourse between their nationals and the nationals of the covenant-breaking State, and the prevention of all financial, commercial or personal intercourse between the nationals of the covenant-breaking State and the nationals of any other State, whether a Member of the League or not.

2. It shall be the duty of the Council in such case to recommend to the several Governments concerned what effective military, naval or air force the Members of the League shall severally contribute to the armed forces to be used to protect the covenants of the League.

Article 22

1. To those colonies and territories which as a consequence of the late war have ceased to be under the sovereignty of the States which formerly governed them and which are inhabited by peoples not yet able to stand by themselves under the strenuous conditions of the modern world, there should be applied the principle that the well-being and development of such peoples form a sacred trust of civilisation and that securities for the performance of this trust should be embodied in this Covenant.

2. The best method of giving practical effect to this principle is that the tutelage of such peoples should be entrusted to advanced nations who by reason of their resources, their experience or their geographical position can best undertake this responsibility, and who are willing to accept it, and that this tutelage should be exercised by them as Mandatories on behalf of the League.

3. The character of the mandate must differ according to the stage of the development of the people, the geographical situation of the territory, its economic conditions and other similar circumstances . . .

Article 23

Subject to and in accordance with the provisions of international conventions existing or hereafter to be agreed upon, the Members of the League:

(a) will endeavour to secure and maintain fair and humane conditions of labour for men, women, and children, both in their own countries and in all countries to which their commercial and industrial relations extend, and for that purpose will establish and maintain the necessary international organisations;

(b) undertake to secure just treatment of the native inhabitants of territories under their control;

(c) will entrust the League with the general supervision over the execution of agreements with regard to the traffic in women and children, and the traffic in opium and other dangerous drugs;

(d) will entrust the League with the general supervision of the trade in arms and ammunition with the countries in which the control of this traffic is necessary in the common interest;

(e) will make provision to secure and maintain freedom of communications and of transit and equitable treatment for the commerce of all Members of the League. In this connection, the special necessities of the regions devastated during the war of 1914–1918 shall be borne in mind;

(f) will endeavour to take steps in matters of international concern for the prevention and control of disease.

Article 25

The Members of the League agree to encourage and promote the establishment and co-operation of duly authorised voluntary national Red Cross organisations having as purposes the improvement of health, the prevention of disease and the mitigation of suffering throughout the world.

Document 5   COULD THE LEAGUE HAVE PREVENTED THE FIRST WORLD WAR?

Philip Noel Baker worked for the League of Nations in a number of capacities. In the following extract he illustrates his conviction that, had the League been in existence, it could have stopped the catastrophe of 1914.

To begin with, if the Covenant had been carried out, the general situation with which Lord Grey was faced would never have existed, for in the Covenant it is provided that the Members of the League shall make a general plan to reduce and limit the national armaments which they each maintain. The Covenant would thus have got rid of the desperate rivalry in preparation for war which poisoned the life of Europe and created the alliances, the counter-alliances and the panic fears by which Lord Grey was beaten. Nor could there have been the constant suspicions that arose before 1914 that nations had in secret even greater armaments than those which they publicly avowed. For under their system of mutual disarmament each member of the League would then have had a right to determine through the international machinery of the League what armaments other Members had actually built up. Such mutual disarmament and control and the abolition of secret treaties would have changed the whole relations of the states of Europe in 1914.

In the second place, the course of events after June 28th, 1914, when the cause of the quarrel actually arose, would have been quite different if the Covenant had existed and had been obeyed. If the purpose of the Austrian Government had been merely reparation for the outrage against her royal citizen, she would have summoned Serbia to the Council of the League, and Serbia could not have refused to come. The Council, with all the Great Powers present and with representatives of both disputing countries sitting as Members and entitled to take full part in the debates, but not entitled to a vote on its conclusions, would have discussed the whole matter with the Press of all the world sitting in the room. In those debates every detail both of Austria's charges against Serbia and of Serbia's defence would have been thrashed out. Probably the matter would have ended by a reference to the Permanent Court of International Justice for a decision on Serbian complicity and on the compensation due, and if so both parties would almost certainly have accepted the verdict as conclusive. In any case, Austria would have had every guarantee for full impartial justice for her claims, and Serbia would have had the same . . .

[B]oth Austria and Serbia would under the Covenant have been under solemn legal obligation not to go to war unless the whole of their dispute had been submitted to this procedure, until the Council had reported its conclusions to their quarrel, and until a still further period of three months had elapsed. That is the minimum delay which under the Covenant is required; and if a country violates its undertakings by not observing this delay it is liable to joint coercive action by all other Members of the League. If, for example, Austria and Germany had refused to have a round-table discussion of their quarrel with Serbia in the Council of the League, and if by mobilizing or by other action, they or any other state had shown that they were bent upon aggressive war, then the other Members of the League would have taken concerted action to maintain the peace. As a first step they would have withdrawn their Ambassadors and Ministers from the capitals of the mobilizing states; if mobilization had been followed by actual aggression, there would have followed too an immediate blockade imposed upon the aggressor state by all the other Members of the League. Under that blockade its supplies from the whole of the rest of the world, its communications with every other country, would almost at a blow have stopped; the tremendous pressure which in the last war was ultimately imposed on Germany by the Allied blockade would have been immediately exercised, and the task of setting it up would have been far easier than it actually was, because no nation in Europe could have remained neutral as of right . . .

Source: P.J. Noel Baker, *The League of Nations at Work*, London: Nisbet & Co., 1926, pp. 9–14.

Document 6   'THE GENEVA RACKET'

Robert Dell was a newspaper man who observed the League of Nations at first hand. He was shocked by the way too many statesmen behaved in Geneva.

It will be seen that in 1933 I already took a cynical view of the League of Nations. It was, unfortunately, almost impossible to follow the proceedings of the League at Geneva without becoming cynical about it. Although they came from so many different countries and represented newspapers with widely different political tendencies, there was a remarkable consensus of opinion among the foreign correspondents in Geneva and they were usually more right than the diplomatists . . .

The fact that Geneva was the centre of international intrigues justifies the title of this book. The behaviour of the great majority of the delegates to the League of Nations did indeed make the League a racket. It became a fraudulent institution betraying the confidence of the public. With certain exceptions, the Government delegates played the game of Power politics without the smallest regard for the general interest of the world and without showing the least vestige of an international spirit. The principles of Machiavelli would have disowned them. They acted in what they believed to be the immediate interests of their respective countries and adopted policies that turned out in the long run to be fatal to those interests. So true it is that the interest of all is the interest of each and that if an individual or a nation refuses to take the general interest into account, the consequences of the refusal are likely to be disastrous to the individual or the nation.

The British Government was one of the most shortsighted. What folly its persistent opposition to any form of collective security is now seen to have been! . . .

Source: Robert Dell, *The Geneva Racket 1920–1939*, London: Robert Hale, 1941, pp. 7–8.

THE VARIOUS DEGREES OF SELF-DETERMINATION   **Document 7**

Jan Smuts discusses the self-determination of nationalities which previously had been subject to European Empires. He argues that different peoples were ready to take on responsibility for their own futures to different extents. This conviction stood behind the idea of mandates – that is, a system whereby the League's Great Powers (such as Britain and France) supervised nations as they worked towards full political independence (see Chapter 5).

Self-determination and the idea of a mandate

What are the fundamental principles which must guide the League in its territorial policy as the general heir or successor of the defunct Empires? They have been summed up for the last two years in the general formula of 'No annexations, and the self-determination of nations'. There is no doubt that behind them is a profound feeling throughout the masses of the European peoples, and any violation of them will meet with stern retribution. It is for the statesmen of Europe to give political form and expression to this deep feeling . . .

So far I have referred only to territories and peoples split off from Russia, Austria and Turkey . . .

When these territories and peoples come to be considered individually it will be found that their conditions for self-determination, autonomy or self-government vary very considerably. Take, in the first place, the cases of Finland, Poland, Czechoslovakia and Jugo-Slavia as instances. They will probably be found sufficiently capable of statehood to be recognised as independent States of the usual type from the beginning. Take again, in the second place, the Transcaucasian or Transcaspian provinces of Russia. It will probably be found that they are as yet deficient in the qualities of statehood and that, whereas they are perhaps capable of internal autonomy, they will in one degree or another require the guiding hand of some external administration. In all these cases the peoples concerned are perhaps sufficiently homogeneous and developed to govern themselves subject to some degree or other of external assistance and control. This will probably be found to be the case also of Upper and Lower Mesopotamia, Lebanon and Syria. Although I mention these ex-Turkish territories together as capable of autonomy but not of complete statehood, it must be clearly understood that there is a great deal of variation among them in this respect. At the one end a territory may be found barely capable of autonomy, at the other end the approach to complete statehood is very close. Mesopotamia would probably be a case of the former kind; Syria the latter.

In the third place, there will be found cases where, owing chiefly to the heterogeneous character of the population and their incapacity for administrative co-operation, autonomy in any real sense would be out of the question, and the administration would have to be undertaken to a very large extent by some external authority. This would be the case, at any rate for some time to come, in Palestine, where the administrative co-operation of the Jewish minority and Arab majority would not be forthcoming; and in the Armenian Vilayets, where Armenian, Turkish and Kurdish populations co-exist in historic enmity, and even the policing of the country would have to be undertaken by some external authority.

In all the above and similar cases where the assistance and control of an external authority is necessary to supplement the local autonomy of the territories in question, the external authority should be the League of Nations. . . . No State should make use of the helpless or weak condition of any of these territories in order to exploit them for its own purposes or acquire rights over them in the manner which has hitherto been a fruitful source of trouble and war . . .

Source: J.C. Smuts, The *League of Nations: A Practical Suggestion*, London: Hodder & Stoughton, 1918. pp. 12–17.

Document 8   BEYOND THE BOWIE KNIFE

This is an extract from a letter to the New York Times *arguing in favour of the USA joining the League of Nations.*

The proposed League of Nations is founded upon precisely the same idea that every civilized community is founded upon – namely the sacrifice of personal rights on behalf of the larger rights of all the people. We enter into a league through the courts and State authority to guard against the lawlessness which the United States Senators plead for. We deny ourselves the rights, the freedom, the independence that members of every savage tribe enjoy, the right of reprisal, the right to do to our neighbour as he does to us, the right to plunder his farm, his house, his granary, if he plunders ours. We found long ago that an eye for an eye, and a tooth for a tooth did not work, however well it may have worked in Israel's time. We appeal to the courts, to the State, to protect us and redress our wrongs. It appears to be no great sacrifice for any of us to do so. It is much the easier course. Out West, years ago, when emigration outran the legal authorities, aggrieved persons took the law into their own hands, and if they were in a mood 'shot up' the whole town. The gun or the bowie knife was the only court of appeal. But that time is past in our communities, and it is high time it were past among the nations.

Source: Letter by John Burroughs in the *New York Times*, 9 March 1919.

TWO VIEWS OF THE ÅLAND ISLANDS   **Document 9**

These two documents show the very different ways the position of the Åland Islands could be interpreted. The one was drafted by the islanders themselves, while the other is a memorandum presented to the League of Nations by the Finnish government. The League had to find a way of responding to these very different arguments. To do this, it set up a special investigation.

(a) Extract from a Memorandum of the Delegation from the Åland Islands which was sent to the League of Nations on 6 June 1920 by J. Eriksson and A. Karlsson in their capacity as accredited members of the Landsting (the Åland Islands' local parliament)

The population of Åland expressed almost unanimously before the nations of the civilised world, its ardent desire for the return of the islands of Åland to Sweden. Their delegates have on several occasions pleaded their cause before the Swedish king and his government as before the allied and associated Powers. In order to explain the reasons for the attachment of the people of Åland to their mother-country, and their resolute determination to renew with her the political ties of former times, we give below a few facts which prove also the obvious justice of their cause.

1. It was from Scandinavia that Åland received its first inhabitants, in the prehistoric times of the Stone Age. During the whole of the following period Åland kept up the ties of ethnology and culture which bound it to its mother country, Sweden. Archaeological researches, the names of localities, the vestiges which remain of ancient times, and manuscript documents, all prove that Åland has never been inhabited by any other race than Swedish. No other language has ever been spoken in the Åland Island than the purest Swedish, first under the ancient Norse form, and then in the successive evolutions which the language underwent in Sweden itself . . .

From the first dawn of history, Åland appears as an ancient Swedish province, forming part of the kingdom of Sweden and possessing like some other provinces, a relative independence, both judicial and administrative. In short, from immemorial times Åland has formed an integral part of the Swedish kingdom.

2. Since the people of Åland were separated from Sweden by violence in 1809, they have remained in much closer economic and intellectual relations with Sweden than with Finland or with Russia. They sell the greater part of their products at Stockholm, which they naturally look upon as their capital. From Sweden comes the strongest influences which direct their intellectual and material development. Thus their feeling of community with their old country is always strong and full of vitality.

3. There is nothing surprising in these close relations between the Åland Islands and Sweden, for a glance at the map shows us that the large island of

Åland is twice as near to Sweden as to Finland, being at 40 kilometres from the Swedish coast and 80 from the Finnish. The islands are thus connected with Sweden even from a geographical point of view.

4. The people of Åland are thus closely connected with the Swedes by their origin, language, history, traditions and their intellectual and economic interests. It is therefore only natural that their character and mentality should bear the national Swedish stamp.

When, therefore, Finnish nationalism tries to stifle all Swedish tradition in the islands and to Finlandize the Swedish population, the Ålanders consider it as an attempt against their very existence.

5. The return of the Åland Islands to Sweden, of which they form an organic part, should clearly and inevitably result from the principle of the Right of Nations to dispose of themselves. The return to Sweden is to Ålanders a natural act of justice, the accomplishment of which cannot be prevented by the will of any oppressor.

Should there be any doubt as to the unanimity of this will of the people, the Ålanders demand that a new plebiscite be taken, the result of which shall be binding both for Finland and Sweden.

(b) Extract of a letter from the Finnish Minister in London, 7 July 1920
The Åland Islands are a continuation of the Finnish mainland, from which they are not geologically distinguished. There is constant communication eastwards with Finland, especially in winter, when ice covers the Narrows, which are very shallow; whilst westwards the Åland Sea, of a depth of from 200 to 300 metres, forms a clearly defined natural frontier between Sweden and the Archipelago.

The Åland Islands form a part of Swedish Finland and their population is connected with the Swedish group in Finland by ties of language, race and culture. The Swedish population of Finland numbers 400,000 souls, of whom the Ålanders form a sixteenth (about 25,000). The economic and cultural progress of the Archipelago is not an outcome of Swedish civilization but is identified, rather, with the civilization of the Swedish element of the Finnish mainland.

From the administrative point of view, the islands have always formed part of the department of Abo, whose capital, the town of the same name, was the ancient capital of Finland. When, for the first time in history, the question of the separation of the Archipelago from Finland was raised, the Swedish Governor of the department of Abo, Stjernstedt, on January 20th 1715 protested to his government at Stockholm . . .

The commercial relations of the Åland Islands have always been much more considerable with Finland than with Sweden. Agriculture, stock-raising, dairy-farming and the fishing industry have none of them received any stimulus from Sweden. The principal Åland industry, ship-building, depends on its connection with Finnish commerce. The Ålanders bring goods and provisions from the mainland, and their own products have always found purchasers on the Finnish coast, with which, from ancient times, the Ålanders have had old-established and continuous relations.

From the political point of view, the Ålanders have constantly proclaimed their Finnish nationality. They have taken part in all national manifestations, and until 1917 the number of votes cast by Ålanders in the elections to the Finnish Diet has continuously increased. The Swedish element of Åland has always shared, within the Finnish nation, the lot of the Swedish element of the Finnish mainland. As the Åland representatives have never suffered any oppression – other than under the regime of Russification – they have never protested to the diet. It is only since 1917 that the Ålanders – expressing a factitious desire, inspired by transient conditions – have demanded the return of the Ålands to Sweden. And this, although independent, Finland has from that time onwards shown herself capable of checking the Bolshevist contagion, and although the Finnish parliament, by the Constitution of July 17th 1919, has given to the Swedish population of Finland, and hence also to the Ålanders, the necessary guarantees to preserve them from denationalisation, and has dismantled the fortifications constructed on the islands by the Russians in 1915–17.

From the strategic point of view, the importance of the Åland Islands is greater for Finland than for Sweden. This Archipelago, which is connected with the Finnish mainland by a bridge of innumerable isles and islets, could more easily form a basis of operations against Finland than against Sweden. In Sweden's possession, the Åland Islands would make a Swedish lake of the Gulf of Bothnia, since there is no good maritime route to the East of Åland, whilst Sweden possesses, near to her coast, a broad and deep navigable channel . . .

In this instance, the rights of the minority are assured by the Finnish constitution . . .

Source: UNOG Library, League of Nations Archives. Extract (a) comes from R545, *The Åland Islands Question*, 11/530/468. Extract (b) comes from R545, *Views of the Finnish Government*, 11/5319/468, 7 July 1920.

TELLINI'S MURDER **Document 10**

This is an extract from the League's report into the murder of General Tellini. Although the Greek investigation of the crime clearly had not been perfect, it was not regarded as improper. Also the report makes plain that a number of bandits were suspected of the crime, although no one was found guilty in the end.

Greek responsibility before the crime

(a) Before the crime, a press campaign of some violence broke out against General Tellini, who was accused of favouring Albania to the detriment of Greece in demarcating the frontier between the two countries.

The Greek Government does not seem to have made any effort to stop this campaign or to moderate the excited condition of public opinion caused by fanatical patriots.

Both the Governor-General of Epirus and the Janina authorities were aware of rumours which were abroad in that town before the crime of August 27th in regard to the appearance of bands of brigands in the frontier region near Kakavia.

A few days before the crime, the Governor-General had advised the Italian Consul not to go unescorted to Santi-Quaranta, where he was to embark for Brindisi.

Under the circumstances it is surprising that no special steps were taken by the same authorities to protect the Delimitation Commission in the suspected region.

Even though General Tellini did not ask for an escort, and even if he had refused it when it was offered, the Greek authorities would, in the opinion of the Commission, have been wiser to insist upon General Tellini's accepting an escort and, if he had persisted refusing, they could have asked him to free them from all responsibility . . .

Greek responsibility in regard to the conduct of the enquiry by the judicial authorities

Generally speaking, the Commission is satisfied that the Greek judicial enquiry was conducted as expeditiously as the normal procedure of the Greek authorities permits. The enquiry shows however certain serious omissions, to which the Commission would draw the attention of the Conference of Ambassadors.

(b) On the day of the crime, the motor-car containing General Tellini and his companions was preceded, at a few minutes' interval, by the Albanian Delegation's car. The latter contained five persons, none of whom were examined by the Janina magistrate, though their evidence might have been of some importance.

Just before the crime, General Tellini's car was stopped by a barricade of branches thrown across the road by the murderers, who had posted themselves close at hand. This barricade constituted a portion of the evidence, and its constituent parts should have been preserved, as they certainly bore finger-prints, which ought to have been taken.

The Greek authorities did indeed give orders to that effect, but their orders were apparently not sufficiently definite. On the evening of the crime the branches had disappeared; they were burnt by the soldiers at the neighbouring Greek post, though there was plenty of firewood to be found in the undergrowth in the immediate vicinity of the post . . .

Conclusions of the Commission

The question at issue is extremely complicated; it must be approached with prudence, and time is needed before a definite opinion can be formed. The mystery of the crime committed on August 27th cannot be cleared up in such a short time as the Commission had at its disposal.

The Commission is not therefore in a position to give any final and definite decision as to where the responsibility really lies . . .

Nevertheless we seem to be getting near the truth.

In the first place the Greek authorities have captured a bandit named Constantine Memos who is notorious in Greece as the author of many crimes, and on whose head a price was set by the Greek Government. There is as yet no evidence that he is one of the murderers, but his past and the fact that he is generally suspected, furnishes a presumption of his guilt.

Secondly, the arrest of the bandit Stefan Corea in Albania gives the Albanian authorities a genuine basis for an enquiry, and there is reason to hope that they are now on the track of the chief of the band, Yani Vancho, whose admissions were heard by a witness. This witness has given sworn evidence.

Before leaving Janina the Commission thought it desirable to notify:

– The Albanian Government of the details which had come to light in Greece with regard to Memos;
– The Greek Government of the information obtained in Albania regarding the Vancho band and the arrest of one of its members, Stefan Corea. This precaution, however, is not enough in itself to bring the truth to light.

If the truth is to be discovered it is essential that there should be full agreement between the Albanian and Greek Governments . . .

Source: UNOG Library, League of Nations Archives: R 615, *The Dispute between Italy and Greece*, 11/32831/30508.

THE RUMBOLD REPORT   **Document 11**

This is an extract from the Rumbold report. It outlines how easily a border incident could get out of control and how, in the 'fog of war' a crisis could escalate to the point of conflict. At issue, ultimately, was the invasion of Bulgarian territory by Greek troops.

Greek Military Action in Bulgarian Territory

The crossing of the frontier was decided upon at Athens on the morning of October 20th. In order to obtain a correct view of this decision it is necessary to get back to the atmosphere which prevailed at the time, determine as accurately as possible the circumstances in which the news from Demir-Kapu was received in Athens and the effect which this news produced on the minds of the members of the Greek Government . . .

Information

In the night of Octiober 19th–20th, at about 3 a.m., the first news was received in Athens regarding the original incident at Demir-Kapu – the death of the sentry and the wounding of Captain Vassiliadis. The despatch added that the incident was premeditated by the Bulgarians and that Captain Vassiliadis had been wounded when, under cover of a white flag, he was going out to meet the Bulgarians.

On October 20th at 9.30 a.m. the Intelligence Officer of the covering battalion sent from Demir-Kapu to the officer commanding his battalion the following information: 'I beg to report that, according to information, Bulgarian forces amount to one battalion. Bulgarians possess machine guns.' The head of the battalion transmitted this news in a slightly altered form: 'The Bulgarians have attacked with a battalion and are occupying the hill-top.' The news which thus assumed an extremely serious aspect was forwarded to Athens, where it was received at 10.30 a.m. At the same time Athens learned the precautionary measures which had been adopted by the 3rd Army Corps.

We have seen that, on the morning of the 20th, the Bulgarian forces amounted to about 160 men, a figure admitted in a Greek report drawn up on October 31st. But at the time, taking into account the natural tendency of combatants to exaggerate, it may be admitted that the information received from the firing line or even the impression obtained by the Intelligence Officer may have so swelled these figures as to lead the Greeks to suppose that a whole battalion was in action. The officer commanding the 4th covering battalion committed the fault of not verifying his information, and above all of not resisting the temptation of improving upon it, whereas in none of the reports drawn up by officers in the firing line was it expressly stated that the Bulgarians were occupying positions in Greek territory. It should also be added that the 3rd Army Corps had, on the evening of October 19th, already received information at second-hand from the neighbouring covering battalion vaguely reporting that the Bulgarians had attacked in considerable force . . .

1. Orders of the 3rd Army Corps [Greece] – On October 20th at 8 a.m., on learning of the death of Captain Vassiliades, the Officer Commanding the 3rd Army Corps sent to the 6th Division, the headquarters of which is at Serres, an order that may be summarised as follows: 'Bulgarians are attacking

in force between Posts 67 and 69. All units are ordered to turn out. One battalion and one mountain battery will stand to.' At 8.30 a.m. there followed another order to guard the Rupel Defile and principal mountain passes and to advance the units up to the frontier . . .

2. Orders of the [Greek] Ministry of War – On October 20th at about 11 a.m., on receiving the telegrams already referred to announcing an attack by a Bulgarian battalion, the Ministry of War sent out the following order: 'The 3rd Army Corps will prepare to advance with all its forces towards Livunovo in the Struma Valley in order to outflank Mount Beles by way of Petrich. The 4th Army Corps will prepare for an invasion with all its forces in the direction of Nevrokop with the object of diverting and containing some of the Bulgarian forces. Both Corps will await further orders before advancing. Aeroplane reconnaissances will be carried out forthwith in the neighbourhood of Demi-Kapu, Petritch, Livunovo, Kula and the Libonovo district.'

All the places mentioned in this order are in Bulgarian territory . . .

3. Orders of the 3rd Army Corps and the 6th Division, and their Execution – In forwarding this order to the 6th Division, the 3rd Army Corps assigned to it the following objectives:

(1) The occupation of the heights north of Kula.
(2) The occupation of the heights south of Petritch.
(3) The outflanking of the Bulgarian forces attacking at Demir-Kapu . . .

In the evening of October 21st, the Commander of the 6th Division gave the following order: 'There is no further information as to enemy movements. The offensive will begin at 6 a.m. on the 22nd and will be carried as far as the objectives fixed. The positions occupied will then be organised.'

On October 22nd, at the hour fixed the execution of these orders began . . .

Source: League of Nations, *Commission of Enquiry into the Incidents on the Frontier between Bulgaria and Greece, Belgrade, November 28th 1925*, C/27/1925/VII (UNOG Library, League of Nations Archives).

MAKING SENSE OF MOSUL   **Document 12**

This extract reports a visit by League staff to towns in Mosul as they attempted to ascertain the political opinions of the inhabitants. It underlines how hard the job could be.

The president [of the Mosul Commission] . . . visited Tel-Afar. The town of Tel-Afar has about 12,300 inhabitants and all of the area has about 25,000. According to the official statistics, the town has about 8,000 Sunni Arabs, 1,950 Turks and 2,300 Kurds. The whole area has about 10,500 Sunni

Arabs, 5,500 Turks and 4,000 Kurds. The town's Kaimakan, a certain Houri de Mosul, maintains nonetheless that there are no Turks in the countryside and so there are 1,950 Turks in the whole area. The president asked him to tell the commission the grounds on which he bases his statistics.

On passing through the town on 16 February [1925], it was notable that the police were very numerous there and that apparently they prevented the public from being on the streets as we passed through.

On the 17th, at about 11.30, when we stopped about 15 minutes away from Tel-Afar, 4 or 5 individuals came running to meet us and pleaded at the top of their voices that the people had been mistreated and injured by the authorities. Immediately after our arrival, pro-Turkish demonstrations took place in front of the government house where we were. The Kaimakan pretended that the events were pro-Iraqi, but he was contradicted by the interpreters who said they were clearly pro-Turk. The British assessor requested the president to authorise the police to disperse the demonstrators in order to avoid trouble between the two communities which (according to him) lived in the town. The president authorised an appeal to the people to stay calm after which the enquiry could continue in tranquillity. We continued the enquiry. The president received members of part of the national defence force, 15 of them who declared that they were all Arab farmers and that they wanted a purely Arab government without any foreigners at all. When the president demanded that the force leave, they declared that they had all the people behind them – almost 50 chiefs of Tel-Afar were said to share their opinion which was also the opinion of the people. While they made this declaration, the people in front of the house cried: long live Turkey, long live Mustafa Kemal. When the committee left, one of its members, Abdel Rahman Effendi, who had participated in the uprising against the English in 1920, but was pardoned subsequently, took a moment and repeated energetically, with a singular expression, that they did not want any foreign influence.

The president then began to question the notables who were presented by the English and Turkish assessors [i.e. officials assisting the commissioner]. Of the eight people questioned, three pronounced themselves in favour of Iraq and four in favour of Turkey, while the eighth declared he was too afraid to express his view openly, although by signals he indicated to us that he was pro-Turk . . .

After the investigation process, the president, accompanied by the assessors, the interpreters and the Kaimakan, went on to the house's terrace. The people who were in part on the roofs and in part in the square in front of the house at once began demonstrating for Turkey as soon as they saw General Djevad Pacha. The British assessor once again demanded that the president authorise that the people be dispersed so that there would not be trouble between the two communities. But the president remarked that there was no second group present and that the demonstration was calm, and so he did not give the requested authorisation. Accompanied by the above mentioned people, the president went to visit a ruin 100 m. away from the house. Descending from the ruin, we passed in front of the crowd which remained in a calm and dignified attitude and acclaimed the General with cries of 'Long live Turkey', 'Long live Mustafa Kemal', 'The hero of Islam' . . .

Source: UNOG Library, League of Nations Archives, D 28, Interviews by Mr Winden, President (translated from French).

EMOTION IN VIENNA   **Document 13**

The following is an eyewitness account providing evidence of the outrage felt by Central Europeans due to their POWs being stuck in Siberia so long after the end of the First World War.

The Rathaus [town hall] last Sunday was crowded to suffocation with men and women who stood for four and a half hours in a state of intense emotion to hear the speeches, which discussed the fate of their relatives and friends. The first of the ex-prisoners who spoke had been five and a half years in Russia and had arrived home just three weeks previously. He had been through awful experiences, which he told in very simple words. He had been shut up in a camp where 'spotted typhus' had broken out and 4,600 men died out of 700 [7000 – error in original]. He escaped with 200 fellow prisoners and got to Petrograd [St Petersburg], found he could not go farther because of the blockade, went to Roumania, then found his way to Poland. 18 of his group were killed, eighty were wounded by Polish guns. In the end he and a few others reached home more dead than alive. The other man's story was much the same and it was a terribly moving experience to listen to them and to study the faces of the crowd.

Source: UNOG Library, League of Nations Archives, Letter from Emmeline Pethick Lawrence to Robert Cecil, 23 June 1920, R 1702, 42/5397/5213, Repatriation of prisoners of war.

NARVA'S TRANSIT SYSTEM   **Document 14**

The following extract tells us something about the transit system used in Narva, Estonia for the repatriation of POWs. It shows that planning constantly had to be updated on account of variables such as the end of summer. Note the reference to 'young girls'. The League's system in fact brought more people out of Russia than just POWs.

Difficulties arising with the advance of the season

The nights are already very fresh. For the most part, the people being repatriated are inadequately clothed (I have seen lots of young girls wearing just cotton smocks). They are disembarked [from the train from Russia] in the open 4 km from Narva. There is no shelter at all during this operation which takes quite a long time. There is a journey on foot followed by a new and long stop without any shelter before they find their accommodation at Ivangorod (tents). At the time of departing from Narva, until embarking on the boat, there is a transshipment journey (14 km) which takes between 5 and 6 hours, and involves being on a barge which is completely without shelter. Everything is slowed down by baggage. It is easy to imagine how things are at the moment, when it rains and there are long periods of waiting without shelter. What will it be like when there is ice and snow, and we have to count on that arriving? I think the following are indispensible: a depot with warm clothing, a building for shelter at the frontier station and before admission to Ivangorod-Narva camp, also on the barge.

Source: UNOG Library, League of Nations Archives, Report to the International Committee of the Red Cross, Geneva by Captain Berdez, 28 August 1920, R 1705, 42/6686/602, Repatriation of prisoners of war (translated from French).

Document 15   INTERVIEW WITH GENERAL WRANGEL

During his visit to the Balkans inspecting Russian refugees, General Thomson (acting on behalf of the International Committee of the Red Cross) met and interviewed the leading 'White' General, Pyotr Wrangel. This extract shows Wrangel's hostility to the idea of repatriation to Bolshevik Russia for his men.

On Wednesday 5 April I had a long conversation with General Wrangel on board 'Lucullus'. Wrangel declared that he has no desire to maintain his army of volunteers as a military force; on the contrary, he would like to give his men the possibility of pursuing their lives right up to the point of being able to return to Russia as individuals or civilians. On the other hand, he is firmly opposed to any of his men returning to the Russia of the Soviets, because he believes they would be executed. Confirming what he said, he indicated that at the time of the evacuation of the Crimea, all of the military and civilian people who could stay in Russia (i.e. those who were not compromised) did so. Personally he had wanted to take 250,000 people with him, but only 150,000 accepted his offer, with 70,000 being soldiers. He maintained that the 10,000 refugees who have already returned to Russia were forced to do so by France. He spoke bitterly about this, saying that the French were guilty of reprehensible conduct (dishonourable) and they have committed an unpardonable crime that respectable (decent) Russians will never forget.

Wrangel does not accept responsibility for the refugees at Constantinople: he has little or no authority among them. The majority of them arrived after the first evacuation from the south of Russia, that is, after the defeat of Denikin.

Source: UNOG Library, League of Nations Archives, Extract from the Report of General Thomson, R 1721, 45/13384/13384, The situation of the Russian refugees in the Balkan countries (translated from French).

OBSERVING BOLSHEVIK SECURITY   **Document 16**

This is an extract from a report by John Gorvin (one of Nansen's men in southern Russia) for T.F. Johnson in Geneva. It provides eyewitness testimony about how repatriated White soldiers were treated upon return to Novorossiysk according to his experiences of the security interviews managed by the local Political Department. The repatriated soldiers in question were Kalmuck. That is to say they were from a tribe with its own culture and language, which practised Buddhism. The questionnaire referred to in the extract was designed to identify the men's political views and to ascertain information about their activities during the First World War, the Revolution and the Civil War.

(2) On the evening of 20 October, I attended the offices of the Political Department (previously house of Governor) to witness the examination of the repatriated men ex Apostolos and Marat [two ships that took former White soldiers back to Russia]. The examination was conducted by Ivanoff, assistant of Kogan [the chief political officer of the region], a short man with small bushy beard and thick lips, of little education but sufficiently agreeable and with a store of rough and ready humour. (I insert these details to give you a little of the atmosphere.) Ivanoff was assisted by two officials of the Political Department. As many of the men examined were Kalmucks, two representatives of the Kalmucks in the camp, one a student, attended as translators; two other repatriated Kalmucks acted as doorkeepers to call the men individually for examination. The examination was a very ordinary affair with an element of drama provided by the general darkness of the room relieved only by an

electric light directly over Ivanoff's head and by the beating of the North east wind (so prevalent in Novorossiysk) and a heavy rain against the one window. In all about 50 men and 2 women were examined. I stayed until 11 p.m. and during these four hours 30 people were examined. Their examination took the form of repeating many of the questions in the enquiry form referred to in my letter to de Watteville of 20 October and checking the verbal replies with the written answers [i.e. reference to a written questionnaire the soldiers had filled in prior to the interview]. I observed that many of them were illiterate and that the written answers to the questions were not in all cases filled in on the form but were contained on separate sheets of paper, many of which had been written at dictation in the offices of the Linpunkt [the welfare station where the soldiers stayed]. A few cases of discrepancies between the written and oral answers were detected by Ivanoff but these were passed over, the men not having understood the questions, and being obviously harmless politically. All the papers of the men and women whom I saw examined were attested as satisfactory. In reply to the question whether the men were prepared to serve with the Red Army, the majority answered that they were prepared to do so if there no alternative, but that they had had enough of armies and were anxious only to return to their homes. Enquiries were also made as to their life abroad but almost without exception the men stated that they had worked there and that seemed to satisfy Ivanoff.

Source: UNOG Library, League of Nations Archives, Letter of 31 October 1922, Gorvin to Johnson, sent from Rostov, R 1744, 45/22278x/22278, Russian refugees: Repatriation of Cossack refugees from various countries.

Document 17　　McDONALD'S RESIGNATION LETTER

This is an extract from the open letter sent by James McDonald on 27 December 1935 as he resigned the post of High Commissioner of Refugees coming from Germany. He stresses the need for the League of Nations to tackle the domestic policies giving rise to the flow of refugees in the first place.

(8) It is being made increasingly difficult for Jews and 'non-Aryans' in Germany to sustain life. Condemned to segregation within the four corners of the legal and social Ghetto which has now closed upon them, they are increasingly prevented from earning their living. Indeed more than half of the Jews remaining in Germany have already been deprived of their livelihood. In many parts of the country there is a systematic attempt at starvation of the Jewish population. In no field of economic activity is there any security whatsoever. For some time it has been impossible for Jewish business men

and shopkeepers to carry on their trades in small towns. The campaign against any dealings with Jews is now systematically prosecuted in the larger towns. Despite the restrictions upon migration from the provinces into the few largest cities where Jewish economic activity is not yet completely excluded, the Jews are fleeing to those cities because there only can they hope to escape, at least for a time, from the more brutal forms of persecution . . .

(15) The efforts of the private organisations and of any League organisation for refugees can only mitigate a problem of growing gravity and complexity. In the present economic conditions of the world, the European States, and even those overseas, have only a limited power of absorption of refugees. The problem must be tackled at its source if disaster is to be avoided . . .

Source: 'Letter of Resignation of James G. McDonald, High Commissioner for Refugees (Jewish and Other) coming from Germany' in N. Bentwich, *The Refugees from Germany, April 1933 to December 1935*, London: Allen & Unwin, 1936, pp. 219–28.

TYPHUS IN POLAND   **Document 18**

This is a section from a report by a US military doctor who was involved in the fight against typhus at an early time. Reports such as these were fed to the League of Nations and helped persuade it to take action. It shows clearly the difficulties caused by the Russo-Polish war.

11 March 1920

From the present indications Poland is threatened with one of the worst typhus fever epidemics in the history of the world, which, unless checked, will prove a danger that will threaten the whole of Europe. The government of Poland is fully alive to the duties incumbent upon her in view of the seriousness of this present epidemic, but cannot conceal the fact of her inability to cope with this grave situation which is developing for the reasons of her lack of financial resources and sufficient sanitary supplies in the present overwhelming emergency.

The typhus epidemic, which, for the fourth year in succession has been raging in Poland has increased in intensity each year, due principally to the large influx of refugees and prisoners of war from Russia, and to the thousands of cases being imported from the Interior of Ukrainia and other eastern territories. The situation at present is getting beyond control.

This western spread has become more and more extensive in measure as the military and political conditions of the Ukraine have become more unsettled. In fact, the breaking up of the armies of General Petlura resulted in tens of thousands of Ukrainians percolating through the frontiers, passing principally through the areas between Tarnopol in the north and Borszow in the south. Sometimes they presented themselves at the quarantine stations in such crowds that they could not be handled and a break-through would result thereby, permitting thousands of cases to be scattered throughout Eastern Galicia.

It is a known fact that the commanders of the Bolshevik armies are ridding themselves of typhus fever cases by sending them in armoured cars . . . [to] Polish territory.

When Denikin's armies retreated before the Bolsheviks, and the Polish armies were invited to occupy the vacant territory, which they are still engaged in, a new and unbelievably large source of typhus fever was opened up. Certain of the larger towns, such as Winnica, were found to harbor thousands of cases without the least care of attention having been given them. As a rule, Denikin's garrisons left behind were garrisons of typhus fever.

The centre of the present typhus epidemic appears to be in Russia and Ukrania, and thousands of refugees entering Poland in their flight from Bolshevism are received in a frightful state. They relate terrible tales as to the number of cases of typhus fever and the suffering resulting therefrom. During the extreme cold those unfortunates, inflicted with the disease and without medical attention of any kind, crowd together in unventilated, heatless buildings, trying to keep warm. They die by the thousands, their bodies being piled in great heaps in adjoining buildings, awaiting burial. Poland realizes these conditions in Russia and Ukrainia, and from a humanitarian standpoint makes no attempt to bar entrance to these refugees. She is thus a rampart against the dangers of this disease which threatens the world, and which, if Europe is allowed to be thoroughly saturated, will result in perhaps one of the world's greatest catastrophes.

Source: UNOG Library, League of Nations Archives, Memorandum by Col. H.L. Gilchrist (USA medical service) attached to the Polish Ministry of Health, R 812, 12/3659/1719, Poland typhus situation and international action.

Document 19   SEIZING OPIUM

This is part of a report detailing the seizure of a consignment of opium in Hong Kong. Clearly the exercise yielded good information about how the illegal trade worked in the region.

On 6th November 1923 Inspector Appleton, attached to the Secretariat for Chinese Affairs on information received, searched the top floor of the house on an arms warrant. As the party at 11 a.m. were going up the stairs they met a man just coming down with a parcel under his arm which proved to contain Chinese raw opium. On reaching the floor they found a hand bag in the passage containing raw opium, and some smaller packages in various parts of the floor also containing the same kind of opium, the total amount being in all 320 taels. Several persons were found on the floor including a Chinese General of high rank; while the party were there 12 persons entered the flat, including 2 small children who were wearing broad pieces of cloth around their waists under their coats, obviously to be used to carry away the opium which was to be purchased by the persons accompanying them. One man tore up and threw away a piece of paper which when recovered proved to be an order for 110 taels of opium and instructions to debit the cost to his current account. A large number of account books and documents were found; the examination proved a very long and tiring task . . . The firm consisted of 5 partners, the capital being $6,500. The floor was occupied nominally as a club. The front room was used as an office in which the accounts were kept and customers entertained. One cubicle was apparently used for the accommodation of friends and customers visiting the Colony. The end room was used for the sale of opium. Six assistants were employed, some of whom brought the opium from the ships and distributed it in Hong Kong. The firm appeared to be composed of natives of the Swatow district. One assistant was permanently stationed at Hoihow, the port for the Island Hainan . . .

The basis of the whole business was the exchange of arms and ammunition for opium. Mauser pistols and revolvers were purchased from various smugglers in Hong Kong with ammunition to fit and forwarded to Hoihow for sale. All the proceeds were used to buy opium. Very little money was actually remitted either way. There appears to have been difficulty in remitting money between the two places owing to the disturbed state of the country. The trade in arms seems to have been very remunerative, the guns fetched $150 to $270 each, and the ammunition made equally good prices. The firm seems to have [been] in the opium trade about one year. In that time they imported roughly 120,000 taels of raw opium from the places mentioned; this opium was retailed here in quantities from 2 taels upwards, mostly in quantities of between 50 and 100 taels. Occasionally a large consignment was forwarded to Swatow, where the firm seems to have been on very good terms with an official bureau called The Opium Suppression Head Bureau. This bureau seems to be another name for the Swatow Opium Farm, who sometimes bought the opium forwarded outright, [or] sometimes sold it on a commission basis. The largest amount imported in any one consignment was 4,299 taels . . . Opium was sold every day in the month preceding the search, and the number of separate sales was over 10 every day . . .

Signed: J.D. Lloyd, Superintendent of Imports and Exports

12 December 1923

Source: UNOG Library, League of Nations Archives, R 762c, 12A/27816/23816x, Opium traffic at Hong Kong and Macao.

Document 20   PERSIAN POPPIES

More effective policing was not the only reaction to the illegal drugs trade. The following document outlines a political response to the problem of opium poppies grown in Persia (Iran). It highlights the attraction of the crop for an underdeveloped country and suggests ways of changing the behaviour.

1. Persia was once the centre of the then-known civilised world, and the chief trade routes to the Far East lay across it. To-day it is off the main trade routes and, at least relatively speaking, is far more inaccessible than formerly . . .

4. While it is probably true that Persia's undeveloped and undiscovered resources are large, the Persian people as a whole are poor – very poor; and this is due to economic conditions which have in the last hundred years been driving her to the wall. During a considerable part of this time, Persia's trade balance has been against her, and the deficit has been in part represented by debt, but more often in the depletion of her capital, in her case of those savings of the past in the form of rare art treasures, beautiful fabrics, tiles, miniatures, and the like, which, to a constantly increasing extent, have gone out of Persia and have found their way into the collections of Europe and America.

5. By reason of famine, disease, civil wars, the causes of which may be traced largely to bad economic conditions, the population of the country has greatly diminished in the last fifty or sixty years, and is to-day, let us say, not in excess of one-third or one-fourth of what the country under more ideal economic conditions might support.

6. Persia, being a country of very scanty rainfall (estimated at from two to twelve inches per year), except in the north-western region and the Caspian Littoral:

(a) The cities and towns are located at the foothills where water from the melting snow is available;

(b) Broadly speaking one-third of the country is a desert, another one-third is mountainous and chiefly suitable for grazing;

(c) The cities are far apart, and as the means of communication are poor, each city is a small empire by itself, only feebly connected with the capital;

(d) Agriculture is chiefly dependent on irrigation, which demands intelligent and industrious labour – but does not permit Persia to compete in the production of raw materials with those countries having abundant rainfall. In addition, Persia is at a disadvantage of distance and high transport costs in reaching world markets . . .

8. There is a lack of security in Persia which accounts to a considerable extent for what is frequently termed by foreigners a lack of initiative of public spirit. For example, the Commission found no disposition to store grain (e.g. in ground silos) in abundant years to carry over to lean years. The reason given

was lack of confidence in the security, the high rates of money, the want of adequate protection of private property . . .

10. Opium poppy is an ideal crop from several points of view, but chiefly because:

(a) It is an autumn-sown crop which can be irrigated in the late fall and early spring when water is plentiful. It is harvested in the late spring or early summer;

(b) It has a high value per pound and money yield per acre, say, four times that of wheat and barley, which are also fall-sown crops;

(c) Its high value per pound (say, $6 to $8) is such that it can bear the terrifically high transport charges prevalent in that country;

(d) Being largely exported, it helps Persia to pay for imports, but it is not by any means certain that Persia would not be better off if she did not buy so largely abroad.

11. A number of industries for which Persia was once famous are dying out and Persia, instead of exporting only manufactured goods having high value (and so able to bear a high transport charge), is attempting to export raw material, such, for example, as wool, cotton (of inferior grade), rice, etc.

12. The industries which are dying out and which might be restored are the production of:

(a) Silk, wool and cotton fabrics;

(b) Pottery, tiles, earthenware, bricks;

(c) Artistic metal-work;

(d) Woodcarving, inlaying, etc.;

(e) Painting miniatures, decorating, engrossing parchment etc.;

(f) Sheep, lamb and goat skins, hides, leather goods.

13. In addition to the industries which are dying out and which may again be put upon their feet, certain other industries can be developed, for example:

(a) Those dependent on the development of mineral oil, of which there is very evidently abundance;

(b) Vegetable oils from oil seed, such as rape seed, peanut oil, castor oil, soya beans, etc.;

(c) Making and distributing dried fruits, preserves, etc.;

(d) Making sugar, especially from sugar cane;

(e) Plaster of Paris, (gypsum), lime and cement.

Conclusions of the Commission

6. The production of opium exists largely by reason of the economic conditions aforesaid. The Persian Government has indicated by its own actions, and by its efforts to prevent the consumption of opium at home (it is absolutely

forbidden in the Government service or in the Army), that it considers the use of opium a serious menace. The Commission came to the conclusion that it was even a more serious menace than was usually appreciated; that it was slowly but surely destroying the manpower of the country; that it was impossible to produce opium for export and not have it also consumed in considerable quantities at home.

Recommendations of the Commission

1. That Persia should allow three years to put its house in order, by which was meant improving its internal economic condition, making a start on building its roads, adjusting its tariffs of import duties, improving its agricultural methods, building up its sources of revenue, before it undertook a reduction in the production of opium and the substitution therefore.

2. That better and more complete methods (indicated in considerable detail) be employed for the control of opium production and distribution.

3. Having taken these preliminary steps, it was believed that the Persian Government could safely undertake to reduce opium production by a reduction of ten per cent annually.

Source: UNOG Library, League of Nations Archives, R 801, 12A/59098/45255, Opium traffic.

Document 21   PEOPLE-TRAFFICKING IN THE FAR EAST

The following is taken from the investigation into people-trafficking in the Far East conducted in the early 1930s. It shows the resilience of the trade.

In the Dutch East Indies, the difficulties put in the way of traffickers by strict Government measures have redoubled efforts by the latter to bring Chinese females into the country under various false pretences, e.g. as adopted children, as famine and flood refugees taken for charitable motives, etc. with the intention of letting them grow up in the Indies until they can be exploited for immoral purposes. Under the pressure of new regulations, the traffickers have been quick to change their methods. According to official information, some years ago, one of the commonest devices employed by them was to introduce Chinese women into the Dutch East Indies as members of waytang troupes (travelling theatrical troupes). As soon as they entered the Dutch East Indies, the women appeared once or twice at performances and were then taken to clandestine brothels. By keeping waytang troupes under observation as they proceeded from place to place, the Government succeeded in checking the practice. Then another device was tried in connection with a recently introduced rule requiring that Chinese marriages must take place before an official of the register office for Chinese immigrants. The traffickers began to use this rule for their purpose in the following manner. A trafficker living abroad would write to an accomplice in the Dutch East Indies, at Semarang for example, that he wanted to smuggle in a Chinese woman. The accomplice would go to the Immigration Office and state that a certain woman coming, say, from Singapore was his wife. If his statement was not credited, he would offer to be married to her by the registrar at Semarang. The ceremony would take place. After some time, the woman, though in possession of an official marriage certificate, would be found in a clandestine brothel. The 'husband' had vanished and would probably be trying to play the same game elsewhere.

As long as the profits in the business may be expected to compensate for the difficulties in smuggling Chinese girls, the traffickers do not seem to be deterred by the most prohibitive immigration procedure. The Commission was informed that Chinese girls destined to be smuggled into the Philippines on the pretext of being minor children of Chinese established in the islands were actually made to live for as long as two years in the village in China which they would later be required to claim as their native place and to undergo a veritable course of instruction in the manner of answering the questions of the immigration officials in Manila.

Source: Summary of the Report to the Council Commission of Enquiry into Traffic in Women and Children in the East, Geneva: League of Nations, 1934. p. 23.

SLAVERY IN ABYSSINIA **Document 22**

This document shows some of the difficulties encountered by anti-slavery drives in Abyssinia (Ethiopia).

9. It would be unfair to the Abyssinian Government to take exception to the fact that it has not yet abolished the status of slavery.

In dealing with Abyssinia, it must never be forgotten that the country was for two centuries cut off from the outside world, that its evolution has been retarded, and that all matters concerning it cannot be judged by the principles governing European nations. Moreover, although Abyssinia signed the 1926 Convention [on slavery], she has not ratified it. Even if she had done so, she would only have been bound, under actual terms of the Convention, to abolish slavery gradually. All that the contracting parties can demand of her is to make every effort to abolish slavery as soon as possible.

Every measure for the liberation of slaves, however, is opposed in Abyssinia by a barrier of ancient traditions. Very many officers of the Empire, including powerful chiefs, are against the abolition of slavery, either simply because they espouse the feelings of the people under their jurisdiction or because they themselves derive benefit from the present situation.

There is surely no need to point to the dangers to which the maintenance of the Government's authority would be exposed, or at all events the political disturbances with which it might be faced, if, contrary to the general feeling and despite the interests which it might harm, it proceeded to abolish the status of slavery too rapidly.

Even supposing that, after abolishing the status of slavery, the Abyssinian Government were able to counteract these dangers in the political sphere, a measure which suddenly transferred vast numbers of persons from the condition of slavery to one of full freedom (as regards the number of the slaves, the Committee has no accurate information) might produce disastrous results in the social and economic fields. Doubtless this consideration played some part in the decision of the Abyssinian Government to refrain from abolishing slavery by a stroke of the pen. It gave as one of the reasons for its Edict of 1924 that, by adopting such a measure, the number of thieves, bandits and criminals would be greatly increased.

It must also be admitted that the mass liberation of slaves would have a considerable effect on the finances of Abyssinia, in that the Government might find itself bound to compensate the former owners, or take steps to ensure that freed slaves were in a position to gain a living, or, lastly, to support those who, owing to age or infirmity, were permanently incapable of earning their own livelihood, for which their master had usually provided until their death.

In short, conditions in Abyssinia make it impossible for the Government, however desirous it may be of abolishing slavery, to do otherwise than advance gradually along this path. If the Government ignored this policy of prudence, it might stir up political, social, economic and financial difficulties which would completely nullify the success already achieved.

Source: Slavery: Report of the Committee of Experts on Slavery provided for by the Assembly Resolution of September 25th, 1931, Geneva: League of Nations, 1932, p. 8.

Document 23   THE CHRISTIE REPORT

The extract shows just a bit of what Christie discovered when he investigated slavery in Liberia – in particular regarding the involvement of government officials in the practice.

B. Oppressive practices restrictive of the freedom of persons, constituting conditions analogous to slavery and tending to acquire the status of classic slavery.

1. Forcible recruiting and shipment of native labour to Fernando Po from the County of Sinoe, with the aid of Frontier Force soldiers, armed messengers, and certain Liberian Government officials proceeded under Samuel Ross of Greenville as late as 1928, when he was appointed Postmaster General of Liberia. After his transfer to the Capital, and as Postmaster General, he continued his recruiting in Monrovia and Montserrado County, sending native boys to Sinoe for transhipment, despite, or in evasion of the law prohibiting exportation of labour out of the country from Montserrado County. There is convincing evidence that forced shipments were made from Sinoe County as early as 1924 when boys were sent down to Mr. Ross by Captain Howard under armed guard, with rice ostensibly for sale, kept under guard until the arrival of the Spanish steamer for Fernando Po and shipped. The incident was reported in that year to the Secretary for the Interior and to the President by P.C. Lemandine, then District Commissioner for Sinoe County, stationed at Sikon. The raiding and forcible recruiting were repeated during the same year until a number estimated as between 600 and 800 had been so delivered. The District Commissioner who protested alleges that he was recalled from his station and eventually relieved of office.

Source: Report of the International Commission of Enquiry into the Existence of Slavery and Forced Labour in the Republic of Liberia, Monrovia, Liberia, 1930.

PROGRESS IN RWANDA-BURUNDI   **Document 24**

This is an extract from a mandates report showing developments experienced in Rwanda-Burundi.

Food Supply

In this domain, progress has been particularly striking.

Formerly, even apart from times of distress when famine was rife – times which are no longer more than an evil memory, the Bahutu were undernourished. Moreover, every year they had to traverse a difficult period during which they had nothing to eat but bananas and sometimes only the leaves of kidney-beans and the roots of various plants. Now they have at least two good meals a day.

The present production of foodstuffs is due to measures which have frequently been explained. It is, in part, due to the introduction of new crops, in particular several varieties of beans affording a yield twice or three times as great as that of native varieties. Wheat is sown to an ever-increasing extent and the notables now eat it in the form of bread. The muhutu is becoming accustomed to eating manioc, which constitutes the staple food throughout almost the whole of the Belgian Congo.

The increase in their resources enables the natives of the lower class from time to time to buy meat, of which they are extremely fond. The number of heads of large cattle slaughtered on the markets has tripled. Foods previously considered taboo, such as the flesh of sheep, goats, pigs and chickens, fish and eggs, are eaten to a continuously increasing extent.

The Family and the Role of Woman
The birth rate has remained very much the same as formerly, but the infant death rate has fallen.

Polygamy is decreasing to a noticeable extent as a result of the increasing influence of missionaries and the standing of a sole wife has improved . . .

Under the influence of civilisation, the woman tends to an increasing extent to become equal to her husband. The latter cannot go away for a long period without her consent. Man and wife eat together, which is rare among black races. Among the chiefs and the principal Batutsi, where this custom was slower in spreading, it is now general, even when strangers are present. The wives of these chief notables, who, formerly, would not show themselves outside the 'rugo', now move about in the neighbourhood of the 'rugo', attend to the cultivation of the family field and often themselves supervise the labourers . . .

Source: Extracts from the Annual report for Rwanda-Burundi, 1938, reproduced in P.W. Anker, *The Mandates System*, Geneva: League of Nations, 1945, pp. 68–9.

Document 25   ARMAMENTS AND THE CAUSES OF WAR

In the following extract from his memoirs, Robert Cecil represents the view that armaments help cause war. Contrast this source with Document 26.

The reduction and, still more, the limitation of armaments I thought vital for peace. It is no doubt easy to argue that war may break out whether the nations are well or badly armed. But even if that be so, unless some way can be found for the international limitation of armaments, an arms race is bound to take place. Each nation on the Continent watches anxiously the extent of the armaments of its neighbours. It knows from bitter experience that as soon as there is a definite armament superiority, the temptation to an ambitious Government to bully its neighbours becomes irresistible. Accordingly, each country is tempted to increase its armaments, with or without alliances, to try to ward off the danger. That leads to increases by its rivals, with all the accompanying growth in the burden of taxation for both countries, and so it goes on. A state of international unrest is created, greatly added to by the necessity for each country to defend its growing expenditure by pointing out the threatening policy of others and by dwelling on the deplorable international characteristics which make them dangerous. Very soon, an atmosphere is produced in which everyone talks of war and when that happens war almost always follows.

This is no fancy picture. People of my age have seen the process going on more than once – a kind of automatic drive towards war, which, when it breaks out, is justified to the peaceful majority in each country as a war of self-defence, as indeed on one side or the other it usually is.

Source: Lord Robert Cecil, *A Great Experiment*, London: Jonathan Cape, 1941, pp. 237–8.

SECURITY BEFORE DISARMAMENT **Document 26**

In a book published later than Robert Cecil's (see Document 25), a senior member of the League responsible for disarmament (Salvador de Madariaga) argues that steps have to be taken to make states feel secure before disarmament can be addressed seriously.

The trouble with disarmament was (it still is) that the problem of war is tackled upside down and at the wrong end. Upside down first; for nations do not arm willingly. Indeed, they are sometimes only too willing to disarm, as the British did to their sorrow in the Baldwin days. Nations don't distrust each other because they are armed; they are armed because they distrust each other. And therefore to want disarmament before a minimum of common agreement on fundamentals is as absurd as to want people to go undressed in winter. Let the weather be warm, and people will discard their clothes readily and without committees to tell them how they are to undress.

Then, disarmament was tackled at the wrong end. A war is the ultima ratio in a conflict; a conflict is the outcome of a dispute that has got out of hand; a dispute is the consequence of a problem that has proved insoluble; a problem is born of a question that has not been tackled in time. Disarmers would avoid wars by reducing armaments. They run to the wrong end of the line. The only way is far more humdrum and modest. It consists in dealing day by day with the business of the world. It follows that disarmament is an irrelevant issue; the true issue being the organisation of the government of the world on a co-operative basis . . .

Source: S. de Madariaga, *Morning without Noon*, Farnborough: Saxon House, 1973, pp. 48–9.

Document 27   LYTTON DISCUSSES THE MUKDEN INCIDENT

In the following extracts from his final report, Lord Lytton judges who was responsible for the explosion at Mukden and its consequences. Notice the balance of his assessment, although it still ends up being critical of Japan.

According to the Japanese versions, Lieutenant Kawamoto, with six men under his command, was on patrol duty on the night of September 18th, practising defence exercises along the track of the South Manchuria Railway to the north of Mukden. They were proceeding southwards in the direction of Mukden. The night was dark but clear and the field of vision was not wide. When they reached a point at which a small road crossed the line, they heard the noise of a loud explosion a little way behind them. They turned and ran back, and after going about 200 yards they discovered that a portion of one of the rails on the down track had been blown out. The explosion took place at the point of junction of two rails; the end of each rail had been cleanly severed, creating a gap in the line of 31 inches. On arrival at the site of the explosion, the patrol was fired upon from the fields on the east side of the line. Lieutenant Kawamoto immediately ordered his men to deploy and return the fire. The attacking body, estimated at about five or six, then stopped firing and retreated northwards. The Japanese patrol at once started in pursuit and, having gone about 200 yards, they were again fired upon by a larger body, estimated at between three and four hundred. Finding himself in danger of being surrounded by this large force, Lieutenant Kawamoto then ordered one of his men to report to the Commander of No. 3 Company, who was also engaged in night manoeuvres some 1,500 yards to the north; at the same time, he ordered another of his men to telephone (by means of a box telephone near the spot) to Battalion Headquarters at Mukden for reinforcements . . .

Lieutenant Kawamoto's patrol, reinforced by Captain Kawashima's Company, was still sustaining the fire of the Chinese troops concealed in the tall kaoliang grass, when the two Companies arrived from Mukden. Although his force was then only 500, and he believed the Chinese army in the North Barracks numbered 10,000, Lieutenant-Colonel Shimamoto at once ordered an attack on the Barracks, believing as he told us, that 'offence is the best defence' . . .

According to the Chinese version, the Japanese attack on the Barracks (Peitaying) was entirely unprovoked and came as a complete surprise. On the night of September 18th, all the soldiers of the 7th Brigade, numbering about 10,000 were in the North Barracks. As instructions had been received from Marshal Chang Hsueh-liang on September 6th that special care was to be taken to avoid any clash with the Japanese troops in the tense state of feeling existing at the time, the sentries at the walls of the Barracks were only armed with dummy rifles. For the same reason, the west gate in the mud wall surrounding the camp which gave access to the railway had been closed . . . As soon as the attack began, the Chief of Staff gave orders for the lights to be extinguished, and again reported to General Wang I-Chen by telephone. The latter replied that no resistance was to be offered . . .

Such are the two stories of the so-called incident of September 18th as they were told to the Commission by the participants on both sides. Clearly, and not unnaturally in the circumstances, they are different and contradictory.

Appreciating the tense situation and high feeling which had preceded this incident, and realising the discrepancies which are bound to occur in accounts of interested persons, especially with regard to an event which took place at night, the Commission, during its stay in the Far East, inter-viewed as many as possible of the representative foreigners who had been in Mukden at the time of the occurrences or soon after, including newspaper correspondents and other persons who had visited the scene of conflict shortly after the event, and to whom the first official Japanese account had been given. After a thorough consideration of such opinions, as well as of the accounts of the interested parties, and after a mature study of the consider-able quantity of written material and a careful weighing of the great mass of evidence which was presented or collected, the Commission has come to the following conclusions:

Tense feelings undoubtedly existed between the Japanese and Chinese military forces. The Japanese, as was explained to the Commission in evidence, had a carefully prepared plan to meet the case of possible hostilities between themselves and the Chinese. On the night of September 18th–19th, this plan was put into operation with swiftness and precision. The Chinese . . . had no plan of attacking the Japanese troops, or of endangering the lives or property of Japanese nationals at this particular time or place. They made no con-certed or authorised attack on the Japanese forces and were surprised by the Japanese attack and subsequent operations. An explosion undoubtedly occurred on or near the railroad between 10 and 10.30 p.m. on Sunday 18th, but the damage, if any, to the railroad did not in fact prevent the punctual arrival of the south-bound train from Changchun, and was not in itself suf-ficient to justify military action. The military operations of the Japanese troops during this night, which have been described above, cannot be regarded as measures of legitimate self-defence. In saying this, the Commission does not exclude the hypothesis that the officers on the spot may have thought they were acting in self-defence.

Source: Appeal by the Chinese Government, Report of the Commission of Enquiry, Geneva: League of Nations, 1932, pp. 67–71.

Document 28   OIL SANCTIONS?

This is an extract from a report by the committee which, during February 1936, looked at the possibility of applying oil sanctions against Italy. They thought the move could have exerted real pressure on the country in due course.

The total stock [of oil available to Italy] at the end of 1934 probably averaged about six weeks' to two months' supply, or 400,000 to 500,000 tons. If to this be added the difference between the purchases and estimated consumption in 1935, amounting to 300,000 tons, a total of 700,000 to 800,000 tons on December 31st, 1935, is obtained. Stocks may have increased during January 1936 by a further 50,000 tons, and, at the end of January, may therefore, have been equivalent to some two and a half to three months' consumption.

If an embargo were imposed, there would be at the moment of its imposition certain supplies en route, representing about half a month's supply to be added to the stocks already in hand . . .

Source: UNOG Library, League of Nations Archives. Box 3681, Folder 1/22440/22392, Extract from the Report of the Committee of Experts for the technical examination of the conditions governing the trade in and transport of petroleum and its derivatives, by-products and residues, Geneva, 12 February 1936.

Document 29   HAILE SELASSIE AT GENEVA

This is an extract from the speech Haile Selassie delivered to the Assembly on 30 June 1936.

I, Haile Selassie I, Emperor of Ethiopia, am here today to claim that justice that is due to my people, and the assistance promised to it eight months ago by fifty-two nations who asserted that an act of aggression had been committed in violation of international treaties. None other than the Emperor can address the appeal of the Ethiopian people to those fifty-two nations.

There is perhaps no precedent for a head of a State himself speaking in this Assembly. But there is certainly no precedent for a people being the victim of such wrongs and being threatened with abandonment to its aggressor. Nor has there ever before been an example of any Government proceeding to the systematic extermination of a nation by barbarous means, in violation of the most solemn promises made to all the nations of the earth that there should be no resort to a war of conquest and that there should not be used against innocent human beings the terrible weapon of poison gas. It is to defend a people struggling for its age-old independence that the Head of the Ethiopian Empire has come to Geneva to fulfil this supreme duty, after having himself fought at the head of his armies . . .

At the outset, towards the end of 1935, Italian aircraft hurled tear-gas bombs upon my armies. They had but slight effect. The soldiers learned to scatter, waiting until the wind had rapidly dispersed the poisonous gases.

The Italian aircraft then resorted to mustard gas. Barrels of liquid were hurled upon armed groups. But this means too was ineffective; the liquid affected only a few soldiers, and the barrels upon the ground themselves gave warning of the danger to the troops and to the population.

It was at the time when the operations for the encirclement of Makale were taking place that the Italian command, fearing a rout, applied the procedure which it is now my duty to denounce to the world.

Sprayers were installed on board aircraft so that they could vaporise, over vast areas of territory, a fine, death-dealing rain. Groups of nine, fifteen, eighteen aircraft followed one another so that the fog issuing from them formed a continuous sheet. It was thus that, from the end of January 1936, soldiers, women, children, cattle, rivers, lakes, and fields were constantly drenched with this deadly rain. In order to kill off systematically all living creatures, in order the more surely to poison waters and pastures, the Italian command made its aircraft pass over and over again. That was its chief method of warfare.

The very refinement of barbarism consisted in carrying devastation and terror into the most densely populated parts of the territory, the points farthest removed from the scenes of hostilities. The object was to scatter horror and death over a great part of the Ethiopian territory . . .

In October 1935, the fifty-two nations who are listening to me to-day gave me an assurance that the aggressor would not triumph, that the resources of the Covenant would be implemented in order to ensure the rule of law and the failure of violence.

I ask the fifty-two nations not to forget to-day the policy upon which they embarked eight months ago, and on the faith of which I directed the resistance of my people against the aggressor whom they had denounced to the world . . .

I ask the great Powers, who have promised the guarantee of collective security to small States – those small States over whom hangs the threat that they may one day suffer the fate of Ethiopia: What measures do they intend to take?

Representatives of the world, I have come to Geneva to discharge in your midst the most painful of the duties of the head of a State. What answer am I to take back to my people?

Source: *League of Nations Official Journal: Special Supplement No. 151*, Geneva 1936, pp. 22–5.

Document 30   THE BRUCE REPORT

This is an extract from the Bruce report which emphasises the importance of social and economic issues for the future stability of the world.

There has never been a time when international action for the promotion of economic and social welfare was more vitally necessary than it is at the present moment. The work of the League in these fields has developed and changed its nature in recent years, and the changes that have taken place necessitate, as we see it, a careful consideration of the means by which the mechanism of international collaboration can be rendered at once more efficient and more easily available to all.

There are two tendencies in the world today which render the need for Governmental co-operation in economic and social questions more urgent than heretofore, and at the same time give greater opportunities for the success of such co-operation.

The world, for all its political severance, is growing daily closer knit; its means of communication daily more rapid; its instruments for the spread of knowledge daily more efficient. At the same time, the constituent parts of the world, for all their diversity and political outlook, are growing in many respects more similar; agricultural States are becoming rapidly industrialised, industrial States are stimulating their agriculture. Nothing is more striking in this connection, or more characteristic, than the swift industrial development of the great Asiatic countries.

These changes inevitably give rise to new problems that can only be solved by joint effort. Thus, trade and personal contacts are facilitated, but simultaneously economic depressions become more widespread; and, were there any relaxation of control, human and animal diseases would spread more widely and more rapidly. Neither the economic nor the physical contagion – nor, indeed the moral – can be checked by national action alone, except by recourse to almost complete isolation . . .

But the fact that the form of economic structure in all countries is tending to become more similar means at once that the problems with which all Governments are faced also acquire greater similarity, and that the opportunities of each country to gain from the experience of others are increased. Countries of the world to-day are, on account of the rapidity of the changes to which we have alluded, in greater need than before of the aid which can be afforded by others, and are more capable of rendering that aid. It is only by joint discussion of the nature of the new problems which these changes present, by exchange of experience, and by co-ordination of national policies, that the adaptations essential to progress can be effected . . .

It is by international discussion, and by the association in the work of independent experts, that Governments can best safeguard themselves against the danger of being pressed by one sectional interest or another to assist it at the expense of the general well-being . . .

We suggest, therefore, that the Assembly should set up a new organism, to be known as the Central Committee for Economic and Social Questions, to which should be entrusted the direction and supervision of the work of the League Committees dealing with economic and social questions . . .

Source: League of Nations, *The Development of International Co-operation in Economic and Social Affairs: Report of the Special Committee*, Geneva: League of Nations Publications, 1939, pp. 6–9, 19.

THE BERNHEIM PETITION   **Document 31**

In 1933, Franz Bernheim, a Jew living in German Upper Silesia, petitioned the League of Nations complaining about anti-Semitic discrimination backed by Hitler's government which was contravening Germany's international obligations. When the German government was challenged, it actually stopped implementing its anti-Jewish policies in Upper Silesia for so long as the League of Nations had rights of supervision in the region. Unfortunately these rights ceased in 1937 and persecution began again. Here is an extract from the original petition.

I. In the Convention of May 15th 1922 between Germany and Poland concerning Upper Silesia the Contracting Parties agreed upon the following provisions:

Article 66. The German Government undertakes to assure full and complete protection of life and liberty to all inhabitants of Germany without distinction of birth, nationality, language, race or religion.

Article 67 para. 1. All German nationals shall be equal before the law and shall enjoy the same civil and political rights without distinction as to race, language or religion.

Article 75 para. 2. Legislative and administrative provisions may not establish any differential treatment of nationals belonging to a minority. Similarly, they may not be interpreted or applied in a discriminatory manner to the detriment of such persons . . .

Article 80. Nationals belonging to minorities shall be treated on the same footing as other nationals as regards the exercise of an agricultural, commercial or industrial calling or of any other calling. They shall only be subject to the provisions in force applied to other nationals.

Article 83. The High Contracting Parties undertake to assure full and complete protection of life and liberty to all the inhabitants of the plebiscite territory without distinction of birth, nationality, language, race or religion.

II. (1) In the Reich Legal Gazette, part 1, issued at Berlin on April 7th 1933, No. 34, a law 'for the Reorganisation of the Civil Service' was promulgated by the Government of the German Reich. Section 3, para. 1 of this law says:

> 'Officials who are of non-Aryan descent are to be placed in retirement; in the case of honorary officials, they shall be discharged from their official position.' . . .

(2) The German Government, in the Reich Legal Gazette Part 1, issued at Berlin on April 10th 1933, No. 36, promulgated a law on 'Admission to the Legal Profession', dated April 7th 1933. Section 1 of this law says:

> 'The admission of lawyers who, within the meaning of the law on the Reorganisation of the Civil Service of April 7th 1933, are of non-Aryan descent can be cancelled up to September 30th 1933.' . . .

On April 1st, 1933, a public boycott of Jewish businesses, lawyers, doctors, etc. was ordered and organised by an office under the authority of the German Chancellor, and they were treated with public contempt as part of this measure. This boycott was carried out by SA and SS formations, also under the orders of the Reich Chancellor as the supreme leader, and the public authorities failed to provide the Jewish subjects of Germany with the protection to which they were entitled by law . . .

The undersigned, Franz Bernheim, born on September 15th, 1899 at Salzburg, Austria, a citizen of Wurtemberg, hence a German national, of Jewish and hence non-Aryan descent, previously residing at Gleiwitz, Schillerstrasse 6b, German Upper Silesia, at present temporarily staying at Prague, Czechoslovakia, employed from 30.9.31 to 30.4.33 by the Deutsches Familien-Kaufhaus, Ltd., Gleiwitz branch, and then discharged for the reason that all Jewish employees had to be dismissed, Passport No. 180/128/30, issued by the Berlin-Charlottenburg Police Office on 28.2.1930, and thus legitimised under Article 147 as a member of the minority in accordance with Part III of the Geneva Convention of 15.5.22.

Hereby submits the petition to the Council of the League of Nations, signed with his own hand, requesting the Council to take such action and give such directions as it may deem proper in order to declare null and void for Upper Silesia the laws, decrees, and administrative measures in contradiction with the above-mentioned fundamental principles and to ensure that they shall have no validity, and further to give instructions that the situation guaranteed by the Convention shall be restored, that the Jews injured by these measures shall be reinstated in their rights and that they shall be given compensation.

VI. The undersigned, Franz Bernheim, further requests the Secretariat of the League of Nations to treat this petition as urgent.

The reason for this request is that, as the above-quoted laws and decrees demonstrate, the application of the principle of inequality to German nationals of non-Aryan i.e. of Jewish descent is being systematically pursued in all the spheres of private and public life, that already an enormous number of Jewish lives have been ruined and that, if the tendencies at present prevailing in Germany continue to hold sway, in a very short time every Jew in Germany will have suffered permanent injury, so that any restoration and reparation will become impossible and thousands and ten thousands will have completely lost their livelihood.

Prague, May 12th, 1933
Signed: Franz Bernheim

Source: UNOG Library, League of Nations Archives, R 3928, 4/4150/3643, Extract from the Bernheim petition, Jews in German Upper Silesia.

Further Reading

General primary sources

The League of Nations Official Journal was published across the life of the organisation and contains a wealth of material about the Council's activities and interests. Hard copies are available at the British Library, and an electronic version is provided by HeinOnline (www.heinonline.org).

Newspapers such as *The Times* and the *New York Times* now offer good quality archives via the internet (www.timesonline.co.uk and www.nytimes.com). It is surprisingly easy to find interesting and colourful articles dealing with the work of the League of Nations.

Introduction: organising the peace of the world

The League of Nations staff were active publicists of the organisation. They have left a thoughtful, instructive literature – although it can, at times, be over-enthusiastic. A good overview of the League's work in the 1920s is *League of Nations, Ten Years of World Co-operation* (London: Hazell, Watson & Viney, 1930). Essays dealing with the problems faced by the organisation can be found in the series *Problems of Peace* (OUP, various dates). Collections of essays looking back on the League's achievements include J.E. Johnsen (ed.), *Reconstituting the League of Nations* (New York: H.W. Wilson, 1943) and H.E. Davis (ed.), *Pioneers in World Order: An American Appraisal of the League of Nations* (New York: Columbia University Press, 1944). Soon after the war, former Deputy Secretary General of the League, F.P. Walters published an overview of his organisation's origins and achievements, *A History of the League of Nations* (OUP, 1952).

Of the more recent titles written by people lacking a personal stake in the organisation, S. Northedge, *The League of Nations: Its Life and Times, 1920–1946* (Leicester: Leicester University Press, 1988) remains a good introduction. A collection of documents about the 'high politics' of the League is provided by R.B. Henig (ed.), *The League of Nations* (London: Longman, 1973), while

Z. Steiner, *The Lights that Failed: European International History 1919–1933* (OUP, 2005) contains much relevant material. Annique H.M. van Ginneken, *Historical Dictionary of the League of Nations* (Lanham, MD: Scarecrow Press, 2006) is a good reference work.

1 What was the league of nations?

There are a number of really thought-provoking classic texts. They include J.C. Smuts, *The League of Nations: A Practical Suggestion* (London: Hodder & Stoughton, 1918) and R. Cecil, *The Moral Basis of the League of Nations* (London: Lindsey Street Press, 1923). Also interesting are Cecil's memoirs, *A Great Experiment* (London: Jonathan Cape, 1941). At some point, anyone interested in the League should also read something by P.J. Noel Baker. Generally accessible is *The League of Nations at Work* (London: Nisbet & Co., 1926).

Those wanting to balance praise with criticism should look at R. Dell, *The Geneva Racket, 1920–1939* (London: Robert Hale, 1941) and E. Bendiner, *A Time for Angels* (London: Weidenfeld & Nicolson, 1975). While both push a particular line, they also contain some genuinely valuable insights and information.

2 How new was the league of nations?

Interesting primary sources about the origins of the League include the Smuts text cited above plus L.S. Woolf, *International Government* (London: Fabian Bookshop, 1916). Also valuable is A. Zimmern, *The League of Nations and the Rule of Law 1918–1935* (London: Macmillan, 1936). Old but lasting discussions which locate the League in historical context include E.C. Mowrer, *International Government* (Boston: D.C. Heath, 1931) and F.H. Hinsley, *Power and the Pursuit of Peace: Theory and Practice in the History of Relations between States* (CUP, 1978 edition).

Newer texts which make their points efficiently include A. Sharp, *The Versailles Settlement: Peacemaking in Paris, 1919* (Basingstoke: Palgrave, 1991) and D. Armstrong, L. Lloyd and J. Redmond, *From Versailles to Maastricht: International Organisation in the Twentieth Century* (Basingstoke: Macmillan, 1996). For a very recent discussion of how the idea for the League grew out of the work of the British foreign office, see P.J. Yearwood, *Guarantee of Peace: The League of Nations in British Policy 1914–1925* (OUP, 2009).

3 A promising start? Disputes, borders and national minorities in the 1920s

The League of Nations Official Journal, *The Times* and the *New York Times* all contain interesting materials about contemporary views of events. An old, but still informative, overview of the League's early security work is F. Kellor, *Security against War, Volumes 1 and 2* (New York: Macmillan, 1924). More detailed, newer studies of specific events are given in James Barros's works, *The Åaland Islands Question: Its Settlement by the League of Nations* (New Haven, CT: Yale University Press, 1968), *The Corfu Incident of 1923: Mussolini and the League of Nations* (Princeton, NJ: Princeton University Press, 1965), and *The League of Nations and the Great Powers: The Greek-Bulgarian Incident, 1925* (Oxford: Clarendon, 1970). The same author also wrote the biography of the first Secretary General, *Office Without Power: Secretary General Sir Eric Drummond 1919–1933* (Oxford: Clarendon, 1979). Zara Steiner's recent book also provides lots of good information.

Regarding the administration of national minorities, some of the older books actually are some of the best. Good titles include J. Robinson, O. Karbach, M.M. Laseron, N. Robinson and M. Vichniak, *Were the Minorities Treaties a Failure?* (New York: Antin Press, 1943), I.L. Claude, *National Minorities: An International Problem* (New York: Greenwood, 1955), O.I. Jankowsky, *Nationalities and National Minorities* (New York: Macmillan, 1945) and C.A. Macartney, *National States and National Minorities* (OUP, 1934). For a modern treatment of the important theme, see C. Fink, *Defending the Rights of Others: The Great Powers, the Jews, and International Minority Protection, 1878–1938* (CUP, 2004).

4 International humanitarian action: refugees and security

You should look at Fridtjof Nansen's books, *Russia and Peace* (New York: Macmillan, 1924) and *Armenia and the Near East* (London: Allen & Unwin, 1928). Readable and also written by a League activist is C.A. Macartney, *Refugees: The Work of the League* (London: League of Nations Union, 1930), while one of Nansen's deputies later wrote his memoirs – T.F. Johnson, *International Tramps: From Chaos to Permanent World Peace* (London: Hutchinson, 1938).

The best recent overview of the refugee question is provided by Claudena Skran, *Refugees in Inter-War Europe: The Emergence of a Regime* (Oxford: Clarendon, 1995). An old but good biography of Nansen is E.E. Reynolds, *Nansen: The Life-Story of the Arctic Explorer and Humanitarian* (London: Penguin, 1949 edition). The Greek refugee experience is captured in D. Pentzopoulos, *The Balkans Exchange of Minorities and its Impact on Greece* (London: Hurst, 2002 edition), while that of both Greece and Turkey is covered in the very readable B. Clark, *Twice a Stranger: How Mass Expulsion forged Modern Greece and Turkey* (London: Granta, 2006). For treatments of refugees leaving Germany and the full text of McDonald's letter of resignation, see N. Bentwich, *The Refugees from Germany: April 1933 to December 1935* (London: Allen & Unwin, 1936).

5 Removing the causes of war: social and economic projects

For the primary sources (reports) used in this chapter, please refer to the list of references. Regarding health and the League, one of the most interesting books is M.A. Balinska, *For the Good of Humanity: Ludwik Rajchman, Medical Statesman* (Budapest: Central European University Press, 1998). There are also relevant articles in P. Weindling (ed.), *International Health Organisations and Movements, 1918–1939* (CUP, 1995). New literature is not so easy to find on drugs trafficking and the League, but older books include W.W. Willoughby, *Opium as an International Problem* (New York: Arno Press, 1976, first published 1925) and B.A. Renborg, *International Drug Control: A Study of International Administration by and through the League of Nations* (Washington: Carnegie Endowment, 1947).

For a good recent study of slavery, see K. Bales, *Understanding Global Slavery: A Reader* (Berkeley: University of California Press, 2005). Literature on the mandates system is voluminous and complex. Good places to start include the old P.M. Anker, *The Mandates System: Origin, Principles, Application* (Geneva: League of Nations, 1945) and the newer M.D. Callahan, *Mandates and Empire: The League of Nations and Africa, 1914–1931* (Brighton: Sussex Academic Press, 2008).

On the International Labour Organization, see J.T. Shotwell (ed.), *The Origins of the International Labor Organization, Volume 1: History* (New York: Columbia University Press, 1934) and Antony Alcock, *History of the International Labor Organization* (New York: Octagon Books, 1971). To get started with international economics, try P. Clavin, 'Europe and the League of Nations' in R. Gerwarth (ed.), *Twisted Paths: Europe 1914–1945* (OUP, 2007).

6 The league betrayed: collective security in the 1930s and disarmament

For the proceedings of an interesting conference about collective security, see M. Bourquin (ed.), *Collective Security: A Record of the Seventh and Eighth International Studies Conferences, Paris 1934, London 1935* (International Institute of Intellectual Co-operation, 1936). For a passionate criticism of the League in the 1930s, see Vigilantes, *Why the League has Failed* (London: Victor Gollancz, 1938).

On disarmament, a book by a senior League member involved in the project is Salvador de Madariaga, *Disarmament* (New York: Coward-McCann, 1929). Much more up to date, however, is Carolyn J. Kitching, *Britain and the Geneva Disarmament Conference: A Study in International History* (Basingstoke: Palgrave, 2003). The following collection of essays is first-rate and contains a number of contributions which are directly relevant: R. Ahmann, A.M. Birke and M. Howard (eds), *The Quest for Stability: Problems of West European Security 1918–1957* (OUP, 1993).

Regarding the crises of the 1930s, the report of the Lytton Commission was published as *Appeal by the Chinese Government: Report of the Commission of Enquiry* (Geneva: League of Nations, 1932). A good, accessible general study about Manchuria remains C. Thorne, *The Limits of Foreign Policy: The West, the League and the Far Eastern Crisis of 1931–1933* (London: Hamish Hamilton, 1972). A great many books indeed discuss Ethiopia, but one of the most readable is R. Lamb, *Mussolini and the British* (London: John Murray, 1997). Finally, for a study of the career of the Secretary General who presided over the decline of the League, see J. Barros, *Betrayal from Within: Joseph Avenol, Secretary General of the League of Nations, 1933–1940* (New Haven, CT and London: Yale University Press, 1969).

References

Primary sources: Archive notes

Archive 0.1: Letter of 28 June 1937 from G. Abraham to S. Heald. R4211. Disarmament General. 7A/29805/29805. United Nations Library, Geneva: League of Nations Archives Collection (hereafter, LoN Archive).

Archive 5.1: Economic Development vis-a-vis the well-being of the natives in Mandated Territories. Memorandum by Sir Frederick D. Lugard of the Permanent Mandates Commission, 19 September 1925. R75. Mandates. Economic progress and moral welfare of natives in mandated territories. 10/46530x/46530. LoN Archive.

Archive 6.1: Temporary Mixed Commission for the Reduction of Armaments. Scheme Suggested by Lord Esher for the Reduction of National Armaments. Presented on 23 February 1922. S 461. Disarmament Conference. Draft Reolutions. 3rd Session. CTA/56. LoN Archive.

Archive 6.2: Danzig. Reports of the High Commissioner to the Council. R3716. 2B/21856/4862. LoN Archive.

Primary sources: League of nations periodicals and reports

Appeal by the Chinese Government: Report of the Commission of Enquiry (1932) Geneva: League of Nations.

Committee on Traffic in Women and Children, Abolition or Licensed Houses (1934) Geneva: League of Nations.

LONOJ: League of Nations Official Journal (various volumes).

Malaria Commission (1924) *Report on its Tour of Investigation in certain European Countries in 1924.* Geneva: League of Nations.

Malaria Commission (1925) *Report on the Tour of Investigation in Palestine in 1925.* Geneva: League of Nations.

Malaria Commission (1937) *The Treatment of Malaria: Fourth General Report of the Malaria Commission and Appendices.* Geneva: League of Nations.

Memorandum Regarding Slavery in the Hukawng Valley in Upper Burma (1925). Geneva: League of Nations.

Report of Preparatory Commission for the Disarmament Conference and Draft Convention (1931). Washington: Department of State.

Report of the International Commission of Enquiry into the Existence of Slavery and Forced Labour in the Republic of Liberia. Monrovia, Liberia, August 1930 (1930). Geneva: League of Nations.

Slavery: Report of the Committee of Experts on Slavery provided for by the Assembly Resolution of September 25th, 1931 (1932). Geneva: League of Nations.

Summary of the Report to the Council: Commission of Enquiry into Traffic in Women and Children in the East (1934). Geneva: League of Nations.

Traffic in Women and Children, Summary of Annual Reports for 1928 prepared by the Secretariat (1930). Geneva: League of Nations.

Primary sources: Books, articles and newspapers

Aims, Methods and Activity of the League of Nations (1935). Geneva: Secretariat of the League of Nations.

Anker, P.M. (1945) *The Mandates System: Origin, Principles, Application*. Geneva: League of Nations.

Azcarate, P. de (1945) *League of Nations and National Minorities: An Experiment*. Washington: Carnegie Endowment.

Bourquin, M. (ed.) (1936) *Collective Security: A Record of the Seventh and Eighth International Studies Conferences, Paris 1934, London 1935*. Paris: International Institute of Intellectual Co-operation.

Brailsford, H.N. (1917) *A League of Nations*. London: Headley Bros.

Castendyck, E. (1944) 'Social Problems', in Davis (ed.) *Pioneers in World Order: An American Appraisal of the League of Nations*. New York: Columbia University Press.

Cecil, R. (1923) *The Moral Basis of the League of Nations*. London: Lindsey Street Press.

Cecil, R. (1941) *A Great Experiment*. London: Jonathan Cape.

Davis, H.E. (ed.) (1944) *Pioneers in World Order: An American Appraisal of the League of Nations*. New York: Columbia University Press.

Goodrich, C. (1944) 'The International Labour Organisation', in Davis (ed.) *Pioneers in World Order: An American Appraisal of the League of Nations*. New York: Columbia University Press.

Greaves, H.R.G. (1931) *The League Committees and World Order: A Study of the Permanent Expert Committees of the League of Nations as an Instrument of International Government*. Oxford: Oxford University Press.

Hitchner, D.G. (1943) 'The Essentials of International Stability', in Johnsen (ed.) *Reconstituting the League of Nations*. New York: H.W. Wilson.

Johnsen, J.E. (ed.) (1943) *Reconstituting the League of Nations*. New York: H.W. Wilson.

Johnson, T.F. (1938) *International Tramps: From Chaos to Permanent World Peace*. London: Hutchinson.

Kellor, F. (1924) *Security against War, Volumes 1 and 2*. New York: Macmillan.

Kershaw, R.N. (1929) *The League and the Protection of Linguistic, Racial and Religious Minorities* ('Problems of Peace' series). Oxford: Oxford University Press.

League of Nations, Ten Years of World Co-operation (1930) London: Hazell, Watson & Viney.

Macartney, C.A. (1930) *Refugees: The Work of the League*. London: League of Nations Union.

McDonald, J.G. (1944) 'Refugees' in Davis (ed.), *Pioneers in World Order: An American Appraisal of the League of Nations*. New York: Columbia University Press.

Nansen, F. (1916) *Through Siberia, the Land of the Future*. London: William Heinemann.

Nasen, F. (1924) *Russia and Peace*. New York: Macmillan.

Nansen, F. (1976) *Armenia and the Near East*. New York: Da Capo Press.

Noel Baker, P.J. (1926) *The League of Nations at Work*. London: Nisbet & Co.

Rappard, W.E. (1931) *The Geneva Experiment*. Oxford: Oxford University Press.

Sitzungsbericht des Kongresses der Organisierten Nationale Gruppen in den Staaten Europas (1931) Leipzig: Wilhelm Braumüller.

Smuts, J.C. (1919) *The League of Nations: A Practical Suggestion*. London: Hodder & Stoughton.

Sweetser, A. (1943a) 'The Non-Political Achievements of the League', in Johnsen (ed.) *Reconstituting the League of Nations*. New York: H.W. Wilson.

Sweetser, A. (1943b) 'Reconstituting the League: Our Future International Society', in Johnsen (ed.) *Reconstituting the League of Nations*. New York: H.W. Wilson.

Sweetser, A. (1944) 'The Framework of Peace' in Davis (ed.) *Pioneers in World Order: An American Appraisal of the League of Nations*. New York: Columbia University Press.

Wilson elibrary. Contains the texts of all the President's main speeches: www.woodrowwilson.org/

Woolf, L.S. (1916) *International Government*. London: Fabian Bookshop.

Woolf, L.S. (1917) *A Durable Settlement after the War by Means of a League of Nations*. London: League of Nations Society.

Zilliacus, M.K. (1929) 'The Nature and Working of the League of Nations' in *Problems of Peace, Fourth Series*. Oxford: Oxford University Press.

Secondary sources: Books and articles

Ahmann, R., Birke, A.M. and Howard, M. (eds) (1993) *The Quest for Stability: Problems of West European Security 1918–1957*. Oxford: Oxford University Press.

Alcock, A. (1971) *History of the International Labor Organization*. New York: Octagon Books.

Alexander, H.G. (1924) *The Revival of Europe: Can the League of Nations Help?* London: Allen & Unwin.

Armstrong, D., Lloyd, L. and Redmond, J. (1996) *From Versailles to Maastricht: International Organisation in the Twentieth Century*. Basingstoke: Macmillan.

Auer, S. (2004) *Liberal Nationalism in Central Europe*. New York: Routledge-Curzon.

Aun, K. (1951) *Der völkerrechtliche Schutz nationaler Minderheiten in Estland von 1917 bis 1940*. Hamburg: Joachim Heitmann.

Bales, K. (2004) *Disposable People: New Slavery in the Global Economy*. Berkeley: University of California Press.

Bales, K. (2005) *Understanding Global Slavery: A Reader*. Berkeley: University of California Press.

Balinska, M.A. (1995) 'Assistance and not mere Relief: the Epidemic Commission of the League of Nations, 1920–1923', in Weindling (ed.) *International Health Organisations and Movements, 1918–1939*. Cambridge: Cambridge University Press.

Balinska, M.A. (1998) *For the Good of Humanity: Ludwik Rajchman, Medical Statesman*. Budapest: Central European University Press.

Barros, J. (1965) *The Corfu Incident of 1923: Mussolini and the League of Nations*. Princeton, NJ: Princeton University Press.

Barros, J. (1968) *The Åland Islands Question: Its Settlement by the League of Nations*. New Haven, CT: Yale University Press.

Barros, J. (1969) *Betrayal from Within: Joseph Avenol, Secretary-General of the League of Nations, 1933–1940*. New Haven, CT and London: Yale University Press.

Barros, J. (1970) *The League of Nations and the Great Powers: The Greek-Bulgarian Incident, 1925*. Oxford: Clarendon.

Barros, J. (1979) *Office Without Power: Secretary-General Sir Eric Drummond 1919–1933*. Oxford: Clarendon.

Bendiner, E. (1975) *A Time for Angels*. London: Weidenfeld & Nicolson.

Bennett, A.L. and Oliver, J.K. (2002) *International Organizations: Principles and Issues*. Upper Saddle River, NJ: Prentice Hall.

Bentwich, N. (1936) *The Refugees from Germany: April 1933 to December 1935*. London: Allen & Unwin.

Brierly, J.L. (1960) 'The League of Nations' in Thomson (ed.) *The New Cambridge Modern History, Volume 12: The Era of Violence, 1898–1945.* Cambridge: Cambridge University Press.

Callahan, M.D. (2008) *Mandates and Empire: The League of Nations and Africa, 1914–1931.* Brighton: Sussex Academic Press.

Carocci, G. (1974) *Italian Fascism.* London: Penguin.

Clark, B. (2006) *Twice a Stranger: How Mass Expulsion Forged Modern Greece and Turkey.* London: Granta.

Claude, I.L. (1955) *National Minorities: An International Problem.* New York: Greenwood.

Clavin, P. (2007) 'Europe and the League of Nations', in Gerwarth (ed.) *Twisted Paths: Europe 1914–1945.* Oxford: Oxford University Press.

Dell, R. (1941) *The Geneva Racket, 1920–1939.* London: Robert Hale.

Dubin, M.D. (1995) 'The League of Nations Health Organisation', in Weindling (ed.) *International Health Organisations and Movements, 1918–1939.* Cambridge: Cambridge University Press.

Dumbuya, P. (1995) *Tanganyika under International Mandate, 1919–1946.* Lanham, MD: University Press of America.

Fink, C. (2004) *Defending the Rights of Others: The Great Powers, the Jews, and International Minority Protection, 1878–1938.* Cambridge: Cambridge University Press.

Firro, K.M. (2003) *Inventing Lebanon: Nationalism and the State under the Mandate.* London: I.B. Tauris.

Gellner, E. (1983) *Nations and Nationalism.* Oxford: Basil Blackwell.

Gerwarth, R. (ed.) (2007) *Twisted Paths: Europe 1914–1945.* Oxford: Oxford University Press.

Ghébali, V-Y. (1970) *La Réforme Bruce, 1939–1940.* Geneva: United Nations.

Ginneken, A.H.M. van (2006) *Historical Dictionary of the League of Nations.* Lanham, MD: Scarecrow Press.

Guigui, A. (1972) *The Contribution of the ILO to Workers Education 1919–1970.* Geneva: International Labour Organization.

Gzoyan, E. (2009) 'The League of Nations and the Question of a Mandate for Armenia', in *Central and Eastern European Review*, www.ceer.org.uk.

Henig, R.B. (ed.) (1973) *The League of Nations.* London: Longman.

Hiden, J. (2006–07) 'The Eesti Pank, the League of Nations Loan and the Bank of England', *Lennuk* 1: 11–13.

Hiden, J. and Smith, D. (2006) 'Looking beyond the Nation State: A Baltic Vision for National Minorities between the Wars', *Journal of Contemporary History* 41: 387–99.

Hinks, P.P., McKivigan, J.R. and Williams, R.O. (2006) *Encyclopedia of Anti-Slavery and Abolition.* Westport, CT: Greenwood.

Hinsley, F.H. (1978) *Power and the Pursuit of Peace: Theory and Practice in the History of Relations between States*. Cambridge: Cambridge University Press.

Housden, M. (2000) 'Ewald Ammende and the Organization of National Minorities in Inter-War Europe', *German History* 18: 439–60.

Housden, M. (2007) 'When the Baltic Sea was a "Bridge" for Humanitarian Action: the League of Nations, the Red Cross and the Repatriation of Prisoners of War between Russia and Central Europe, 1920–22', *Journal of Baltic Studies* 38: 61–83.

Housden, M. (2009) 'International Security and the Fight against Epidemics: Lithuania and the European Campaign against Typhus, 1920–23', *Tiltas* 10: 22–5.

Housden, M. (2010) 'White Russians crossing the Black Sea: Fridtjof Nansen, Constantinople and the First Modern Repatriation of Refugees displaced by Civil Conflict, 1922–3', *Slavonic and East European Review* 88: 495–524.

Huber, V. (2006) 'The Unification of the Globe by Disease? The International Sanitary Conferences on Cholera, 1851–1894', *Historical Journal* 49: 453–76.

Jackson Preece, J. (1998) *National Minorities and the European Nation States System*. Oxford: Clarendon.

Jankowsky, O.I. (1945) *Nationalities and National Minorities*. New York: Macmillan.

Jones, R. and Sherman, S.S. (1927) *The League of Nations: From Idea to Reality*. London: Sir Isaac Pitman & Sons.

Kitching, C.J. (1999) *Britain and the Problem of International Disarmament 1919–34*. London: Routledge.

Kitching, C.J. (2003) *Britain and the Geneva Disarmament Conference: A Study in International History*. Basingstoke: Palgrave.

Likhovski, A. (2006) *Law and Identity in Mandate Palestine*. Chapel Hill: University of North Carolina Press.

Lamb, R. (1997) *Mussolini and the British*. London: John Murray.

Lloyd, L. (1995) 'The League of Nations and the Settlement of Disputes', *World Affairs* 157.

Madariaga, S. de (1929) *Disarmament*. New York: Coward-McCann.

Manderson, L. (1995) 'Wireless Ward in the Eastern Arena: Epidemiological Surveillance, Disease Prevention and the Work of the Eastern Bureau of the League of Nations Health Organisation, 1925–1942', in Weindling (ed.) *International Health Organisations and Movements, 1918–1939*. Cambridge: Cambridge University Press.

McKercher, B.J.C. (1992) 'Of Horns and Teeth: The Preparatory Commission and the World Disarmament Conference, 1926–1934' in McKercher (ed.) *Arms Limitation and Disarmament: Restraints on War, 1899–1939*. Westport, CT: Praeger.

Morgan, P. (1995) *Italian Fascism 1919–1945*. Basingstoke: Macmillan.

Mowrer, E.C. (1931) *International Government*. Boston: D.C. Heath & Co.

Nish, I. (1977) *Japanese Foreign Policy 1869–1942: Kasumigaseki to Miyakezaka*. London: Routledge & Kegan Paul.

Northcroft, D.M. (1926) *Women at Work in the League of Nations*. Keighley: Wadsworth Press.

Northedge, S. (1988) *The League of Nations: Its Life and Times 1920–1946*. Leicester: Leicester University Press.

Pentzopoulos, D. (2002) *The Balkans Exchange of Minorities and its Impact on Greece*. London: Hurst.

Renborg, B.A. (1947) *International Drug Control: A Study of International Administration by and through the League of Nations*. Washington, DC: Carnegie Endowment.

Reynolds, E.E. (1949) *Nansen: The Life-Story of the Arctic Explorer and Humanitarian*. London: Penguin.

Robinson, J., Karbach, O., Laseron, M.M, Robinson, N. and Vichniak, M. (1943) *Were the Minorities Treaties a Failure?* New York: Antin Press.

Scheuermann, M. (2000) *Minderheitenschutz contra Konfliktverhütung?* Marburg: Herder Institute.

Sederholm, J.J. (1920) *The Åland Question from a Swedish Finlander's Point of View*. Helsinki: Government Printing Office.

Sharp, A. (1991) *The Versailles Settlement: Peacemaking in Paris, 1919*. Basingstoke: Palgrave.

Shotwell, J.T. (ed.) (1934) *The Origins of the International Labor Organization, Volume 1: History*. New York: Columbia University Press.

Simpson, J.H. (1939) *The Refugee Problem: Report of a Survey*. Oxford: Oxford University Press.

Skran, C.M. (1995) *Refugees in Inter-War Europe: The Emergence of a Regime*. Oxford: Clarendon.

Smith, A.D. (2000) *The Nation in History: Historiographical Debates about Ethnicity and Nationalism*. Cambridge: Polity Press.

Spaull, H. (1924) *Women Peace-Makers*. London: George G. Harrap.

Steiner, Z. (2005) *The Lights that Failed: European International History 1919–1933*. Oxford: Oxford University Press.

Stone, R.A. (ed.) (1978) *Wilson and the League of Nations: Why America's Rejection?* New York: R.E. Krieger.

Thomson, D. (ed.) (1960) *The New Cambridge Modern History, Volume 12: The Era of Violence, 1898–1945*. Cambridge: Cambridge University Press.

Thorne, C. (1972) *The Limits of Foreign Policy: The West, the League and the Far Eastern Crisis of 1931–1933*. London: Hamish Hamilton.

Tooley, T.H. (1997) *National Identity and Weimar Germany: Upper Silesia and the Eastern Border, 1918–1922*. Lincoln: University of Nebraska Press.

Towle, P. (1993) 'British Security and Disarmament Policy in Europe in the 1920s' in Ahmann, Birke and Howard (eds) *The Quest for Stability: Problems of West European Security 1918–1957*. Oxford: Oxford University Press.

Vigilantes (1938) *Why the League has Failed*. London: Victor Gollancz.

Walters, F.P. (1952) *A History of the League of Nations*. Oxford: Oxford University Press.

Weindling, P. (ed.) (1995) *International Health Organisations and Movements, 1918–1939*. Cambridge: Cambridge University Press.

Whittam, J. (1995) *Fascist Italy*. Manchester: Manchester University Press.

Willoughby, W.W. (1976) *Opium as an International Problem*. New York: Arno Press (first published 1925).

Yearwood, P.J. (2009) *Guarantee of Peace: The League of Nations in British Policy 1914–1925*. Oxford: Oxford University Press.

Zimmern, A. (1936) *The League of Nations and the Rule of Law 1918–1935*. London: Macmillan.

Index